LIBRARY AUTOMATION

LIBRARY AUTOMATION

Manohar Nanda

ANMOL PUBLICATIONS PVT. LTD.
NEW DELHI - 110 002 (INDIA)

ANMOL PUBLICATIONS PVT. LTD.
H.O.: 4374/4B, Ansari Road, Daryaganj
New Delhi - 110 002
Ph.: 23261597, 23278000
B.O.: No. 1015, Ist Main Road, BSK III Stage
III Phase, III Block
Bangalore - 560 085 (India)
Visit us at: www.anmolpublications.com

Library Automation

First Published, 2006

PRINTED IN INDIA

Published by J.L. Kumar for Anmol Publications Pvt. Ltd., New Delhi - 110 002 and Printed at Mehra Offset Press, Delhi.

Contents

Preface

"Library Automation" as a paper is being taught at B.L.I.Sc. and M.L.I.Sc. in 'Library Science' at various universities and institutions. This book is designed as an introductory text to the above paper, encompassing vital information on all pertinent aspects. Thus the material presented here would be of interest as well as of great use to the students, teachers and professionals of Library Science. This book will provide complete knowledge of the history of automation in libraries, functions reference services, acquisition system, online technical support systems, automated cataloguing, role of computers, electronic media in library, bibliographical classification, periodical indexing etc. to the students.

The major topics dealt in this book are—Automation in Libraries; Automated Reference Service; Acquisition System; Automated Circulation Control Systems; Automated Serials Control; Abstracts: Types and Functions; Online Technical Support Systems; Functions Automated Acquisitions; Automated Cataloguing; Multimedia Catalogue; Cataloguing Department; Role of Computers; Electronic Media in Library; Bibliographical Classification; Periodical Indexing; Indexing in Library.

It is hoped that all those will benefit from the contents of this book for whom it is meant. The author will feel amply rewarded, if motive is achieved.

Editor

1

Automation in Libraries

Since the advent of the term automation in 1936, plethora of definitions are found in library literature. Sometime the terms 'mechanization and automation' looked overlapped, although there is a difference of one degree between the two. Mechanization was aimed at handling problems of bulk, weight and distance at replacing muscle and movement with machines. Automation is the name given to an automatic system of working. A few meaningful definitions are examined hereunder.

Encyclopaedia of Britannica Defines Automation. "The name given to an automatic system of working. The difference between automation and mechanization, a related term, is being mainly one of degree".

Mr. Harder introduced automation in 1936. He defined it initially as "the automatic handling of parts between progressive production processes".

Since then the term has been applied to a wide variety of automatic machinery and automatic systems, and is commonly used to describe any operation in which there has been a substantial substitution of controlled action for human efforts or intelligence.

Encyclopaedia of Library and Information Science

Library automation is the use of automatic and semi-automatic data processing machines to perform such traditional library activities as acquisitions, cataloguing, and circulation. Although these activities are not necessarily performed in traditional ways, the activities themselves are those traditionally associated with libraries; library automation may thus be distinguished from related fields such as information retrieval, automatic indexing and abstracting, and automatic textual analysis.

Linguistic purists have argued rightly that the term "automation" applies more correctly and narrowly to automatic process control, and indeed this was historically the first use of the term. The broader meaning, however, has had the sanction of widespread usage for a number of years, and "library automation" is now by far the most commonly used term for mechanization of library activities using data processing equipment.

General Characteristics

The characteristics of an automated system are:

1. The operations/processes are carried out automatically.
2. Avoids or reduces human action and thus saves labour.
3. It accelerates efficiency and speed in operation.

HISTORY AND DEVELOPMENT OF AUTOMATION

From centuries together libraries have sought technological aid to facilitate and augment their service to readers. For example the introduction of a simple typewriter into libraries dates back to the late 1800s. Historically the phrase "Library automation" too has been used many a time synonymously with "Library Mechanization" which from some quarter was not considered quite accurate. On the other hand it was felt convenient to simply equate library automation with "computerization". But today without any controversy the term 'Library automation' is used extensively to refer primarily to the use of computers to perform some of the traditional library activities such as acquisition, cataloguing, circulation, and serial control etc. Conventionally the related fields such as information storage and retrieval (ISR) automatic indexing and abstracting, automatic text analysis etc. did not fall within the purview of 'Library automation'. This distinction has now almost disappeared. Information systems, is included in the context of automation. Although computers are playing primary roles in library automation today, the roles played by tele-communication technology, video technology, micrography, and reprography are of great significance because of the magnitude of support they offer to library automation.

Punched Cards Systems

Before the advent of computers, International Business Machines (IBM) and Remington Rand led the way to business technology by introducing equipment such as keypunch machines and electro-mechanical card sorters and collators. Although these devices were not computers, they had certain similar qualities such as they could read, compute, and manipulate data recorded in reusable form. William Saffady mentioned that as early as the 1930s and extending into the 1960s, a number of libraries in the United States had used punched cards in combination with sorters, collators, and other equipment as an alternative to manual record keeping.

In the United States Ralph Parker installed a Hollerith punched-card system for circulation control at the University of Texas in 1936 and by the middle 1940s had also experimented with its use in serial record control. In 1942 the Montclair Public Library of Montclair, New Jersey, installed "two specially designed book charging machines" which recorded individual transactions automatically in punched cards. The Library of Congress produced a book catalogue using punched cards in 1950, and the King Country (Washington) Public Library another one in 1951.

These were scattered instances of mechanized systems, however. More were installed in the late 1950s and early 1960s, but most of these were in small, specialized libraries. Typically, such systems used standard punched-card equipment, sometimes called "unit record" equipment because the punched card as a unit record was central to its operation.

Computerized Library Systems

Computers were not used before about 1961, and in this respect library automation lagged behind business, industry, and science. The lag was not due to lack of interest and enthusiasm on the part of librarians, however; computers were still assumed by most people to be satisfactory only for numerical work, and computer programmes were still oriented business and scientific applications. Even unit record equipment was difficult for most libraries to obtain until their parent institutions-universities, local governments, and businesses-had obtained computers.

The general purpose computers that were widely available in the 1960s opened new era of library automation systems. Punched card equipment remained in use, but played only secondary and insignificant role. Most of the computer systems common in the 1960s used punched cards for input and thus the information was fed into the system in a way like unit record systems. But once the data were entered many other operation could be performed during a single processing. More important aspect was that the system could "remember", storing information regarding book orders in progress, books held or on loan, periodicals received and so forth all on magnetic tape. Moreover, the information could be transferred automatically in and out of the computer "core" storage as needed for complete operations.

Availability of computers on wider scale, subsequent improvement in data processing capability, and reduced cost together gave impetus to growth and rapid development of library automation in the 1960s. Another realization that computer could be used effectively for non-numerical work further augmented interest in computer use.

While the 1960s saw the emergence of computer applications in libraries and the 1970s ushered in the online era, it, has only been in the 1980s that automation has become a feasibility rather than a goal for the future for large number of libraries in the world. It makes the first half of the 1980s quite different from the previous decades but the later half added new dimension providing unimaginable facilities through variety of automated methods used for library operations.

NEED FOR AUTOMATION

Various factors have contributed to bring about change from conventional to automated library operation. Broadly speaking the main reasons behind this change are as under:

1. Growth of Document. The amazing growth of documents especially in areas of sciences, social sciences and technology in the form of book and non-book material forced the library planners to utilize new technology for the organization of information since the traditional library methods failed to cope with the task.

2. Users Services. Heavy influx of documents added new dimension to user's needs. It is only the computers which can ensure improved and quick service. For example the manual work of housekeeping such as acquisition, cataloguing, circulation, serials control, etc. can be done with greater speed and efficiency with no arrear and backlog kept pending. Automated cataloguing provides variety of access points to a greater volume of information. Online catalogue has made it possible for a reader to press the key of the typewriter like terminal and have access to large bibliographical databases and obtain information in whatever field. It can be viewed on screen and if it is needed a printout can also be obtained. Mode on services such as current awareness service and selective dissemination of information can also be introduced efficiently.

3. Greater Efficiency. The workflow in the library may be made more rapid, more systematic and efficient with the help of the computer. The records in the computerized store are more accurate, more reliable and more accessible than the manually prepared records. All sorts of housekeeping jobs and information works can be performed with more speed, accuracy and greater efficiency.

4. Cooperation And Resource-sharing. No single institution, however resourceful can now collect, organize all documents available all over the world even in a specific field. Nor anyone organization can collect all documents in the areas of inter-disciplinary and multidisciplinary subjects. During the last two decades there has been an increase in cooperation and resource-sharing on the part of libraries by developing computer-based systems. It has two advantages: *(a)* access to more documents and information sources due to coordination and cooperation of many libraries in a system and *(b)* less expenditure, because the total cost is shared by a number of library in the system. The computer-based library systems, such as Online Computer-based library centre (OCLC) in the United States, the University of Toronto Library Automation System (UTLAS) in Canada and the Birmingham Libraries Cooperative Mechanization Project (BLCMP) in the U.K. are functioning successfully with increasing databases and multidimensional services.

The advantages of library automation are far-reaching. Housekeeping jobs aside, the facilities of time-sharing and online services have made library automation more effective for efficient and appropriate service. Today only computerized library can take part in computer networking and information networks at national and internatioal levels. It is the only way in which efficient standardised and faster service is assured, besides access to a world of information and data.

COMPUTER APPLICATIONS IN LIBRARIES

The application of the computer to library operation has two aspects namely housekeeping routines and information storage and retrieval. The housekeeping routines include acquisition and ordering work, cataloguing, circulation control, serial control, and keeping of records, statistics for overall management purpose. The application of computer to information service comprises generation and collection of information, information retrieval, current awareness services, selective dissemination of information, computerized databases, information transfer and distribution etc.

In the field of housekeeping routines, the job description amenable to computerization in each area is outlined as follows:

1. Acquisition Work

(i) Selection of Material

(ii) Checking of duplication

(iii) Ordering work

(iv) Preparation of order cards/slips

(v) Verification of books with order file and invoices

(vi) Accession work

(vii) Sending orders (offline or online) to suppliers/vendors

(viii) Updating record file

(ix) Print out of received and non-supplied documents

(x) Control of book budget *i.e.* expenditure incurred and balance.

2. Cataloguing

(i) Preparation of Authority file/thesaurus or subject Heading list

(ii) Arrangement of catalogue cards into classified, alphabetical or subjectwise alphabetical

(iii) Preparation of shelf-list

(iv) Original cataloguing (offline or online)

(v) Preparation of list of catalogued item (accession list) in any desirable form

(vi) Centralized/cooperative and shared cataloguing possible

(vii) Provision of access points in a variety of ways and in an appropriate physical form.

3. Circulation Control

(i) Registration of members

(ii) Issuance of borrower cards

(iii) Charging and discharging of items

(iv) Preparation of overdue and recall notices

(v) Detection of problem borrower at the point of issue.

(vi) Maintaining statistics in variety of forms.

(vii) Updating of record file

(viii) Managing of book reservation system

(ix) Calculation of necessary fines for overdue books.

4. Serial Control

(i) Selecting suitable title for purchase

(ii) Generating purchase orders; renewal and new

(iii) Receiving issues and claiming issues not received

(iv) Allowing access to details of current holdings

(v) Routeing individual issues to various members

(vi) Preparing catalogues of serials and other records

(vii) Keeping current and accurate details of serials holdings

(x) Exercising budget control and producing management information

(ix) Organizing completed volumes of serials for binding.

In the area of information retrieval process three tasks are generally performed by the computer, *i.e.* indexing, storage or organization of information in a desired format, and retrieval or recall of information whenever required. Job description amenable to computerization is outline as under:

Information Retrieval Process

(i) Indexing of documents

(ii) Preparation of Thesaurus

(iii) Abstracting

(iv) Compilation of Union Catalogue

(v) Bibliographic work

(vi) Inter-library loan

(vii) Reproduction of documents

(vii) Searching and providing printouts of relevant information.

In order to meet demand of the user, libraries have to build up their own databases with the help of computers. Catalogues, indexes, bibliographies, union catalogues are in a sense example of databases. They only need conversion into machine-readable form. These jobs are now widely done in libraries. Databases on specific subjects, interdisciplinary and multidisciplinary areas are also being created in the library for anticipated and potential use of the patrons. The kinds of databases prepared in the library are usually known as in-house databases.

Libraries too have access to external databases. These databases are created, promoted, and maintained by local organization, national and international agencies to provide access to comprehensive information resources on specific areas for their own research and need. Some scientific and technical organizations also establish databases and make them available to customers on commercial basis. The only condition for the libraries to have access to the external databases is that they must have a compatible computer system, be prepared to process software packages or be connected by online facility within the country or outside the country.

The databases may be divided broadly into four groups according to their purposes and contents, *viz.*, bibliographic databases, non-bibliographic databases, textual/numeric bases, and catalogue record databases. The bibliographic databases such as INSPEC, SCISEARCH, COMPENDEX, CHEMABS, MEDLAR, BIOSIS hold comprehensive data on science, science citation index, engineering index, chemical abstracts, medicine, biological sciences respectively. There are many other such computerised bibliographic databases. The non-bibliographic databases are of the directory type. They hold actual text or information rather than references in machine-readable form.

They mostly concern with business, financial statistics, industrial data, social sciences, economics, banking, marketing etc. Librarians are closely concerned with these databases. Such databases are accessible *via* the similar channels as bibliographic databases. Textual/ numeric databases are also non-bibliographic and include numeric, textual-numeric, properties and full text databases. The catalogue record databases are online computerised catalogues of national libraries like the Library of Congress, National Library of Canada etc. These are all machine-readable catalogues (MARC). If, a library has a set of compatible computer, the MARC tapes can be used in great variety of purposes. For example printed catalogue for public use can be obtained out of the MARC tape mechanically.

In the United States and Europe, computer is heavily used for current awareness service. The users are kept informed of the latest information in their respective field. Selective dissemination of information (SDI) has been computerized in number of libraries. The service comprises two kinds of jobs: description of documents received and preparation of users profiles indicating their areas of interest. Computer easily does matching function and transmits information with the least human involvement.

Thus the use of computer in various library activities has proved Landau's concept of 'Library-in-a disk' a reality. This revolutionary concept which envisages 'Paperless Information System' or according to Lancaster 'Paperless Society' has brought about drastic changes in library outlook. As stated before, in developed countries manual library operations are fast vanishing giving way to automated systems, These modern and dynamic innovations are providing library service as "Libraries without walls" with an ability of free access (or paid) to world information. But the role of librarian has not diminished in this changed scenario; it is being modified to make him an Information Specialist.

❐

2

Automated Reference Service

From the very beginning reference service has been defined in variety of ways. Wyer defined reference service as "that part of library administration which deals with the assistance given to the readers in their use of the resources of the library". Margaret Hutchins narrates "reference service includes the direct aid within a library to persons in search of information for whatever purpose and also various other library activities especially aimed at making information as easily available as possible". Broadly speaking the function of reference service is to assist library users in obtaining access to required information. It is entirely a public service activity in which the librarian functions as a professionally trained information specialist. Much of the reference work entails two types of transactions. Firstly it is a ready reference question which requires a factual response. Secondly, it is literature searching activity which demands more time to prepare bibliographies on specific topics.

Methodologies employed to answer both the queries are the same. The reference librarian interviews the enquirer to clalify the question; formulates strategy, and then appropriate sources are identified. In response, the enquirer is directed to these sources. In other words the librarian actually does the search and provides factual information or bibliographic citations to the enquirer.

Before 1940s all types of reference activities were manually operated, that is the preparation of bibliographies in specific topics relied on printed indexing and abstracting journals. Bibliographic listings and other sources providing access to monographs, periodical literature, technical reports etc., were manually prepared. In 1950 punched cards were used for data processing and information storage. These are the immediate predecessors of computer-based systems of 1960s.

Machine-Readable Reference Sources

For an automated reference service, the availability of machine-readable reference sources is an indispensable prerequisite. The early 1960s witnesses the era of offiine computer-based systems. During this period (1960s-1970s) many publishers of printed bibliographies and indexes started using computer-based text-editing and photosetting techniques. Saffady states that in the late 1960s and early 1970s, publishers of indexing and abstracting journals and bibliographies began to sell machine-readable versions of their products in addition to or in place of their printed equivalents. This data was and is still offered on the reels of magnetic tape. MARC tapes are among the earliest examples of such machine-readable bibliographic data products. Today many printed indexing and abstracting journals and bibliographies are available in machine-readable versions and commonly used in computerized online information retrieval systems. These machine-readable products are sometimes called bibliographic data base.

DATABASE

The term data-base denotes an integrated accumulation of computer-processible data organized in a manner suited to a wide range of applications. It is synonym today for a collection of printed or numeric records which have been transformed and stored in a computer. A database may range everything from a standard Index, to an encyclopaedia, to a statistical collection such as census reports etc.

Databases may be classified into the following categories:

1. Bibliographic (or Reference) databases
2. Non-bibliographic or (source) databases

Generally speaking, bibliographic databases are a series of linked bibliographic records, with each record containing some combination or permutation of the following components:

(a) document number

(b) title

(c) author

(d) abstract

(e) full text

(f) source reference

(g) indexing words or phrases

(h) citation, or number of references

(i) organization originating the document, or author's address, or both

(k) local information, *e.g.* location, special classification numbers

(j) language of the document.

These components constitute a document reference which contribute to bibliographic control by facilitating the retrieval of relevant documents when they are needed. Such a document reference does not normally give the information itself, but rather indicates documents in which information might be located.

Bibliographic databases may be created by local information units. In addition, there are larger, internationally accessible data bases which can be searched with the aid of international telecommunications networks.

Most machine readable bibliographic databases have their origin to an abstracting or indexing journal. Some databases and their printed equivalents are:

Database	*Printed Equivalent*
MEDLARS (Medical Literature and Retrieval system).	Index Medicus
INSPEC (Information service in Physics, Electro-technology, Computers and control)	Science Abstract
COMPENDEX (Computerized Engineering Index.)	Engineering Index
ERIC (Educational Resources Information Service).	Resources in Education
BIOSIS (Bioscience informtion service)	Biological Abstracts
SCISEARCH	Science Citation Index.

Some of the available machine-readable bibliographic databases are interdisciplinary in nature and can be considered general reference sources. For example LC MARC, UK MARC CANMARC which contain cataloguing records pertaining to published materials regardless of field. News and current affairs databases are also interdisciplinary scope. Examples include NATIONAL NEWSPAPER INDEX, NEWS SEARCH AND MAGAZINE INDEX, the NEWSPAPER INDEX. Other examples of interdisciplinary bibliographic database include:

1. Books in Print.
2. British Books in Print.
3. Comprehensive Dissertation Index.
4. Ulrich's International Periodicals Directory.
5. Monthly Catalogue of U.S. Government Publication.
6. British Official Publications.

Data bases dealing with single scientific or technical discipline are more numerous. MEDLARS, BIOSIS PREVIEWS, CA SEARCH; INDEX CHEMICUS.

Some highly specialized scientific disciplines are served by a number of machine-readable bibliographic databases. Examples include AQUACULTURE, WATER RESOURCES ABSTRACTS, WATERNET. Field of Engineering is covered by two important databases such as COMPENDEX and INSPEC.

Broadly defined nonbibliographic database contains data other than citations to books, articles, or other library materials. Non-bibliographic database is further divided into two groups: *(1)* Textual data bases which contain information equivalent to that found in printed reference sources as encyclopaedias, directories, and periodical publications; and *(2)* Numeric data bases or other quantitative information. Numeric databases consist of information expressed as numbers presented in the form of tables or time-series'. They usually comprise a measurement (population or quantity), a time-series (months, years etc.) and a variable (production, imports, exports etc. of a specific commodity).

Today the Academic American Encyclopaedia, the Encyclopaedia Britannia, Everyman's Encyclopaedia and many other are available as machine-readable data-base accessible through the online search services. The ACADEMIC AMERICAN ENCYCLOPAEDIA is also available in CD-ROM and videodisk format.

Directory type data-bases are among the most common nonbibliographic reference sources available in machinereadable form. ENCYCLOPAEDIA OF ASSOCIATIONS is an example. BIOGRAPHY MASTER INDEX is a mixed bibliographic and nonbibliographic data base which serves as a master index to biographical information found in directories, dictionaries, and other published sources. The number of bibliographic and nonbibliographic databases is growing all the time. CD-ROM is being heavily used for this purpose alongwith other optical storage devices.

Multidisciplinary and specialized search services share a common operating methodology. The commercial organizations purchase or otherwise obtain bibliographic and nonbibliographic databases in machine-readable form from their producers; convert the databases to a desirable form for storage on their computers, and allow libraries or other subscribers to perform various retrieval operations on such data using prewritten databases management software. (Saffady).

ON-LINE INFORMATION RETRIEVAL SERVICE

During the late 1960s and early 1970 information retrieval service remained offline. After receiving query, reference librarian used to formulate suitable search strategy consisting of a combination of commands and, search terms. These search requests were then key-punched and batched for processing against one or more data bases at predetermined schedule. When processed, the computer used to produce printed lists of citations for each request. The search results consisting of these retrieved citations (output) would be mailed to the enquirer or the originating library.

But from the mid 1970s the era of online information retrieval starts. In an online system, machine-readable bibliographic data base is maintained on disc for interactive searching by librarians working at local terminals. The computer terminal in the library is usually linked by telephone to a large mainframe computer in a city which may be 20 to 3000 or more miles away. In this mainframe computer is stored the needed information in a database. The Librarian or the searcher analyses query and formulates search strategy consisting of a commands and search terms. While interacting, he just enters the commands with the help of terminal keyboard and the result is seen on the video display unit or cathods ray tube. The print out is not possible by the VDU unless the matter is 'printed by the connecting printer. Here if the user needs a printed record of citations, he just pushes a button and the records are immediately printed out.

Online computer search is just like two way conversation between searcher and computer system. Therefore, online system is also referred to as interactive *i.e.*, conversational or real time which means as they occur'. This interaction takes place through terminal connected to computer through communication lines. Thousands of abstracts and indexes, bibliographic and nonbibliographic data are stored on discs and used online.

Some government bodies and corporate libraries in the United States and Europe have developed their own online search capabilities, using machine-readable bibliographic data bases created locally or purchased from publishers of printed indexes and abstracting services. Most libraries, however, use the external online search services for retrieving details of published items on a particular subject whereas previously they have used printed abstracting and indexing journals.

A computer search is neither complicated nor difficult. Anyone can learn, although it takes time to be skilled searcher. Here comes the reference librarian who acts as intermediary because the average user has neither the skill nor the time to search.

Essential Components

Computerized online information retrieval systems have now taken several forms and have numerous components. According to Katz the basic delivery system for online service consists of:

1. Hardware which is usually a terminal connected via telephone lines to a mainframe large computer.
2. Software or instruction to computer which makes it possible to effectively and quickly search for specific bits of information.
3. Databases which are the electronic equivalent of the printed reference works and are searched by a computer. These are available from vendors and/or publishers, some are fee-based.
4. Databases on CD-ROM or other form of disc which can be searched by the library on its own microcomputer.

Besides this, there is an area of electronic networks which tie together the libraries and can be operated by individuals out of their homes or office.

TYPES OF REFERENCE SERVICE AVAILABLE ONLINE

Types of information services online varied greatly. Many types of searches are possible many times more than with manual methods. The following are some of the types of searches that can be done using online services:

1. Retrospective Search. It is a common search which goes back to the earliest dates covered for one or more databases. A retrospective search may cover a specific topic a certain author, a specific document type, a specific journal or some other particular area, but more often it is exhaustive.

2. Selective Search. By selective search means a bibliography of recent research about a specific author or ongoing research conducted by a specific organization. A list of newspaper articles on a recent event or on specific topic is another example. Online search is more amenable in such case than that of manual methods.

3. Comprehensive Search. Comprehensive search is usually done on a specific topic. It typically covers all documents types, all author and all time periods covered by the appropriate databases. For examples a comprehensive search may pertain to patents, government activities, legislation etc. It also ensures exhaustivity.

4. State-of-the Art Search. The state-of-the art search identifies the current status of an area of research in a particularly industry. It helps to discover what an organization or individual is doing presently.

5. SDI Search. Online SDI (Selective Dissemination of Information) search is considered ideal. A search profile can be stored indefinitely on an online retrieval system and search profile is updated automatically on many databases. The user simply enters the profile and citations are retrieved, then automatically mailed periodically to the user.

6. Ready Reference Search. Many quick-reference questions can be answered by using online services. This is because online data-bases contain large amount of primary information in machine-readable form. Bibliographic data-bases may be used for citation verification for inter-library loan purpose. Directory or numeric, textual type databases available online provide immediate answer.

7. Patent Search. Patent search is popular in business, commercial and industrial libraries. Manual patent search is highly time consuming and labour-intensive. Online patent search takes far less time and is less expensive. Patent issues and applications are both searchable.

Online reference services reviewed as above, are commonly met by the users in the libraries. There are many other types of searches that may be performed using online databases. Vendors like DIALOG, BRS, SDC and others can provide long list of online reference services available with them.

Advantages

Tedd discusses some of the advantages of this online approach for the librarians. They are briefly described as follow:

1. Immediate access to a wide range of information running into millions of records is possible.
2. The larger number of access points provide more effective and exhaustive search. It offers coordinate terms, freetext searching and many other features which allow the searcher to go beyond the subject and/or another approach. Here Boolean logic operates.
3. Automatic printing of retrieved references (citations) and the ability to order a copy of the original document eliminates clerical hurdles.
4. Since online databases are readily updated than the printed version, currency automatically prevails.
5. Searching is much faster and response instantaneous.
6. Some databases are available online which have no equivalent printed product.

BIBLIOGRAPHIC SEARCH SERVICES

A number of notable online bibliographic search services are available. Some are discussed here briefly.

(1) BLAISE. The British Library Automated Information Service (BLAISE) was introduced in 1977. It is a cataloguing service which includes both current and retrospective online access to UK and LC MARC records. Together the files contain over two million bibliographic records of books and serials. In addition to this, access to databases such as British Education Index and Eighteenth Century Short Title Catalogue is provided. This whole online search service is known as BLAISE - LINE and is used by libraries all over the world.

(2) BRS. Bibliographic Retrieval Services (BRS) was introduced in 1976 in New York. The purpose was to provide innovative and cost-effective online search services. Its major service provides online access to bibliographic and full-text databases (mainly scientific and technical). Other services include facilities for the design, development and maintenance of private files and the design and implementation of specialist information retrieval software. BRS offers SDI service. It also makes available a cross data base for multifile searching, online accounting and an online catalogue service. It is owned by Information Handling Services.

(3) ESA-IRS. The Information Retrieval Service (IRS) of the European Space Agency (ESA) at Frascati, Italy offers online search service in the early 1970s via a special telecommunications network-ESANET. Previously it used ESA/RECON, but the present software used is known as QUEST. The ESA-IRS database system provides access via online process to more than twenty databases mainly on nuclear and space sciences. In Britain, the Department of Industry has provided a dial-up technical information service known as DIAL TECH. ESA-IRS is one of the most used search services available on Euronet.

(4) DIALOG. The DIALOG information retrieval service is run by Lockheed Information Services at Palo Alto in California. It is one of the first online search services which started operation in 1972. The search software was prepared from the RECON (Remote Console) "developed by Lockheed for the National Aeronautics and Space Agency USA. The online services of DIALOG comprise 175 databases of which half can be categorised as scientific and technical. The other half includes subjects like, agriculture, humanities, social sciences, the arts, management, business, economics and information science etc. It has databases, both bibliographic and non-bibliographic, American and European. It charges access fee, telecommunication charges and prices for printouts of retrieved citations. Some of the databases are AGRICOLA, LISA SOCIAL SCISEARCH, COMPENDEX, ERIC etc. DIALOG has made tremendous contribution to online service in Europe. It contains over 16 million bibliographic citations available online and these are constantly reviewed and updated. It has online current awareness and SDI services.

(5) SDC ORBIT. The System Development Corporation (SDC) started offering an online search service in 1972. Located at Sauta Monica, California, SDC and the Lockheed's Dialog are the largest online database organization in the world. Currently SDC has about eighty databases which cover a wide variety of subjects such as business and economics, chemistry, engineering, electronics, energy and environment, industrial science, petroleum and fossil fuels, US government reports and legislation, patents and social sciences. SDC prepared a software package for online search in 1968. It is known as ORBIT (OnIine Retrieval of Bibliographic Information Time-shared) some of the well known databases available through ORBIT are ACCOUNTANTS, AGRICOLA, BIOSIS, CHEMDEX, ENVIROLINE, ERIC, INSPEC, TITUS etc. Both DIALOG and ORBIT can be accessed via Telenet, Tymenet and other networks.

ORBIT also offers certain special services. These include SDI service and the facilities for users to establish and maintain their own private databases.

In addition to the few discussed above, several other online information systems in the United States' have been developed.

OCLC (Online Computer Library Centre) BALLOTS (Bibliographic Automation of Large Library Operations using a Time-sharing system) at Standford University, WLN (Washington Library Network at Olympia, RLIN (Research Libraries Information Network) are few examples. In Canada the largest online computerized library system is UTLAS (University of Toronto Library Automation). In Britain, the largest online system is BLAISE. It offers online services through a large number of databases under various names and styles, such as MEDLINE, SDI-LINE, TOXLIN, CHEMLINE, CANCERLINE. The second longest online system in the United Kingdom is called BLCMP (Birmingham Libraries Cooperative Mechanisation Project.) In Europe, online access is available to ESA (European Space Agency) and DIMDI (Deutsches Institute for Medizinische Dokumentation and Information).

Tymnet and Telenet

The member libraries to online search services as discussed above or any institution willing to pay the fees are using the online databases. No special telephone lines are required. The conventional telephone network provides access. But this dial-up method is recommended for those libraries which are located in the geographic vicinity of the given online database. For long distance communication, the use of online database by the libraries was expensive.

This obstacle was partially overcome during 1970s with introduction of publicly accessible packet-switching networks such as TYMNET and TELENET. Telenet and Tymnet are computer-controlled networks consisting of leased telephone lines which link geographically dispersed time-sharing computer services with access nodes in major and medium-sized cities. For example a library in New York wishing to access the DIALOG computer at Palo Alto in California. would dial a local Telenet or Tymnet telephone number and type a series of commands. This will cause the network's computers to route the call to the DIALOG computer. In most cases, Telenet and Tymnet charges are considerably lower than those incurred in conventional long-distance telephone communication. They have over 200 nodes in Europe and other parts of the world.

Both provide access to almost all the major American online service. EURONET provides online service to EEC countries mainly but it is being extended to other countries also by interconnecting with the host computer systems of such countries.

Document Delivery Systems

By document delivecy means the process in which libraries provide to the users the books articles, reports and other documents indexed in online databases, albeit in most of the cases it consists of citations and abstracts rather than the full text of the requested material. However to make the service complete the libraries have to evolve mechanism which enable them to deliver a document or a photo copy of the desired material into the users hand. The conventional interlibrary loan systems are highly time-consuming which offset the very purpose of online search. It is not unusual for U.S. Libraries to process backlogs of several days or even weeks and respond to those requests by means of efficient postal services. Thus in order to expedite the services it is thought necessary to investigate means of either supplying hard copy ordered during the search and retrieval process or supplying the full text as part of the retrieval process. It is well realized that in the long run, the keys to more rapid document delivery will be the expansion of online databases to include full text of documents and the use of other technologies such as optical disc, either in conjunction with or apart from online delivery. The trend toward online full-text database is already evident.

As Reynolds has pointed out that online full-text databases are not now nor will they ever be an all-encompassing solution to the problem of document delivery in libraries. The current publications might be available online, there will still be large amount of retrospective materials published only in hard copy not converted to machine-readable form.

To address this problem consistent efforts have been made toward the development of alternative document delivery methodologies. For this purpose, several avenues have been attempted to facilitate library resources sharing activities. Efforts are also made to improve and speed up interlibrary loan processing through technological intervention. Also many libraries have sought solution in the use of COM to provide more convenient and speedy access to documents.

The present situation is that libraries are interested in more efficient and faster means of documents delivery at a time when full-text online databases and other advanced technologies are only beginning to address those needs. Libraries are using two methods to secure documents from remote locations. These are commercial document delivery service and digital telefacsimile technology. Many library consortia have established formal or informal courier services for document delivery. (Reynolds). The need to send message speedily and accurately, telex systems are widely used which are invariably known as electronic mail, electronic messaging or teletex. Teletex is an enhanced telex system. A teletex terminal is a device similar to a word processor with a keyboard, screen, printer and internal storage. Some word processors, such as IBM's Display writer, are capable of receiving and transmitting teletex data. Project Hermes established in 1984 is a teletex-based document-delivery service which incorporates: document ordering, automatic document delivery, regular delivery of pre-specified documents, electronic mail, transfer of documents between participants.

Another technique which is used for document delivery is telefacsimile which is also known as facsimile or fax. There are both analog and digital facsimile machines and facsimile can be sent via cable, telephone lines, microwave and other means. Usually they are sent over telephone lines because that is more economical. Another latest device is known as LDX (Long Distance Xerox). It is a telefacsimile system which provides 135 lines per inch and electrostatic printing on paper. Only single pages (not directly from books) can be transmitted. It is costly but is speedy one.

From an operator's point of view, the procedure for transmitting copies on a digital machine is similar to that required for the analog modules. A page of a document is placed on a surface similar in appearance to the surface of a photocopying machine. After a telephone connection has been established with the receiving site, the sending machine scans a page and converts the image into electronic signals, which are transmitted over the telephone line to the machine at the receiving site. A facsimile of the original is produced in hardcopy form based on the pattern of signals received. Digital telefacsimile machine can transmit an image of a page in less than 60 seconds. Although not widely used in libraries, it is being experimented as a means of document delivery in US and Europe.

There are several other electronic document delivery systems being planned. A consortium of five major publishers comprising Elsevior, Pergaman, Wiley, Academic, Springer and Black-Wells Scientific planned to implement a system under the name of ADONIS (Article Delivery Over Network Information Systems). Started in 1981 it aimed to supply facsimile images of pages from Video disc. It uses a combination of laser scanning and printing, and digital optical storage of the complete page of scientific, technical and medical journal articles. Requests for copies are sent to Adonis from the BLLD (British Library Lending Division).

❑

3

Acquisition System

Automated library acquisition systems are designed to handle the considerable amount of paperwork involved in buying books. Typically they print purchase orders; maintain book fund accounts and print book fund reports of various types; provide information on orders outstanding, and sometimes on works in process-that is, books received but not yet catalogued; prepare vouchers or checks to pay for the books. Many also print other reports derived from the order information; one system described below, for example, produces 32 separate products. These may include lists of orders by order number, by author, by country, by language or by any other element of data that has previously been coded and entered into the system; claims or cancellation notices to be sent to a dealer when the book has not been received within a predetermined period of time; and notices of the original requester of a book that it has been ordered or received. Some of the more elaborate systems also provide for such functions as conversion of foreign currencies to dollars; automatic checking for possible duplicate orders; reordering from a second vendor if the first cannot fill the order; computation of such dealer performance measures as average length of time to fill an order, or average discount; and provision of information for cataloguing or circulation functions.

Acquisition systems also vary in other respects:

1. By type of material handled (most handle monographs, but many do not handle serials).

2. By type of orders handled (many do not handle standing, blanket or approval orders, or gifts and exchanges).

3. By type of payment possible (some cannot accommodate payments in advance, deposit accounts, or memberships).
4. By type of language representable (most cannot deal with non-alphabetic languages such as Chinese, and many do not provide for diacritics).

One of three major technical catalogues are:

1. Those based exclusively or primarily on unit record equipment.
2. Off-line, batch-processing systems using computers
3. On-line systems using various types of remote terminals for communication with a computer.

Acquisition Systems Based on Unit Record Equipment

The typical punched-card or unit record acquisition system uses a keypunch, a sorter, a collator, and a tabulating machine such as the IBM 402, 403, or 407. Cards are punched with order information, and are then sorted and passed through the tabulator to print orders. The punched cards are then placed, with the help of the collator, in the file of cards used for previous orders, to create an order outstanding file; this file may also be printed out in list form on the tabulator.

When the books are received, the price paid for each item is punched into one of the cards, which then serves to update financial records, and in some cases to write vouchers or checks. The public libraries of Decatur, Illinois and Lake Country, Indiana provide early uexamples of such systems. Decatur began late in 1959 with an inexpensive set of equipment (the IBM Series 50) costing $ 375 per month, and used it to produce not only purchase orders but 14 other products as well, including accounting records, statistics, shelflist cards, and book cards. By 1963/1964, the cost for machine rental, material, and equipment had risen to $798 per month, but payroll, budgeting, and circulation functions had been added, the total staff of the library had been reduced, and the library was operating on less money then it had five years previously.

Among university libraries, the University of Missouri, St. Louis University, and the Joint University Libraries of Vanderbilt, Peabody, and Scarritt were early pioneers with punched-card systems. The Missouri system was unique in its use of an IBM machine no longer being manufactured, the "Cardatype," rather than the customary accounting machine. The Cardatype combined a typewriter-like keyboard and printing platen with the ability to read unit record cards, punch them, and perform modest computational chores.

Data entered though the keyboard, read from punched cards, or computed in the arithmetic unit could be utilised in the production of printed orders and other records, and as many as four additional typewriter units could be attached to the central unit, each preparing distinctive documents. The application at Missouri is an excellent example of a unit record system in which the same punched cards are used repeatedly to produce various products.

The Cardatype, used at the beginning of the process to prepare purchase orders, also produced temporary cards for the public catalogue, Library of Congress card orders, order records, and report slips. A collator was used periodically to search the file of cards for the books on order, and if items were not received within a specified period of time the same cards were used to produce cancellation notices or claim notices. If the items were reported out of print, the card could also be used to request quotations from out-of-print book dealers, in which case a copy of the request from was again placed in the public catalogue as well as in a desiderata file.

In the St. Louis University application, the order date was recorded in so-called "Julian" or "shop" date from-that is, the number of the day of the year-and this was used to trigger claim notices. The files were so arranged that if the items ordered were not received within ninety days of the time ordered, a claim notice was automatically produced. After operating for several years, the system was abandoned for lack of sufficient volume to justify its cost.

The Joint University Libraries system handled fund accounting, produced orders for Library of Congress catalogue cards as well as for books, printed lists of books on order and in process, and produced temporary cards to be field in the public catalogue. A special card punch, the IBM 526 summary punch, was connected to the 402 tabulator so that when purchase orders were printed, cards could be punched with the total amounts of each order for use in encumbering funds. The system was converted to a computer operation in 1966 using IBM 1401 and 7072 computers, and is still in operation at this writing. Numerous special libraries had also begun such systems by the mid-1960s, typically using company equipment for a few hours per week. The one at IBM'S Watson Research Laboratory is of particular interests. As books moved from one step to another, the appropriate cards were manually shifted. Three times a week, an IBM 407 tabular was used to print the file, creating a "Processing Information List," or "PIL," which made information on the processing status of any item readily available. The system was later transferred to an IBM 1401 computer, with "recent additions" in one list and the other five categories combined in a second list, still called "PIL"

The status of each item was noted in columns corresponding to the five categories, with "Julian" or "shop" date shown for the day each item moved into each category. By observing which column had the most recent date, one could see at a glance the status of each item. The computer was programmed to identify items which stayed too long in one category, and produced notices of items that required claiming or exporting. "PIL" lists, increasing in sophistication of typography and production, were to become a common feature of later systems until superseded in the 1970s by terminal displays of the same information.

Off-line Computerised Acquisition Systems

As general purpose computers become widely available in the 1960s, off-line, batch-processing computerised systems became (and as for this writing, remain) the most common and popular form of acquisition system. Most such systems still use punched-card input, feeding order information into the system in a way not greatly different from unit record systems, but once data input has taken place information is normally transferred back and forth between magnetic tape or magnetic disk files without the necessity of repeated manual handling of cards.

The typical acquisition system of this type, in addition to printing orders, automatically updates the file of information on orders out standing, encumbers the necessary funds and updates the appropriate financial records, stores the bibliographic information for later use, and gathers statistics. Two public library systems are of interest as examples of the transition from unit record systems to computers. Both used a Univac machine, the 1004 Card Processing System, which had 'capabilities about halfway between the unit record systems and a small computer as the IBM 1401. The Suffolk County (New York) Cooperative System began with an IBM 403 tabulating system in 1963, and switched to the Univac 1004 a year later, adding tape drives for storage. A unique feature was the use of mark-sensing pencils to record and input some elements of data, such as the list price and discount in lieu of keypunching, the information. The magnetic tape drives allowed the system to store fiscal data and bibliographic information for production of catalogue cards. The Nassau County (New York) Library System began with a similar system in 1964; the system was transferred to a Univac 1005 with magnetic tape drives in 1968 so that order and other reports could be printed faster and the information for them stored more conveniently.

By far the most popular computers for acquisition systems in the mid-1960s, however, were those in IBM's 1004 series, particularly the 1401. The University of Illinois at Chicago Circle began using a 1401 for an offline acquisition system in 1964, incorporating the "Processing Information List" feature pioneered at the IBM Watson Research Library. The UICC was arranged not strictly alphabetically, but according to a computer-generated code work composed of the first four letters of the author's last name, the author's initials, and the initials of the first two words of the title.

Order were printed on three-by-five-inch slips, which were manually sorted by vendor and attached to vendor and attached to cover letters for mailing. Pennsylvania State University implemented a similar system the same year, using a 407 tabulator as well as a 1401 and a 7074 computer. A unique feature was the use of "change cards," five cards punched with the order number each time an order was prepared, and later used to report changes in the status of a book on order or in process. These cards were placed in cardboard packets and kept in a manually arranged file; if the status of an order changed, one of the card was withdrawn, a code for the change was written on the card, the card was sent to a keypunching section where the code was punched in the card, and the card was then used by the computer to update the master magnetic tape record of orders outstanding.

Codes were established for some twenty-five different changes, including "not yet published," "out of print," "book in cataloguing," and "processing completed." In addition to a listing of orders in process, with the status of each order shown, the system produced daily lists of books requested by faculty but not yet ordered for each university department or separate fund, about 250 lists in all; when the system was later redesigned, however, this feature was dropped.

Perhaps the example of an off-line batch-processing system of the mid-1960s is the one at the University of Michigan, implemented in 1965 on an IBM 1401, converted a year later to a 1460 and soon after to an IBM 360, and still running strong at this writing. A ten-part order form is generated, which includes slips for the official and public catalogues. The orders outstanding file is automatically updated, but instead of printing it out the university now produces it on a computer-output microfiche (COM) for both economy and ease of handling.

Entries for Slavic language works have "Slavic" punched at the beginning of each entry, and orders for music recordings similarly begin with the word "Recording" in order to create separate sections in the list for such works; other entires are alphabetised through the first 83 characters. The Michigan system is one of the few projects for which good cost figures are available. About a year after the initial implementation, an analyst from outside the library evaluated the system in terms of both overall efficiency and costs.

The results indicated that the system did indeed perform efficiently and economically; almost fifty percent more orders were handled by the automated system than by the previous manual system, and the cost per order, when like activities were compared, dropped by seven cents over a two-year span. The librarian principally involved with development of the system has cautioned, however, that "while the information gathered was informative, it can, at best, only be considered as a guide since it is impossible to compare accurately an existing system with something that might have been."

In the same year that Michigan's systems was first implemented, Washington University in St. Louis designed a system to control technical processing routines after books left the Acquisitions Department and until they had been fully catalogued and processed. Building on Penn State's "change card" idea, the system was designed to generate "process control cards" that could be inserted in IBM 357 terminals along with a plastic prepunched "badge" indicating the particular change in status to be recorded: for example, that the book has been received, or reported not yet published, or canceled, or forwarded to a particular cataloguing station, or to the card preparation unit, or (finally) that the book was under central of the public catalogue and could be removed from the system.

The information would be automatically recorded by a high-speed card-punch (an IBM 1034) in a remote location, and then be transmitted to the computer. Two years earlier, in 1966, Yale University packed up the idea of "process control" and used it in the design of an acquisition system that later served as a model for the automated acquisition system at the Library of Congress. As implemented at Yale, the technical processing "monitor" checks the status of each order during each day's run, and notifies the library of orders delayed past a predetermined length of time, and of other actions that need to be taken as a result of changes in status.

The system represents an improvement in communications for off-line systems, presaging tlle later development of no-line system; the insertion of prepunched cards in remote terminals eliminates the necessity of manually punching the information in a data processing department and carrying the cards to the computer, and the computer "talks back" by automatically printing action reports regarding particular items when needed. A remarkable thirty-two different outputs were originally produced by the Yale system, including notices to requesters of the status of their orders and large inprocess and order number listings, both of which were changed to microfilm form in 1971 because of their size and cost. First implemented on an IBM 6094-7040 "directcoupled system," the system was converted in 1972 to run on an' IBM 360 Model 67 and a short time later to an IBM 370 Model 155. IBM 357 data collection devices are still used for recording status and location of items, and IBM 826s are used to prepare order forms while simultaneously punching the same information into cards.

Other example of batch-processing off-line systems in university libraries are legion. By 1966, the Joint University Libraries system had converted to a 1401 and the University of Missouri had converted its unit record system to a 1440 computer, in this case not a university computer but one used solely by the library. In California, the Honnold Library, which serves the six Claremont Colleges, implemented a computerised acquisition system using an IBM Model 40.

The fullest bibliographic information available was entered as early in processing as possible, and a book catalogue was produced as the final step in the system. The University of Maryland, which had a unit record system modeled after Missouri's, Converted to an off-line system using several computers in succession, most recently a Univac 9300.

Other Ivy League universities were not to be outdone by Yale. Harvard implemented a successful system in 1967, Cornell in 1968, and Columbia between 1968 and 1971. The Harvard system automatically edits order information for obvious mistakes such as lack of vendor, unusually high price, and invalid fund coding before producing orders.

Prices need not be in United States dollars, since the computer has been programmed to convert all foreign currencies into dollars at the current rate of exchange, which can be altered daily if needed. The system checks the outstanding order file periodically, and claims are automatically produced if orders have not been received in the time specified by the selecting librarians; if an item has still not been received after two claims have been produced and a third survey of the files made, the order is automatically cancelled.

The Columbia system is remarkable particularly for the size and power of the equipment used: two IBM 360s, a Model 91 coupled with a Model 7, one of the most powerful complexes in the world at the time it was installed. Input is prepared on IBM magnetic tape Electric typewriter (MTSTS) and converted to machine-readable from on a Digidata System 30 converter. Records for aterials in all Roman alphabet languages and in transliterated Cyrillic languages are handled by the system, as are microforms, maps, and speech records, but not serials; and material received through purchase, blanket order, standing order, gift, exchange, deposit, and cooperative acquisition programmes are all included. As in the Yale system, the flow of materials in monitored through acquisitions and cataloguing departments and until catalogue cards are field in the public catalogue. About 65,000 order are processed annually for a impressed annually for a impressively low 93 cents per order.

An acquisition system differing from others in its extensive use of paper tape was implemented in 1968 at the University of British Columbia. Friden Flexowriters were used to punch the paper tapes as a by-product of such activities as typing orders, processing invoices, and receiving books. The paper tape then served as input to a PDP-ll computer which, in conjunction with a Honeywell 200, did the processing. The usual orders outstanding lists, claims, cancellation notices, and fund reports were produced, as was a list of current accessions, later discontinued for lack of user interest.

A system originally developed in 1968 at Florida Atlantic University for use on an IBM 360 was transferred to Arizona State University and implemented there, on a Honey well 200, in 1971. Of later off-line, batch processing system, one in particular may be noted because of the unusually small size of both the system and the institution involved. This is the acquisition system implemented in 1971 on an IBM 360 Model 30 at Parkland College, a two-year community college in Champaign, Illinois. The system has required the addition of an extra staff member for keypunching, plus $170 per month for a model 129 keypunch, $400 per year for punch cards and magnetic tape, and several hundred dollars more per year for specially printed forms, but the library staff apparently believes these costs are offset to some extent by the fact that it no longer orders items preprocessed at a cost of $2.05 per item. Among special libraries, perhaps the best-known batch-processing system is at the Washington University School of Medicine Library in St. Louis.

The system was begun in 1965 in conjunction with a book catalogue project. The cards were then used to update the magnetic tape record of orders outstanding and orders received, using the university's 1401 computer, Later changes in the status of particular orders were indicated on copies of the order form, them punched into cards, which again were used to update the magnetic tape file. Some seventeen different lists were printed out from the file at periodic intervals.

Very few computerised acquisition of this type have been reported in public libraries. Several that developed from unit record systems have already been noted, but only one that was initiated as a computerised system of the Orange County (California) Public Library. It began as a straight forward book purchasing system in 1966, using an IBM 1460 computer.

After converting the system to run on a 360 Model 30 and then on an RCA Spectra 70 Model 45 computer, the library decided to redesign the system entirely in order to incorporate additional features, including a book catalogue. Both library staff and a commercial software firm were used to accomplish the design and programming tasks. The new system, termed BIBLIOS (for Book Inventory Building Library Information Oriented System) was implemented in 1969, also on the RCA Spectra 70 computer owned by the county. Development costs were just over $100,000 for the acquisitions portion of the system, and the cost of ordering and receiving a title under the system has been calculated at approximately $ 2.23.

On-line Interactive Systems

In 1967, Connie Dunlap, developer of the University of Michigan system and at that time head of their acquisitions department, spoke to an ALA Pre-conference on Library Automation regarding the status of acquisition systems. No no-line systems were then in use, she pointed out and although several were planned, it appeared likely that most institutions would find such systems too expensive. By 1975, however, the costs of online storage and the necessary terminal equipment had declined dramatically, and over a dozen such systems were in operation. Perhaps the earliest to be implemented was at Washington State University in 1968, using three IBM 1O50s on-line to an IBM Model 67. Paper-tape readers and punches are attached to the 1050s to provide an alternative means of entry, and as backup to the on-line system.

As purchase order information is entered, each field of information is "tagged'/ (assigned a unique code) by the terminal operator, and the computer edits each field for valid order number, correct budget information, and so forth. When the information has been entered the operator visually edits the resulting typed version and makes any necessary corrections on the spot. A code indicating that the record has been edited is then entered on the record, without which the record cannot be processed. The entry and editing process requires an average of about three minutes per title.

The 1050 terminals are also used to input receiving and involve information, to enter accession numbers, and to indicate that can be cleared from the in-process file. Washington State has adopted the Washington University-Yale University process control technique, and as a by-product of the order entry procedure a book card is created for insertion in IBM 357 card readers to indicate when a book is received and moves through various stages in processing.

Because both on-line and off-line input are possible the library has made comparative studies of the two methods. The results indicate that operators prefer to work on-line, and make fewer errors as a result. Most errors are identified immediately by the computer, or are recognised by the operator, so they can be corrected at once and the most of erroneous information flowing through the system is drastically reduced. The increased efficiency made possible by improved communication between man and machine is thus concretely demonstrated.

The use of the terminal was limited to a seven-day period beginning on the 17th of the month, however, and appears to have been merely a means of avoiding the necessity for correcting the paper tapes and re-inputting them. No searching was done via the terminal, and although the device could print out information from the computer no real interaction appears to have taken place or been intended. The project was funded through the Computer Center, not the library, and when the funds were cut off in September of 1972 the system was discontinued.

Meanwhile, also in 1969 and also in Massachusetts, terminals with visual display screens were being used for the first time in an acquisition system. The "Book Order and selection System" (BOSS) of the University of Massachusetts in Amherst uses for such devices on-line to an IBM 370/145 computer. Design of the system began in 1968, and less than twelve months elapsed before the system was operational.

Currently BOSS processes about 90,000 orders per year, maintains the on-order file, provides both receiving and invoicing information, and produces claims for items not, received. The original order information as well as changes are entered *via* the terminal; since the visual display shows an outline or "mask" of the information to be entered, no special coding forms are required. If a keying error is caught by the computer, the visual display screen immediately indicates it.

After the error is corrected and the computer determines that all required information has been entered, a mask for the next order is displayed. The order outstanding file can be searched on the 2260 by order number, author, title, or Library of Congress card number. The unit cost for acquisition of an item has been calculated at $2.55, which includes that cost of searching (not normally a function handled by a batch-processing system) and some costs properly assignable to cataloguing. Manual file maintenance has been substantially reduced, and the backlog of processing eliminated.

A smaller system was implemented at Oregon State University in 1970 using a CDC 3300 computer and a CDC 210 (later 211) terminal with a visual display screen as well as a 3 KSR teletype (keyboard) terminal. Dubbed LOLITA, the system was developed over a three-year period for around $90,000, a modest figure compared to most other early on-line systems.

In part this low cost was possible because an existing time-sharing system at the university's computer center was used, and "programming efforts could be concentrated exclusively on the design of LOLITA and an earlier pilot project... No time was needed to design, debug or redesign the operating system software, as was necessary at Washington State University and the University of Chicago."

One report indicates that "acquisitions personnel have been transferred to other duties, book-keeping loads on the college book-keeping operation have been reduced, list of new books are more, complete and are produced with less labour, and the system provides input to the cataloguing operation which has resulted in some further saving there. The fund accounting system is sound is now accepted by the state for legal accounting purposes. An interesting feature is as provision for entering orders into the system and "holding" them until funds become available. In a recent fiscal year, the library received enough funds in the last ten days to double'monographic purchases for the year, and despite the shortness of time the library was able to encumber the funds using this capability.

Syracuse and Northwestern Universities both implemented on-line acquisition systems during 1971 using keyboard terminals in the IBM 2740 series, and both connected to IBM 370 computers. Despite some similarity in equipment, however, the systems have marked differences. Northwestern's provides input from MARC tapes, converts foreign currency, and writes checks, whereas Syracuse's does not; on the other hand, Syracuse's system automatically issues cancellation notices, checks for duplicate billing and duplicate orders, assigns funds based on the subject matter of the item being ordered, produces accession lists and delinquent order lists, and provides a wide variety of other management information, none of which is provide at Northwestern. Unfortunately, no costs for either system have been published.

Perhaps the most sophisticated system presently in operation is Stanford University's BALLOTS. BALLOTS is a combined or "integrated" technical processing system, and includes both acquisition and cataloguing functions. By 1975, over $2.5 million in grants from the Office of Education, the Council on Library Resources, and the National Endowment for the Humanities had been spent on its development. Design began in 1967, but the first production operations did not occur until 1972, when the first part of the acquisition system (the "MARC module") was implemented.

The first segment provided the capability of searching machine-readable cataloguing data supplied by the Library of Congress, and using it to order and catalogue books. During the first year only MARC titles could be handled, but by late 1973 other parts of the system had been implemented, and non-MARC titles could also be acquired and catalogued. Serials, standing orders, and approval orders are also now handled by the system, although in contrast to most other acquisition systems fund accounting is not.

The equipment used is a large IBM 360 Model 67 computer, a small PDP 11 computer as an intermediary, and a number of Sanders 804 programmable display terminals; cataloguing and acquisition departments share 11 terminals, and others are located at the reference desks in the main and undergraduate libraries, where library staff assist the public in searching the files.

The searching capabilities of the system are in fact its most elegant feature, with many indexes on-line and numerous automatic hints and instructions from the computer as a search progresses. There is also a programme for training new users of the system *via* the terminal itself. A similarly sophisticated system implemented the same year at Dartmouth College is also of interest. Two cathode-ray tube terminals and two Model 33 teletype machines are used for communication with the computer. Searching is performed primarily on two files, an in-process file and a vendor file, the latter providing such vendor performance statistics as the average time to fill an order, average number of claims, and average discount Perhaps because the number of orders in process at anyone time is relatively low (compared to the large university and public libraries in which such on-line systems are more commonly found) an in-process list is still printed out weekly, even though the same information is available through terminal inquiry.

The relatively low volume may also account in part for the fact that the costs of the automated system appear substantially higher than for the previous manual system: about $8.75 per item processed, versus $6.12 before. One observer has commented the "a tauter, less complex system could provide adequate speed and control at a substantially lower cost," and it is possible that the library is paying a significant premium for the sophistication or the system.

A useful contrast, to cite one final example, is the one-line system in operation since 1972 at the Cleveland Public Library.

Cleveland had previously used batch-processing systems: an IBM 1401 system from 1968, and an IBM 360 Model 20 system from 1968 to 1972. In 1972 it purchased not one, but two LIBS 100 minicomputer systems from Computer Library Services Inc. (CLSI), complete with all programmes necessary to run the systems, for a total price of $57,000 per system.

Cleveland's objectives in switching to on-line mini-computer were "to escape from a batch processing system" with separate data processing and acquisitions departments and the many problems arising from split responsibilities, "to get away from the massive generation of reports and listings that were of little value for management purposes, "and" to keep track of the flow of materials and dollars at a reasonable price."

❐

4

Automated Circulation Control Systems

Circulation of books and other materials is an important part of library public services. This section deals very delicately with the reader's community. Here one finds flow of reading materials, but the flow must be controlled by library operation so as to serve the users in the best possible way with the available resources. It is the duty of this section to check misuse and promote proper use of library documents. Simultaneously, it is necessary to record the movement of material, maintain statistics in order to display strength and weakness of stock and provide guidance for collection development in future.

It is also expected that circulation should be as simple, speedy and effective as possible. All the stage of movement must be recorded and records cumulated. The books requested for reservation must be trapped and the user served.

The objectives of circulation control may be summarised as follows:

1. To get information about the books to be borrowed, whether they are in the library or not.

2. To identify the document to be borrowed, such as call number, ISBN, other identification number, author, title, edition, year etc.

3. To identify the borrower by particulars, such as name, address, borrower number, category, whether membership is lapsed, present status, borrower's signature, etc.

4. To record the borrowing with particulars, such as the date of loan, the date of return, to whom it is loaned, any restriction regarding the loan, category of the loan, etc.
5. To keep records of the number of books on loan to individuals.
6. To check overdue books and to prepare reminders.
7. To ensure rapid charging and discharging of documents.
8. To trap the reserved documents.
9. To update loan files.
10. To prepare statistics.

DEVELOPMENT OF AUTOMATED CIRCULATION

Circulation control is one of the most widely automated library operation, and it is often the first activity that libraries consider automating. There are several reasons for this. For example most circulation control operations are clerical in nature. Their routine is error-prone in filing and related record keeping activities. Charging and discharging of library materials with an annual circulation of over 200,000 is highly labour-intensive. In most cases accurate maintenance of circulation statistics is impossible.

Saffady has pointed out that as early as the 1930s and extending into the 1960s a number of libraries in the United States used punched cards in combination with sortors, collators, and other "Unit record" equipment as an alternative to manual record keeping. Such "precomputer" data processing systems were typically based on inventory control models used in business. But in the mid-1960, with the introduction of computers for business applications, a number of libraries developed computerized circulation control systems based on offline (batch-processing) technique.

Basic Systems

A computer-based circulation, control system should perform the following functions:

1. Provision of information on the location of circulating items- either all items or only those items on loan or elsewhere, *i.e.* at the bindery, on reserve, being re-catalogued, etc.
2. Identification of items on loan: to a particular borrower or class of borrowers (namely, off-campus users).
3. Printing recall notices for items on long-term loan.
4. Renewal of loans.
5. Notification to the library staff of overdue items and printing of overdue notices.
6. Recording of holds or personal reserves for items on loan but desired by another borrower, often with additional provision for notifying the library staff when the item is returned and printing a book available notice for mailing to the person who requested the item.
7. Notification to the library staff or problem borrowers (*i.e.*, those with unpaid fines, or overdue books) either at the time of an attempted loan, or at the time a borrower is leaving the institution or on request from the library.
8. Calculation and printing of statistics of various types.
9. Analysis of both summary statistics and statistics for the circulation of particular items for use in acquisitions, planning of services and for other administrative purposes.
10. Calculation of fines, printing of fine notices, recording receipt of fines, and sometimes printing of fine receipts.
11. Provision for handling special categories of borrowers and special types of materials, and
12. Provision for printing due date slips, automatically generating orders for lost books or needed (additional) copies and printing mailing labels for remote borrowers.

These functions may not be considered necessary for all libraries. The outline just elucidates the possible features of an automated circulation control.

FILE

1. Main File. Main file is the main component of circulation control. It records all loans and contains the record of each book not available in the library stock. Every record contains at least the minimum information, such as the book number, the borrower number and the date of borrowing. The main file is the loan file. If bibliographic information is not included in the loan file, another file called the book fine is maintained.

2. Borrower File. In. addition to main file, a borrower file is also maintained on magnetic tape. It includes one record for each authorized borrower. Like the manual card file each borrower's record consists of such fields as identification number, name, address, telephone, privilege category, registration date, and expiration date. The identification number may be a random number with alphabetical digital character or it may be structured number with certain information about the borrower. Coded information in the borrower number allows analysis of the use made of the library or to impose limit on the number of books to be loaned and the loan period etc. On the tape, borrower records are usually arranged in identification number order.

3. Document File. Some libraries maintain document file which contains information about Document Identification Number (DIN), author, title, edition (if any) volume, year of publication, name of publishers, and place of publication etc.

The Document identification number (DIN) can be anyone of the following:

(1) Call number, *(2)* Accession number, *(3)* Alphabetic random code, *(4)* ISBN and copy number, *(5)* Random number, *(6)* Any other locally structured number.

TRANSACTION AT CIRCULATION DESK (OFFLINE)

At the charging desk, the input is made to the computer. It relates primarily the book number and the borrower number. Both are assigned and identified uniquely. In the offline computer, the input is made in the batch processing system and in the online computer, it is made in the random access processing system. In the batch processing system, the data capture device transmit data to the paper tape or the magnetic tape cassette or floppy disc at the issue desk and then processed periodically. The computer may hold a trapping store to indicate reserved or problem borrowers. Trapping-store system consists of some electronic store which is capable of holding a document identification number (DIN). When the book is returned, the DIN is checked against the numbers held in the trapping-store. If the number is present, then a lamp glows which indicates that the document is reserved.

If the off line computer is used and no device for trapping the reserved books is attached to it, the computer printouts with the previous input of such lists that may be used as check lists. In case more than one copy is available in the library for a book requested for reservation, the book numbers may be linked to catch the book borrowed or information of other copies obtained from the main: file. The computer can check the dates of returns of the books and thus prepare reminders for overdue books. These can be produced by line-printers. In the offline computer, over-borrowing can be checked after the due date is over. The updated transaction records prepare printouts with borrowers numbers. Updating of loan files from time to time prepares the corresponding records also from time to time. The statistical records can be kept on the basis of the transactions.

Although batch-processing circulation systems can eliminate the maintenance of paper file and time-consuming preparation of overdue and recall notices associated with manual system, there exists a gap in time between the action (counter transaction) and the computer's processing and reporting of information. The result is that some, of the information contained in batch-processed lists become outdated. Also in batch processing circulation systems "hold" function for reservation of book is not automatic. A separate card file or list is maintained manually and consulted for each item reserved etc.

On-line System. In an on-line system the details of transactions are entered through a terminal connected to a computer directly. One can obtain up-to-the-minute information through the terminal. But, the main problem with mot of the libraries is the lack of continuous on-line facility even with parent authority's computer.

Hybrid Approach. Tedd reveals that some circulation systems whilst being predominantly batch do allow online access to the files of items on loan, etc., but such a file would only be accurate as of the last time it was updated. This mixture of batch and online processing is sometimes referred to as 'hybrid'. The majority of currently available systems, especially the turnkey systems, are online and real-time; this, means that as soon as an item is issued or returned the relevant files are instantly updated and the most current information is immediately available.

DATA-CAPTURE DEVICES

The data capture devices are used in the library, either offline or online, to record transcription of books and the borrower on the pre-printed form. Then these data are converted to the machine-readable form and made input to the computer.

1. VDU Terminals. The recent innovation is visual display unit terminals or tele-typewriter terminals. In this case, self-adhesive labels with sensitive bar codes are required for each book. The data capture terminal 'read' the book card and the borrower card and 'write' data as required.

2. Label Based Systems. The Automated library system (ALS) UK has developed a label based system. This system is based on cards. The book number and the borrower number are punched on two cards. Both the cards are placed in a reader at the time of borrowing, and the information is transferred to the paper tape. The

ALS system has also a label based device. In this device, a non-magnetic metallic label is placed on the book. The label has metallic dots. At the time of borrowing, the borrower card having a similar label is passed over the sensing device with the book label. Thus, the data is written on some machine-readable medium.

3. Light Pen System. The 'Plessey' developed a lightpen system in 1972. It is a device for the graphical input and consists of a photo detector mounted on a pen-shaped holder. As the pen is held over the displayed element, it senses the light created on the patterns of the bars printed on the self-adhesive label, while the electron beams projected on them are picked up and sent to the computer as signals. As the computer knows the elements of signals, the data is written in the computer. The label with bar is transformed into the digital number. Every book in the library is assigned a given label with a unique number of identification, and a similar label with the borrower number having unique identification is held on the identification card of the borrower. The light pen method eliminates all cumbersome procedures of keeping the hand copy record or input media. No book card is required because identification is made by the unique label. By holding the light pen on the book label and on the borrower label, the transaction is made within seconds, the fastest job in circulation control. The Plessey light pen system is a widely used device. The book and the borrower numbers are encoded on labels as thick and thin bar or line code. The light-sensitive pen does the job quickly. (Mahapatra)

4. Stored Programme Control System. Another device is the Telepen consisting of the teletypewriter and the light pen. Both alphabetic and digital characters are encoded on labels. It incorporates a minicomputer that can be linked to a mainframe. It can also record transactions independently on the magnetic tape. It may also be equipped with a trapping store. The Stored Programme Control (SPC) is a hybrid system which provides added facilities. The system has a minicomputer to act as and enlarged trapping store and it is also connected with a large computer for processing data on the magnetic tape.

In some automated systems where issuing and returning of items is not very high, the labelling of the stock is not necessary. It is also a problem that some labelling systems require special 'readers' in order to convert the data into the appropriate bits for input to the computer system. Other systems require special sensing devices. For example, as mentioned before, bar-coded labels are usually 'read' using light pens which includes a light sensitive device which can be used to decode the pattern of thick and thin lines in the bar code. OCR labels are usually 'read' by a hand-held OCR wand.

DEVELOPMENT FROM 1970s TO DATE

Batch-processing, circulation systems reflected the situation prevailing in the 1960s and early 1970s. Through the mid-1970s, most automated circulation control systems were customed-developed for a single library or library system. As stated before, in batch processing keypunch or key-to-tape devices were used to convert information about individual circulation transactions to computer-processible form. The resulting data were then batched for processing at predetermined intervals etc.

By the mid-1970s, library automation specialists had begun to concentrate on the development of online, real-time circulation control systems. which process circulation transactions as they occur. Since data files are updated immediately, such real-time systems accurately reflect the status of a library's circulation collection. Printed lists are replaced by online terminal inquiries to determine the circulation status of specific items.

While real-time circulation control system are custom-developed (inhouse) for individual libraries, some vendors in D.S. offer generalized preformulated approaches to automated circulation control that eliminate the need for customized system. Such preformulated approaches, according to Saffady, fall into two groups: *(1)* pre-written circulation control software meant for execution on a computer system; and *(2)* turnkey systems, consisting of pre-configured combinations of hardware and software. It is marked as self-contained products.

The early (1970s) prewritten circulation control software packages and turnkey circulation systems were single purpose products. But later on the domain experts developed integrated, multifunctional turnkey systems and software packages which combines circulation control with other capabilities. In addition to circulation control, the most complete integrated system comprises application modules for Cataloguing, online catalogue' access by library users and/or staff, acquisitions, and serials control, a community bulletin board system, and electronic message transmission.

Whether designed as single purpose products or as integrated systems components, prewritten circulation software packages and turnkey systems can be implemented for more quickly than customized circulation control systems which may require months or perhaps years to develop. Likewise prewritten software packages and turnkey systems minimize or eliminate requirements for local software expertise. Library using them don't need to hire programmers.

While pre-written circulation control software, packages are available for computers of all types and sizes, libraries, medium-sized or large have typically relied on mainframe and minicomputer-based products. Examples of IBM mainframes include the NOTIS software package; IBM's own DOBIS/LIBIS programme; and the TECHLIB/STATS implementation of the BASIS software package. Minicomputer-based turnkey circulation control systems are available from CLSI, Geac, Data Research Associates (DRA), OCLC, Universal Library Systems and other vendors in U.S. (Saffady).

❐

5

Automated Serials Control

The problem of controlling serials by computer remained a challenge for a long time. Some believed that it was one of the most difficult housekeeping operations to be automated mainly due to the unpredictable nature of serial publications. Serials control systems are indeed distinct from monograph systems in a number of ways. A monograph is a single entity at hand whereas serials are published at regular or irregular intervals; their contents usually vary from issue to issue. An article as a single bibliographic unit may be published in more than one issue and even in more than one volume. Secondly an issue of a serial may not be a bibliographic unit in itself but a bibliographic unit embodied in a particular article comprising more than one issue or volume. Obviously, users may be interested in an issue of a serial as a bibliographic unit or an article spread over a number of issues as a bibliographic unit. This conflict between the physical unit and the bibliographic unit and their management problem make serials control a complex task. Computers were first used to assist in the control of serials in the 1960s. The systems depended on punched cards and batch processed. Even today the majority of the automated serials control are batch processed run on a mainframe computer. In 1970s a number of libraries in the D.S. attempted online real-time integrated serials control systems. Many developments are now seen in this area. The serial services are being offered by library cooperatives, and special serial subscription agencies. More software for serial control are being developed.

AUTOMATED SERIAL CONTROL SYSTEM

Computerised serials control system comprises several sub-systems. They are:

1. INVENTORY. Preparation of lists of serials in cards and to make input to the computer, designing and implementation of data files.

2. ORDERING AND ACQUISITION. Selection, ordering and acquisition of serials newly subscribed.

3. CATALOGUING. Preparation of catalogues of serials and other records designed to meet the needs of users.

4. ACCESSIONS. Receiving of serials, checking-in, placing claims if not received, renewal of subscription, checking gaps, if any, updating of holding records, placing orders for back volumes, preparation of data files, record maintenance, etc.

5. CIRCULATION. Making available serials issues in separate volumes in the bound form, keeping records of circulation, checking and making arrangements for binding, preparation of lists of titles or lists of articles, etc. (Mahapatra)

Inventory

Inventories of serials may be prepared primarily in the card form under the title and the subject with cross references from previous files, if any. Each title is recorded by the date of the first volume and subsequent volumes indicating any missing issues. Location is indicated by the call number given to periodical title or the shelf mark. While inventories are prepared in any form as required in the individual library, these may be edited and recorded in the required format. The records then may be kept in the computer in punched cards, or magnetic tape or disk. The magnetic tape file may be sorted for preparing various kins of inventories and printout obtained from the computer. Once main files or database files are input to the computer, updating with keypunching will be simpler and easier. The updating of input data may be of three kinds-additions, deletions, and changes. Higher degree of accuracy is achieved by the computer.

Ordering And Acquisition

The initial ordering of a serial is akin to ordering a monograph. Ordering entails processes like requesting, approving, checking, ordering and accounting in respect of each new serial title.

In the accounting system, the total amount of money to be spent on serial is usually called the serials fund which is divided among subjects or departments. The serials fund is further sub-divided under a number of heads, such as back-sets and duplicate volumes purchases, and binding etc. Financial data file is maintained which shows in general two kinds of transactions: *(1)* those made under each head and *(2)* those made with each of the suppliers and/ or the parties with whom any transaction is made. New orders are input to computer with all details of price, cost invoice, amount paid or ready for payment.

The acquisitions function may be divided into two parts *i.e.* receiving and claiming. When an issue is received, it must be checked to ensure that this is the correct or latest item received and then the main data file must be amended to show new receipts. Typically a file of punched cards should be created for all the serials to be received. When the issue arrives the card file is searched and extracted and a new card prepared if no appropriate card is present in the file. All cards relevant to the issues received are eventually processed in a batch and the computer-held main data file is updated. The remaining cards, if any, serve to alert the librarian to the non-receipt of certain issues. (J.E. Rowley).

The claiming function is a smaller but a complex job. The point at which the claiming procedures should start, mainly depends upon the professional judgment of the librarian. The computer easily provides list of outstanding issues that the librarian needs in order to send claims.

Preparing record for renewal of subscription is a routine job. The data file for acquisitions may include the details of the dates when subscriptions fall due to be renewed and the amounts to be paid. The printouts of such records may be produced at regular intervals for perusal and action. Renewal notices may be printed by the computer. After making payment in each case of renewal, the account to show balance should be updated.

Accessions

Each new issue of the serial is recorded in the library. If it is a new serial, it should be input to the data file with bibliographic detail. When all the records are input and the files are updated, the issue may be sent to the reading room or the place where to send. The next useful job which is performed by the computerised accessioning subsystem is the production of a current list of recent arrivals of journals. It may be used as a part of current awareness service.

Integrated System

It may be mentioned that in computer- based networks (*e.g.* OCLC, WLN or RLIN) ordering, acquisition or check-in system depends upon centrally located full bibliographic data base. The member libraries use this facility only through their nodes. They are directed to adhere strictly to the practice/standard approved by the system and create files accordingly at their respective centres.

Cataloguing

In an automated serials Cataloguing Work, the bliographic data is recorded in machine-readable form. As stated earlier computer-based serials system generates, from the master file, lists in several orders, *e.g.* title, subject, location, supplier, etc. Here, there is no difference between a monograph and serial automated work. Then the serials catalogues may be printed in book-form or COM. The frequency of updating the lists varies but usually lies between the limits defied by monthly and annually. (J.E. Rowley).

Circulation And Binding

Circulation of serials is practised on limited scale. For an ordinary loan circulation-control system for monograph can suffice for serials. However routing of serials is important in special library and must be computerized. To operate such a system a list of users, their location, department and details of the serials they would like to see are input and lists of readers for each issue of a serial are produced. Ideally the list should be produced in an order which minimizes the movement of an issue between different departments and locations and also reflects the priorities. The bound issues or back-sets of a serial may be loaned to readers in some libraries. The technique for circulation is usually the same as for lending books.

Binding

The primary objectives of automated bindery control include:

1. Production of binding slip.
2. Identification of volumes ready to bind.
3. A record of volumes at the bindery from which the volumes not returned on schedule may be identified.

The computer-based bindery control modules are either part of an automated check-in system or are a standalone (local) bindery control system. Each bindery system works slightly different. In all cases, however, binding slips or lists are produced to accompany the volumes sent to the bindery. These binding slips and/or lists are created from records which generally contain the following data: title (or author and title), binding colour, class of binding, colour of lettering and its style, size and location (for title, volume, and call number), instructions for handling advertisements, indexes, and title page. Most of the systems have the binding data coded in fixed length fields. Some bindery records also contain issue, frequency, number of issues bound together, and binding frequency.

The identification of the volumes to be bound can be accomplished automatically using the issue frequency and the number of issues bound together or using the frequency of binding. Several bindery control systems allow the production of binding slips (lists) on request. These systems allow the request as part of the serial check-in system.

The third function of a bindery control system is to provide a record of volumes at the bindery. This record is made accessible by call number and title as well as the bindery shipment. Online circulation systems can be used to charge volumes to the bindery and to provide overdue notices when volumes at the bindery are not returned on schedule.

The Control System

All these subsystems must be integrated in one serials control system. Each of the subsystems must have a main file or master file and other working files. All these files must be integrated in one file in the serials control system which constitutes the core file. The core file is the master file of the system and all other files and records are subordinate to this core file. The central control, data record, decision making, management production of printouts in desired sequences, accounts, statistics and every routine and management job will be controlled by this system with the core file. It may be designated Master Serial Control File. It will hold all the records centrally with connections to the following data files-selection data, ordering data, acquisition data, accessioning data, cataloguing data, description data, circulation data, users data, binding data, binders data, suppliers, data, holding data, statistical data, non-receiving data, accounting data, financial data, claims data, renewal data, cancellation data, etc. These data can produce printout lists for various purposes. (Mahapatra)

The core file should include the following information:

Identification number

International Standard Serial Number (ISSN)

Title and abbreviated title

Call number or shelf number

Frequency

Expected dates of receiving issues

Library holdings and wants

Volumes bound and unbound

Supplier

Subscription rate in rupees and foreign currency, if any.
Subject (may be coded)
Language (may be coded)
Nature of the serial (whether abstracting or indexing journal or having other special feature). (Mahapatra).

For the serials control system, it is better to start with key punching and unit card methods. The punched cards in file or deck can be used. If possible, the paper tape and magnetic media can be used as with handling books etc. In serials control department batch-processing is the most convenient method for record and operation. But an online integrated system is highly desirable for all sorts of quick references.

INTERNATIONAL SERIALS CONTROL SYSTEMS

Computerisation in libraries has created immense potentialities in standardisation of data at the international level and opened up a new vista for transfer of and access to information and documents. The capabilities of the computer have been increased enormously. All these situations have contributed to making transfer of software packages across geographical barriers and national boundaries. Attempts have been being made for controlling data at the international level by the machine-readable form.

ISBD(s)

To create and maintain international standards in bibliographic descriptions for easy flow of information, IFLA started the programme of the International Standard Bibliographic Description (ISBD) to be applied to national bibliographies, library catalogues and other information sources. The aim of ISBD is to provide standard descriptions for library materials of different kinds, and to ensure international propagation of bibliographic information. The functions of ISBD's are to make records from different sources interchangeable, so that, records produced in one country can be easily accepted in library Catalogues and/or other bibliographic lists in any other country and to assist in the interpretation of records transcending language barriers, so that records produced for users of one language can be interpreted by users of other languages. By the application of the International Standard Bibliographic Description, the bibliographic records can be converted to the machine-readable form. The bibliographic descriptions of serials are made by the International Standard Bibliographic Description (Serials), ISBD(S), which can be used in the machine-readable format.

ISSN

The use of International Standard Book Number (ISBN) in publications makes it possible to identify them. In countries where ISBN has been accepted, all the recent publications are marked with the International Standard Book Numbers. For identification ordering and processing of serial publications; the International Standard Serial Number (lSSN) is being used. There are many national centres established in different countries, and they register and allocate the International Standard Serial Numbers. These unique International Standard Serial Numbers (ISSN's) facilitate computerisation of serials catalogue records by providing machine-readable serials records. These ISSN's act as access points to the international network of serials publications. They also promote computer-based information service on the strength of holdings of serials in various libraries at the international level. (Mahapatra)

CODEN

ISSN is not the only serial numbering system. Twenty year older is CODEN system developed by the American Society for Testing and Materials, fully titled CODEN FOR PERIODICAL TITLES. It is controlled by the Chemical Abstracts Service and covers mainly scientific and technical literature. Details of titles. covered are given in the INTERNATIONAL CODEN DIRECTORY. In a sense, of course, ISSN and CODEN are rivals; in practice, both are frequently cited on the same publication.

ISDS

The International Serial Data System (ISDS) was set up in 1971 under the world science information programme. UNISIST, recognising the fact that an internationally accepted coding system for serial was essential for machine-readable records. It was also felt that an effective system for compilation and dissemination of information on serials was essential. For these reasons an international centre, ISDS, was established in Paris. (Mahapatra)

THE INTERNATIONAL SERIAL DATA SYSTEM acts as a central node in an international network of national centres with the aim at meeting the need for an internationally accepted coding system for periodical titles for collecting, recording and disseminating accurate information on the periodical literature. The general aims of the ISDS are to:

1. Develop and maintain an international register of serial publications.
2. Define and promote the use of international standard serial numbers.
3. Facilitate the retrieval of scientific and technical information in serials.
4. Establish a communications network between libraries, secondary information services, publishers of serial literature and international organizations.
5. Make this information currently available to all countries, organizations or individual users.
6. Promote international standards for bibliographic descriptions, communication formats, and information exchange in the area of serials publications. (Tedd).

The International Serial Data System records conform to the MARC standards. It uniquely identifies the serial title whether the International Standard Serial Number has been used or not. The components of the ISDS are:

ISSN
Key title

Variant Title, if any
Abbreviated title
Imprint
Frequency
Country of origin
Former and later title, if any
Language edition, if any
Related title, if any

The ISDS records may be used in computer-based libraries. They are available in the MARC exchange format. The ISDS, ISBD(s) and ISSN have made serials control most effective and efficient both at the national and international levels. They too have promoted international exchange of information and software package transfer in the machine readable form.

CONSER

Conversion of Serials Records project (CONSER) was initiated by the United States in 1974. Now it is a cooperative project undertaken by the Library of Congress, the National Library of Canada, the National Library of Medicine and the National Agricultural Library and other participating libraries. The retrospective and current serials records are being converted to the machine-readable form. The National Serial Database has been established in the Library of Congress, under the National Serial Data Programme (NSDP) as a part of CONSER. The serial database is accessible *via* the Online Computerised Library Centre (OCLC, formerly Ohio College Library Centre) network. CONSER records may be used in union lists, bibliographies, information retrieval and as a basis for selection and acquisition. Products available from CONSER includes: *(a)* weekly tapes of serials records; *(b)* a keyword-out of context index of serials titles; and *(c)* a microfiche of authenticated records. (Rowley)

SUBSCRIPTION AGENCY SERVICES

Many of the serials subscription agencies have started offering services to libraries to assist serials control. This is quite similar to the services being provided to assist libraries in the fields of ordering and acquisition of monographs. In Europe and U.S. many such agencies have developed inhouse computer-based systems for ordering, claiming and supplying their customer libraries with serials. Humphreys in Potter and Sirkin work *"Serials Automation in the U.S."*, categorizes the services offered by the subscription agencies in the following way:

1. **Subscription Handling.** This is the primary service offered by the agencies. A basic subscription handling service includes contacting the publishers to determine rates, ordering, preparing invoices and dealing with renewals.

2. **Bibliographic Information Related to Serials.** This service is really a by-product of the subscription handling service. The quality of bibliographic data provided varies, and some agencies are considering acquiring the CONSER database. Some agencies provide the bibliographic data in a variety of physical forms and some provide online access.

3. **Issue Handling and Check-in.** This can either be carried out directly by the agency or software for this purpose may be developed by the agency for use on a library's inhouse computer system.

4. **Budgetary Details.** This includes providing libraries with details of expenditure on serials by fund account, budget code, subject parameters and so on.

5. **Production of Union List. (Tedd).**

The following four agencies are extensively providing subscription services to libraries in U.S., U.K and elsewhere:

i. Ebsco, Birmingham; Alabama, U.S.

ii. Frown, Massachusetts, U.S.

iii. Swets and Zeittinger, Lisse, Netherlands.

iv. Blackwell's Oxford, U.K

COMPUTER CATALOGUING FOR SERIALS

Automation is doing a good deal with serials cataloguing data which facilities search and retrieval. There is complete access to everything in the record from all possible angles. This increase in access points per bibliographic item is a great achievement of computer in cataloguing work.

Cataloguing serials is now easier than ever before. It has solved many problems of automated serials cataloguing. A few relatively minor differences exist for descriptive cataloguing of monographs and serials. ISBD provides a framework for describing any type of material libraries collect and that framework is the basis for Part 1 of AACR2. The rules laid down make cataloguing aspect of serial consistent with the description of other materials. The other part of descriptive cataloguing is the application of Part II of AACR2. These rules apply equally to any materials; seriality is no longer a factors. Moreover the use of computer has relegated the concept of main entry to background. It does not depend upon a particular entry point. A good consolation for serials cataloguers.

The bibliographic elements suggested in AACR2 as appropriate to serial cataloguing are confined to eight areas. The cataloguer does not face any problem in doing manual or automated serial cataloguing. The trouble arises with blending these entries in a computer system. The "entry" in a computer system may drive from a MARC record or from a CONSER (Conversion of Serials). Individual serials cataloguers may disagree on statements of responsibility, series formation, title proper, or other information in the area of description. Another point of interest is that if a serial is entered on MARC/ CONSER record in a way which differs from local practice it is a must for local library using a system, to change the entry and adhere to the practice displayed in the data base being used, may it be CONSER or WLN or any other.

Osborn gives the following instructions to serials cataloguers.

1. Since AACR2 calls for inclusion of the ISSN and key title in the catalogue entry for serials, these should be followed.

2. Should CODEN or another symbol be employed, the other coding should be substituted for ISSN in the catalogue entry.

3. Key titles be recorded in abbreviated form. The standards employed in abstracting and indexing services can be adopted, otherwise recourse should be had to two publications of the International Organization for Standardization: International Code for the Abbreviation of Title of Periodicals (Geneva 1972) and International List of Periodical Titles Word Abbreviations (Geneva 1973).

4. Abbreviated key titles should be followed for headings on visible index cards, computer check-in listings, as well as on catalogue entries. Libraries which do not have a computer programme need not add identifiers or key titles to their catalogue entries.

5. If a computer-based catalogue is basically a record of items in a library; if it is intended to help readers and staff to find those items, then a clear, simple entry will suffice.

Bibliographic records as approved by CONSER are the records which OCLC participants are directed to use for serial cataloguing and for the construction of other files, such as the on-line serial check-in file. Originated at OCLC, the CONSER programme is located in the Serial Record Division at Library of Congress. Other users of this programme are a select group of research libraries.

CONSER records are distributed through MARC serial tapes and LC cards and also through CONSER microfiche.

❐

6

Abstracts: Types and Functions

An extract is an abbreviated version of a document created by drawing sentences from the document itself. For example, two or three sentences from the introduction followed by two or three from the Conclusions or summary might provide a good indication of what a certain journal article is about. A true abstract, while it may include words occurring in the document, is a piece of text created by the abstractor rather than a direct quotation from the author.

Abstracts can be characterized in a number of different ways including length. There is absolutely no reason why all abstracts should be approximately the same length. Factors affecting the length of an abstract include the following:

1. The length of the item being abstracted;
2. The complexity of the subject "tatter;
3. The importance of the item to the organization preparing the abstract. As with the exhaustivity of indexing, an industrial information centre may want to prepare longer abstracts for the company's own reports than it does for other items;
4. The diversity of the subject matter. For example, an abstract prepared for the proceedings of a conference may need to be rather long if the papers presented cover a wide range of topics;

5. The "accessibility" of the subject matter in a published abstracting service, in particular, it might be sensible to prepare more complete abstracts for items that are less accessible physically (*e.g.*, limited distribution reports or papers presented at conferences) or intellectually (*e.g.*, those written in obscure languages);

6. Cost Longer abstracts are not necessarily more expensive to prepare than short ones. Indeed, it may take much longer to prepare a good condensation of 200 words than one of 500. Nevertheless, it is obvious that the cost of a published abstracting service would increase significantly if the average length of an abstract was increased by say, 50 percent. Typesetting, paper, and mailing costs would all be affected;

7. Purpose. An abstract used primarily to provide access to a document for retrieval purposes might need to be longer to provide sufficient access points.

A very brief abstract (*e.g.*, one that attempts to describe a document by means of a single sentence) is sometimes referred to as an annotation, but this is a rather imprecise term.

A distinction is frequently made between indicative abstracts (sometimes called descriptive abstracts) and informative abstracts. The distinction is illustrated in figure 1 and 2 which show two different types of abstract prepared for the item first depicted. The indicative abstract simply describes (indicates) what the document is about, whereas the informative abstract attempts to summarize the substance of the document, including the results.

That is, an indicative abstract might mention what types of results are achieved in a study but the informative abstract would summarize the results themselves. Cremmins explains that indicative abstracts may contain information on purpose, scope or methodology but not on results, conclusions, or recommendations. On the other hand, the informative abstract may include information on purpose;

scope, and methods but must also contain results, conclusions, or recommendations.

For some purposes, a good informative abstract might act as a reasonable substitute for reading a document. An indicative abstract is unlikely to serve as a substitute in this way. Its main purpose would be to indicate to the reader of the abstract whether or not he would be likely to want to read the original. For obvious reasons, informative abstracts tend to be longer than indicative. They are also more difficult to write. Indeed, while it will usually be possible to write an informative abstract for an experimental study, it may be almost impossible to do so for a theoretical study or an opinion piece. For this reason, informative abstracts occur more frequently in science and technology than they do in the social sciences or humanities.

A single abstract may incorporate indicative and informative elements depending on the interests of the intended readers. For example, consider a report on air pollution abstracted in a publication intended for chemists. Much of the abstract, covering the environmental aspects, is merely indicative, but a part of it may be truly informative (*e.g.*, presenting results from analyses performed on atmospheric samples).

Indicative and informative abstracts may both be included in a single published abstracting service. In general, however, indicative abstracts are more common. Fedosyuk describes detailed procedures for distinguishing between indicative and informative abstracts using linguistic criteria and even presents an algorithm for this task.

While this is ingenious, it is not clear why one would want formal procedures for making such distinctions. The term subject slanting is sometimes used in connection with abstracts. The implication of the term is that the abstract should be "slanted" to the interests of the intended users. That is, in abstracting, as in indexing, a guiding question should be, "Why are our users likely to be interested in this item?" Abstracts prepared by an organization for its own internal use should always be slanted to local needs and interests.

The situation is a little more complicated in the case of published abstracting services.

A distinction can be made between services that are discipline-oriented and those that are mission-oriented. The former attempt to serve the needs of a particular discipline (*e.g.*, chemistry, biology, the social sciences) while the latter try to meet the needs of a particular industry or group of individuals (*e.g.*, abstracts for the rubber industry or abstracts for nurses).

Subject slanting is more relevant and feasible in the case of mission-oriented services than it is for discipline-oriented, because the interests of users of the former tend to be more homogeneous and specialized than the interests of users of the latter. At least one study has indicated that rather little slanting occurs in published services.

Figure 1: Indicative Abstract

> *Telephone interviews were conducted in 1985 with 655 Americans sampled probabilistically. Opinions are expressed on whether: (1) the establishment of a Palestinian state is essential for peace in the region; (2) US aid to Israel and to Egypt should be reduced; (3) the US should (a) participate in a peace conference that includes the PLO, (b) favour neither Israel nor the Arab nations, (c) maintain friendly relations with both. Respondents indicated whether or not they had sufficient information concerning various national groups in the region.*

Another type of abstract is the critical abstract. Such an abstract is really a "condensed critical review."

Applied to reports, journal articles, and other relatively brief items, a critical abstract serves much the same purpose as a critical book review. A critical abstract is evaluative. The abstractor expresses views on the quality of the work of the author and perhaps contrasts it with the work of others. For example, a critical abstract of the item might mention weaknesses of the methodology used-the way the population was sampled, the size of the sample, the wording of the questions-or compare the results with those of earlier surveys. Because the writers must be true experts, critical abstracts are rather uncommon. Two publications that do include critical abstracts are Mathematical Reviews and Applied Mechanics Reviews ("R).

An examination of AMR reveals, however, that true critical abstracts are very much the exception rather than the rule.

Figure 2: Informative Abstract

Telephone interviews conducted in 1985 with 655 Americans, sampled probabilistically, brought these results: most (54-56%) think U.S. aid to Israel and Egypt should be reduced; most (65%) favour U.S. participation in a peace conference that includes the PLO; more than 80% consider it important that the U.S. should maintain friendly relations with both Israel and the Arab countries; 70% believe that the U.S. should favour neither side; most (55%) think that the establishment of a Palestinian state is essential to peace in the region. The Israelis are the best known of the national groups and the Syrians the least known. The Arab-Israeli situation is second only to the conflict in Central America among the most serious international problems faced by the U.S.

Nowadays abstracts frequently appear in scholarly journals along with the articles to which they relate; they are usually written by the authors of the articles. In many cases these abstracts are picked up and reproduced by the indexing and abstracting services. Some journals include abstracts in more than one language. For example, several Russian and Japanese journals include English abstracts.

Purpose of Abstracts

Many different purposes of abstracts could be mentioned. First and foremost, perhaps, abstracts facilitate selection. That is, they help the reader decide whether a particular item is likely to be of interest or not. In this way, they save the time of the reader-*e.g.*, by preventing him from acquiring articles that would not be of any interest. In some cases, too, a good informative abstract may actually substitute for the reading of an item that is of interest to the user. Abstracts are particularly useful in illuminating the content of items written in languages unfamiliar to a particular reader.

The printihg and distribution of abstracts is effective in keeping people informed of newly published literature in their fields of interest (*i.e.*, providing for current awareness). Abstracts appearing within the articles or reports to which they relate are useful to an indexer in helping him identify the central subject matter of the item as rapidly as possible. Borko, and Bernier limply that abstracts can substitute for the full text in indexing activities, but this may not always be a desirable practice. Finally, abstracts now play an important role in computer-based retrieval systems by facilitating the identification of pertinent items and by providing access to stored items (in systems in which the text of abstracts is stored in searchable form). For certain purposes, a structured abstract may be preferred to one in the form of narrative text.

Abstracting involves putting the appropriate "values" into the frame. That is, for each article, the type of irrigation, soil type, crops involved, climatic conditions, and location are indicated, and codes are used to represent the type of results achieved. This type of abstract has value in the compilation of handbooks summarizing a large number of studies performed in a particular field. However, it would only work for a subject area in which the essential elements would remain more or less the same from one study to another. Zholkova describes how facet analysis might be used to create a structured abstract but is somewhat unconvincing on the value of this approach.

Terse Literatures

Bernier and Yerkey have described and illustrated the use of highly abbreviated statements each of which encapsulates the major "point" of some publication. They refer to these generically as "terse literatures" and to the most condensed of these as ultra terse literatures." One variety is the ultraterse conclusion, a very brief statement on the major conclusion reached in some piece of research. For example:

> Theoretical linguistics has had no significant impact on information science

This type of summarisation is not an abstract in the conventional sense; nevertheless, terse literatures are certainly related to abstracts. They have a number of potential applications. For example, it would be possible to produce a handbook summarizing what is known about some phenomenon (*e.g.*, disease) as a series of ultra terse statements, each statement linked to a bibliographic reference identifying the source from which it is derived.

Modular Abstracts

In 1964. Hemer and Company undertook a study for the National Science Foundation on the feasibility of "modular content analyses". These had two components: modular. 'abstracts and modular index entries. Modular abstracts were intended as full content descriptions of current documents. Each abstract consists of five parts: a citation, an annotation, an indicative abstract, an informative abstract, and a critical abstract. The set was so designed that an abstracting service could process it to conform to its own unique requirements with a minimum of effort: anyone of the abstracts could be used intact, or the modules edited to form, for example, a partially indicative, partially informative abstract, or a partially informative, partially critical abstract.

Physical and Mathematical System
Axismmetric and Blunt Body Systems
Re-entry Bodies

Environment
Atmospheric Entry

Re-entry Conditions
Space Flight.

Mass Transfer
Ablation, Analytical
Ablation, Charring
Ablation, Melting
Ablation of Glasses
Chemical Reaction Effects
Thermal Thickness
Reaction Zone
Reaction Thickness

Figure 3: Modular Index Entries

The prime purpose of modular abstracts was to eliminate the duplication and waste of intellectual effort involved in the independent abstracting of the same documents by several services, without any attempt to force "standardized" abstracts on services whose requirements may vary considerably as to form and subject slant. Both abstracts and index entries were prepared by subject specialists, and it was intended that they would reconcile the requirements for speed of publication with the thoroughness of abstracts prepared by experts. Their standardized format and treatment would also reduce repetitive handling and speed the flow of work within recipient abstracting services.

1. A method is described for the determination of strontium and barium in human bone by radioactivation analysis.
2. Results of analyses of 35 bone samples, from normal persons of both sexes and different ages, are given. The concentrations of barium and strontium were found to be of the order of 7 and 100 pg./g. of ashed tissue respectively.
3. No relationship between sex or disease of individuals with strontium and barium concentration was noted. The

concentration of strontium in the age group 0-13 years was significantly lower than that in the group 19-74 years.

4. No significant difference was found in the concentrations of strontium and barium in the various bones of those individuals examined.

5. Results obtained in this survey are discussed and compared with those of other workers.

/00193/

/Method/Determ/Strontium/Bone/Humans/Radioactivation/ Analysis/00193/

/No Relat betw/Stroncium/Humans/and/Sex/or/Disease/00193/

/No Relat betw/Barium/Humans/and/Sex/or/Disease/00193/

/Method/Determ/Barium/Bone/Humans/Radioactivational analysis/

/00193/

Determ/Stroncium/Bone/Humans/Radioactivational analysis/100 UG per G ashed tissue

/00193/

/Determ/ Barium/Bone/Humans /Radioactivational analysis/l00 UG per G ashed tissue/

/00193/

/INCR/Stroncium/Humans/ Adults/age 19-74/CompW/ Children/0-13/

Comparison of mini-abstract, author's summary and abstracts from Chemical Abstracts and Biological Abstracts. Reproduced from Lunin by permission of Drexel University. The abstract from Biochemical journal is reprinted by permission of the Biochemical Society, Portland Scientific

Press; the abstract from Biological Abstracts by permission of biosis and the abstract from Chemical Abstracts by permission of Chemical Abstracts Service. Note that one abstract follows the author's summary very closely and the other is merely a further abbreviation of it.

BA 32118857,1958

18857. Sowden, Elenor M., and B. R. Stitch. (Med. Res. Council Radiobiol. Res. Unit, Atomic Energy Res. Establishment, Harwell, Didcot, Berks, Eng.) Trace elements in human tissue. 2. Estimation of the concentrations of stable strontium and barium in human bone. Biochem. Jour. 67(1): 104109. 1957. A method is described for the determination of strontium and barium in human bone by radioactivation analysis. Results of analyses of 35 bone samples, from normal persons of both sexes and different ages, are given. The concentrations of Ba and Sr were of the order of 7 and 100 pg/ g of ashed tissue respectively. No relationship between sex or disease of individuals with Sr and Ba concentration was noted. The concentration of Sr in the age group 1-13 years was significantly lower than that in the group 19-74 years. No significant difference was found in the concentrations of Sr and Ba in the various bones of those individuals examined. Results obtained in this survey are discussed and compared with those of other workers.-Auth summ.

CA 51: 18184,1957

11. Estimation of the concentrations of stable strontium and barium in human bone. Eleanor M. Sow-den and S. R. Stitch. Ibid. 104-9. A method based on the technique of Harrison and Raymond has been used for the demo of Sr and Ba in human bone by radioactivation analysis. Results of analyses of 35 bone samples, from normal persons of both sexes and different ages, are given. The concns. of

Ba and Sr were found to be of the order of 7 and 100-/g. of ashed tissue, resp. No relation between sex or disease of individuals age group 0-13 yrs. was significantly lower than in the group 19-74 yrs. No significant difference was found in the concns of Sr and Ba in the various bones of those individuals examined. The results obtained in this survey are discussed and compared with those of other workers.

The modular index entries would suggest descriptive terms, drawn from representative index vocabularies, that could be used intact, with refinement or with augmentation, to index the abstract derived from the modular package. The representative index vocabularies used as sources for the modular index entries were to be derived from the current indexes or authority lists of the recipient abstracting and indexing services and would thus be reflective of the indexing styles and policies of these services. A test of the concept was performed in the field of heat transfer, this being a highly interdisciplinary subject of potential interest to a large number of abstracting services.

Sets of abstracts/index entries were prepared and submitted to several services for routine processing. The services completed questionnaires to evaluate the concept. It was concluded that it was possible to produce a content analysis, in modular form, that could be used as input to a variety of abstracting services, but that the majority of services were reluctant to relinquish their autonomy in order to participate in the type of clearing house implied by the modular approach.

Mini-abstracts

The term "mini-abstract" is rather imprecise. It could mean merely a short abstract. As used by Lunin, however, the term refers to a highly structured abstract designed primarily for searching by computer. It is, in fact, a kind of cross between an abstract and an index entry, and Lunin defines it as a "machine-readable index-abstract" The terms used in the abstract are drawn from a controlled vocabulary and are put together in a specified sequence. For example, the statement "There is a decreased amount of zinc in the blood of humans with cirrhosis of the liver" would be written:

/Decr/Zinc/Blood/Humans/Cirrahosis/Liver

Note that the abstractor tries to keep to a sequence of terms as close as possible to the normal sentence structure. The contents of a document may be described in some detail through the use of a series of such stylized statements. While intended primarily to facilitate searching by computer, Lunin's mini-abstracts can also make sense to the intelligent reader.

Telegraphic abstract is also imprecise. It implies a document representation that is presented very parsimoniously: not in complete sentences and resembling a telegram. Indeed it might just be a string of terms without syntax. Lunin's mini-abstracts are telegraphic in style. The term "telegraphic abstract" was used to refer to an essential component in the early computerized retrieval system developed at Western Reserve University.

❒

7

Online Technical Support Systems

The use of computers and the creation of a standardized MARC format were significant achievements in the evolution of library automation, but their full impact was best realized within the context of other important development occurring between the aid-1960s and the mid-1970s. The cornerstone of these development was a radical change in mass market computer technology, characterized by faster processing, increase storage capability, and decreasing hardware prices. Systems such as the IBM 1401, popular in library use during the early and mid-1960s, comprised what came to be known as second-generation computers. Faster and incorporating far greater memory in less physical space than the vacuum table based computers of the 1950s, The rapid and quantum advances were made in solid state computer technology that even by the mid-1960s, newer models of computers were so much more powerful than the IBM 1401 that a third generation was hailed. The magnitude of technological advancement even within the third generation can be shown by comparing two disk transport systems, the IBM 2314 and the IBM 3330, from the late 1961s and early 1970s. The 2314 utilized removable pack; a piece of information could be assessed in an average of 75 milliseconds, and information could be read into memory at a rate in excess of 800,000 characters per second.

As processing speeds and storage capabilities were increasing, the size and price of the machinery were decreasing. By the early 1970s, computers appeared on the market that were comparatively so small and inexpensive that they warranted the label of "minicomputer." Slower and less powerful than their contemporary larger counterparts, minicomputers processed capabilities that matched and exceeded the most sopnisticated second-generation computer of barely a decade before, and at a mere fraction of the price. In a 1977 issue of Library Technology Reports, William Scholtz put the comparison in perspective:

> In 1960, the IBM 1620 computer needed a room that was approximately 20 by 30 feet... In 1974, a similar machine in terms of capability took up.a space that was approximately 3 feet by 3 feet. [and] could perform identical tasks to those performed by the IBM 1620 in about one quarter the time. And finally, the cost to buy the 1974 machine was about what it cost to rent the IBM 1620 for one month.

The chief implication of these technological advancements in terms of library application was to usher in the era of online automation. Although the mini-computer would play its own role in this development, earlier online library systems in the last 1960s were based on use of the larger third generation computers. The computers for these systems were shared among a number of users and invariably were located outside the library in a centralised data processing facility.

Another difference between second-and third generation facilities was the extent of the latter's timesharing capacity. Second-generation systems were generally not capable of timesharing; the computer processed one job before moving to the next job in the queue. The remarkable advancements in speed, all tasks associated with design, and storage capacity in third generation systems allowed them to process a number of jobs simultaneously or so it seemed. In actual fact, the computer still performed one task at a time, but could handle several jobs coincidentally and execute tasks so quickly that it appeared to each user that the computer was interacting exclusively with their programmes, files, and commands.

Although the technological environment for online library systems has been in place since the late 1960s, their realization by the late 1970s was still in a stage of infancy if viewed within the context of the totality of libraries in the United States. Despite the decrease in computer hardware prices that characterised the late 1960s, the design, implementation, and maintenance of an online system were still prohibitively expensive for all but a few libraries during the late 1970s, and even most of these required special grant funding.

Between the late 1960s and late 1970s, three trends evolved in the development of online library systems. The first consisted of pioneering in-house projects in single institutions. The second centered around the evolution of what came to be known as "bibliographic utilities." The third trend was the emergence of private enterprises developing prepackaged "turnkey" automated library systems. These three trends are discussed in the remainder of this chapter.

In-house Circulation Developments

Much as with unit-record equipment and computerized online batch processing, the earliest online library system focused on circulation.

Illinois State Library System

One of the first online systems was at the Illinois State Library in Springfield, in late 1966, at a time when many other libraries were designing full offline systems. The backbone of the system was an IBM 1620 computer located in the state processing facility. The equipment in the library consisted of IBM 1033 prints and 1031 card readers, which were similar in operation to the 357 Data Collection System, requiring insertion of machine-readable book cards and borrower identification badges. Rather than producing transaction cards or recording transaction data on tape, however, the 1031 at the Illinois State Library transmitted data directly to the computer.

By later standard, the online system at the library was primitive. Although transaction information was conveyed directly to the computer as it occurred, it was stored on a separate daily transaction pack and was merged with the main circulation file only on a once-a-day batch processing basis. The system did not include item-specific online query, so that it was still necessary to use offline batch-produced circulation lists to trace circulation information pertaining to a given item. For these purposes, the system was much like wholly offline batch processing systems. What set it apart from those, however, was its ability to perform two important functions online: checking borrower registration numbers for validity and checking each returned item against an online holds file. Each time a borrower identification card was inserted into the designated slot of the 1031, the borrower number was automatically checked against a computer-stored file of valid borrower numbers. If the borrower's number did not have a counterpart in the file, that fact was generated immediately on the 1033 printer. This was a major improvement over completely offline operations. Where such validation, if done at all, could be performed only by manual look up in a printed directory of borrower numbers.

The other important online function of the Illinois State Library system was checking holds, and that had equally important implications. When the book card of a returned item was placed in the 1031 for discharge, the call number was checked against an online list of call numbers of items placed on hold. If the cell number of the returned item matched a call number in the holds file, a message was automatically generated on the 1033 printer showing call number, identification number of the patron who had placed the item on hold, and the data when the hold had been placed. In this manner, greater control over holds was realized than was possible in offline batch processing computerized circulation systems.

Midwestern University System

Another early online circulation system was implemented in late 1967 at Midwestern University in Wichita Falls, Texas. The Midwestern system was unique in that it was, at least insofar as its designers know, the first and perhaps only online circulation system to operate on an IBM 1401 computer, a decidedly second-generation machine.

Like the Illinois State Library system, Midwestern used IBM 1031 input stations and 1033 printers, validated borrower identification numbers, and checked items against an online holds file. But it went further than the Illinois system in several important respects. Not only did the Midwestern systems check borrower numbers during a charging operation for general validation, but it also determined if a borrower had any outstanding overdue items or unpaid fines. If so, the computer generated an immediate list of the charges on the 1033 printer. The Midwestern system had an online query capability, albeit restricted to searching on a borrower number. The keying in of a number prompted the computer to respond by printing a list on the 1033 containing all items charged to that borrower. But perhaps the fundamental difference in the Midwestern system was that the main circulation file was online in the strict sense of the term, with the file being updated immediately upon completion of each transaction, rather than in a batch mode.

Eastern Illinois University System

In September 1968, the Booth Library at Eastern Illinois University in Charleston began to operate its own version of a online circulation system using a third generation IBM 360/Model 50 computer and the IBM 1031 input stations and 1033 printers. The Booth system had the basic functional characteristic of the Midwestern system, but with an important additional query feature. The Midwestern system had query capability by patron number; the Booth system supplemented this with item query by call number. By entering a particular two-digit code followed by a call number, a terminal operator could retrieve bibliographic information and current circulation data about a specific item.

A further extension of this search capability was a scanning command that displayed bibliographic entries in call number-sequence. Since the Booth Library online file was an inventory file containing an abbreviated bibliographic record for nearly even item in the library not just items currently charged out-the scanning capability allowed shelflist searching of the entire library collection. The structure and search capabilities of this system suggested possible extension as a public-access tool, and in fact plans were announced to locate a public access CRT terminal near the card catalogue in fall 1971. Still, the known item query capability of the Eastern. Illinois system allowed more immediate information about the circulation status of an item-ever if the query had to be generated by a circulation attendant-than was possible in an offline system.

Mini-computer-Based Hybrids

In the early 1970s, a number of academic libraries began to incorporate minicomputers in their circulation operations. A significant feature of these systems was that at least part of the processing hardware was located in the library itself, although a larger computer, outside the library, still played an integral role. Typically, the minicomputer in the library contained certain files for immediate online access and captured transaction data for later batch transmission to as larger computer located outside the library on which the main circulation file was stored.

One of the most common mini-computers in this type of configuration was the IBM System/7 in use in circulation control in at least six libraries by early 1974. In the system operational at the University of Pennsylvania in Philadelphia, five online files were stored in the minicomputer. Each of these contained critical information against which various types of transactions were checked. There were three item files against which renewal attempts and discharges were checked. A call number file contained the call number of all items placed on hold, the access number file contained a list of all items recalled, and a reserve book file contained all items for which in request had been placed to transfer the item to a reserve book collection upon its return. Another file, against which all patron identification numbers were checked, was the restricted patron file, containing a lost of borrower identification numbers of all users whose further attempts to charge materials were to be blocked for some reason. The fifth online file was the daily transaction file, which recorded the day's activity. Once a day, this file was transmitted to the main computer, an IBM 370/Model 168, located at the university data processing center, for batch updating of the main circulation file. This transmission, usually involving information for about 3,000 transactions, required about 30 minutes.

For the most part, improvements, gained in the Online circulation systems of the late 1960s and early 1970s over what was possible in an offline system were focused on immediate access to information about restricted items, such as holds, and better control of patron privilege. Although improvements regarding access to information about restricted items enhanced public service by allowing more rapid reshelving of returned items and a better system for regulating holds and ensuring identification upon return, these benefits were not always immediately evident to the average library user. The second common capability, immediate access to Online delinquent patron files, could as likely cause ill feelings as goodwill between the library and its users. The lack of reliable backup measures, inexperience in dealing with online systems, and continued reliance on batch-produced circulation lists combined to make early online circulation systems less than revolutionary in terms of public service. At least one fadlity, the Simon Fraser University Library, had so many problems and so much user discontent with its online system that it abandoned on line and reverted to its earlier offline system.

Ohio State University System

Perhaps the outstanding example during the early 1970s of online circulation system that could, in fact, facilitate user services to a degree not possible in an offline system was demonstrated by Ohio State University's Library Control System. The entire philosophy behind the design and 'application of the system for the Ohio State University libraries was, as described by Hugh Atkinson, "that the system should be one which would speak to the problems of its users rather than simply the problems of the library." These problems included, among others, a decentralized library structure consisting of a main library and more than 20 branches. Only one catalogue-the main library's—contained complete information for all items in all 21 libraries.

Similar to several earlier online circulation systems, Ohio State opted for an "inventory" file approach in which the main machine-readable database contained records for all items in the libraries rather than an "absence" file, which would have contained records only for those items in circulation. This principles as fundamental at Ohio State since the system was to be used as a locator file as well as for circulation operations. A massive conversion effort-perhaps the largest of its kind carried out by any library to that date-was contracted to a vendor, which put into machine-readable form records containing call number, unique item number, author, title, date of publication. Library of Congress card number, language code, from of publication code, and holding for each of 1 million distinct titles and 2.5 million items.

The key to the Ohio State system was its items query capability. Searching was possible by call number, title key, and a combination author / title key. When the desired item was retrieved, it was possible to see which library or libraries on campus owned a copy of the item, and whether each copy was charged out. Search terminals were available in the main library and in most of the branches. Thus, the entire union catalogue of the libraries' holdings could be assessed from any library in the system. Although this in itself was a fundamental improvement over the single union catalogue in the main library. An item not already checked out in one library could be charged on terminals located in any a copy was found to be available in a different branch library, the circulation attendant could issue a command that would generate a charge slip in the branch library that had the copy. The item would be retrieved in that library and placed on a shelf to await later pickup by the patron. The online union catalogue, showing location and circulation status of each item throughout the system, combined with the capability of remote charging to remove much of the patron uncertainty that was inherent under prior circumstances.

The Ohio State University library system, like all other online system, was not entirely free of problems, but many of them could eventually be alleviated by design changes and the system was such an improvement over earlier conditions that the problems were of comparatively minor consequence. The impact of this system on library service was probably best exemplified by the fact that, during the first 18 months it was in operation, circulation at the Ohio State University libraries increased by more than 40 percent. The system was an important achievement owing to its scale of implementation, its query capabilities, and its emphasis on public service problem solving. The same system was later taken by Atkinson to the University of Illinois and implemented; today it is the basis of an important networking system in libraries throughout Illinois.

Apart from circulation, the late 1960s and early 1970s saw the development of a number of online technical processing systems. One of the earliest acquisitions systems was designed at the Washington State University Library in Pullman and was implemented in 1968; an on line serials control system was up and running at University Level in Quebec the same year. Predating both of these was the beginning of a comprehensive online library system at the Redstone Scientific Information Center in Alabama. Some parts of the system. were operational as early as 1966. And by the early 1970s, acquisitions, cataloguing, authority control, serials check-in, and circulation were online.

Offline computerization had been an important development in acquisitions, providing for machineassisted production of purchase orders, improved methods of fiscal control, and more timely updating and generation of status lists. Still, a significant amount of from handling and paper file maintenance remained in many of these systems. The online acquisitions systems developed in the late 1960s and early 1970s represented major improvements by reducing the amount of manual handling and maintenance of paper products, as well as further enhanced those functions that had been performed well in offline computerized system.

Acquisitions

One of the more ambitious projects in the late 1960s was carried out at the Oregon State University Library at Corvallis.

Christened LOLITA, this online acquisitions system required nearly seven "staff years" in programming, systems, and clerical labour to develop. It contained three Online files: order / in-process file contained three display screens of information input when an order was placed, and updated as an item passed through the acquisitions and cataloguing procedures. The first screen included basic bibliographic data, the second screen contained accounting data, and the third screen allowed for local cataloguing information such as call number and location. The amount of time and file maintenance that this system saved the staff, particularly when compared with a manual system, was considerable.

LOLITA generated four paper copies of each order, two going to the vendor, one later used as a cataloguing workshop, and one retained as a general hard copy record for the library. The two copies for library use were a reduction over most offline systems, and some libraries went even further. With the online acquisitions systems in use at the University of Massachusetts Library and the Dartmouth College Library, neither library retained any paper copies of the order form in technical processing at all.

One of the greatest contributions made by online systems in general was the expansion of access points, and these early acquisition systems were no exception. It was possible with an offline system to produce lists or maintain paper copies of order forms by more than one point of access, such as by order number, author, and title if desired, but that merely increased the number of' lists to be consulted or files to be maintained. As a result, the number of listing parameters was usually minimized in offline systems. In online systems, all files and their indexes could be maintained in the computer, and multiple access points to a single record would not mean an increase in hard copy materials to be consulted or maintained. LOLITA, however, only provided to access points, order number and author, to each record in the system

The early online acquisitions systems retained some of the capabilities that had been included in their offline predecessors, but the newer systems were much improved in quality, speed, and ease of handling. LOLITA, along with several other early systems, provided for handling of partial shipments and authorization of partial invoice payments, capabilities that were handled, if at all, only with some difficult by offline systems. The fund accounting component of LOLITA was also successful. A year-end encumbrance report could be generated in 20 minutes, and LOLITA was to only much faster, not also judged more accurate and detailed in a controlled comparison with manual ledgers.

Perhaps the most important characteristic of online acquisitions systems was that, in most cases, it was only one part of a broader integrated technical processing system that brought the acquisitions and cataloguing functions closer together. The online order record, upon receipt of an item, became an online cataloguing record. This greatly reduced duplication between acquisitions and cataloguing and also provided an end product consisting of a machine-readable bibliographic record for each item entering the collection. In LOLITA, the final steps in the online processing after an item had been received were for a cataloguer to verify the bibliographic information originally entered by the acquisitions department and the complete the record by adding local cataloguing data. The completed record was removed from the online file, but not before it had been copied onto magnetic tape as a permanent machine-readable record.

One of the most comprehensive uses of MARC records evolved in the University of Chicago Library Data Management System. Orders could be searched against the MARC files, and there was a retrospective searching capability whereby incoming MARC records were searched against the local bibliographic file to identify previously created local records as potential candidates for bibliographic upgrading by the new matching MARC record. These features in one from or another could be found in other systems, but an interesting feature of the Chicago systems was its use of MARC tapes as a collection development tool. Subject profiles, defined by Library Congress classification numbers and ranges of numbers, could be maintained online, and each incoming MARC tape was matched against them.

The result was an offline list of items falling into each subject profile for use in identifying potential orders for the library. The system also allowed access to these lists online if a bibliographer wished. The system also allowed access to these lists online if a bibliographer wished. Supplementing the LC class number profiles were certain national bibliography online profiles used to identify potential orders from an area studies prospective. In addition to profiles designed to identify items of potential interest for the library, the University of Chicago system also included a capability designed to assist in better control over blanket orders from publishers. The first four digits of an International Standard Book Number (ISBN), MARC field 020/ are unique to each publisher. Each record on the MARC tapes was automatically searched on these first four digits at Chicago. The system could then generate lists of items published by each publisher with whom Chicago had a blanket order arrangement, and these lists could be used to assist in monitoring receipt of blanket order items.

Ballots

Several of the largest research libraries in the United States were interested in the concept of an online integrated technical processing system as early as the mid-1960s, although actual systems could be implemented at these institutions only after several years of planning, design, and experimentation. These of the more well publicized of these large-scale efforts included the Northwestern Online. Total Integrated System (NOTIS), the University of Chicago Library Data Management System mentioned earlier, and Standford University's Bibliographic Automation of Large Library Operations using a Time sharing System (BALLOTS). Without minimizing the importance of achievements elsewhere, BALLOTS was perhaps the most sophisticated online technical processing system developed in the early 1970s. Because of its later adoption as the online bibliographic component of the Research Libraries Group (RLG), its impact on American librarianship during the 1970s and early 1980s has been greater than any other system originally designed for use by a single institution. An experimental version of BALLOTS was brought online as early as 1969, but it was not until 1972, after further design and modification, that the system was dully implemented. It ran on the Standford University campus computer, an IBM 360/Model 67, with a Digital Equipment Corporation PDP 11 mini-computer in the library as a front-end communications processor.

The hardware for BALLOTS was in itself an important achievement. The selection of terminals with a programmable capability was based on the design requirements for the terminal display features desired. Two important functional considerations were to allow for protected fields in an online record that could not be modified by a terminal operator, and at the same time to permit line insertion to allow expansion in length of certain non protected fields. At the time BALLOTS was being designed, either one of these further could be incorporated by using a non-programmable terminal, but not a combination of the two. Only a programmable terminal, such as the Sanders model could allow both protected and expandable fields. In addition, it was possible for several programmable terminals to share a single communications line rather than each requiring its own dedicated line.

BALLOTS was designed around several modules and contained four online files critical to technical processing. One was a MARC file, which held the most recent 6 to 12 months of MARC records from the Library of Congress. A second was an In-Process File (IPF), which contained a record for each item anywhere in the processing stage from initiation of an order to final cataloguing. Once received and catalogued, the record was transferred into a third file, the Catalogue Data File (CDF), which contained an online record for each item fully processed on BALLOTS. Fourth was a Reference File (REF), which included see references, see also references, and explanatory and history references.

When a request for an order was submitted a terminal operator first searched the MARC file to see if as corresponding MARC record was available. If a match was found, the operator requested an online ordering work form, which contained mnemonic fields into which information could be entered. Appropriate bibliographic data were automatically transferred from the MARC record to the work form, requiring the terminal operator to input only the additional information pertaining to the order, such as vendor code and accounting data. An online order record could easily be created for an item where there was no available MARC record, but this naturally required more time since bibliographic information had to be supplied from other sources and typed onto the Online work from offline products, such as purchase orders, a cataloguing workslip, and a temporary order slip, were printed each evening for all items entered into the In-Process File during the day. Stanford found the traditional 3" x 5" slip too small for its purposes and, as described by Veaner, "because copies of certain forms no longer had to be filed, the forms themselves could be designed around their data requirements rather than a filing cabinet size."

The online order from was updated as its status changed, such as when an item was received. After receipt was indicated the item was given to the cataloguing department for final processing. One of the helpful features of BALLOTS was its tracing procedure; the location of an item within the processing unit was kept up-to-date online ever to the name of the specific cataloguer handling the final processing. It was the responsibility of the cataloguing department, with item in hand, to verify and, if necessary, modify the information on the online record created in acquisitions and to add any additional pertinent data. Catalogue cards and spine labels were then printed offline, with the day's production of all cataloguing cards sorted into filing order sequence.

BALLOTS had a number of built-in features that made input and modification of records easy for a terminal operator and at the same time reduced the likelihood of operator error. Fields that were inappropriate for operator- input or modification were automatically protected so the operator could not even place the cursor in those positions on the screen display. After entering information into a nonprotected field, the operator could move the cursor to the next nonprotected field simply by depressing the shift and tab keys. Throughout the procedure were default protocols that assumed the operator's next most logical step but these could be overridden by the operator if an item required a typical treatment.

The system also had validation capabilities for certain types of information such as account codes. When an account code was entered by an operator onto the online order work from, the system checked the code validity. This check did not prevent a valid inaccurate code from being assigned to an item, but it did insure that nonexistent accounts could not be charged.

Ordering selected volumes of a multipart set hard always been a problem in acquisitions systems, but BALLOTS handled this in a way that minimized the work of the terminal operator and still allowed flexibility in subsequent processing. If, for example, volumes 1, 2, 3, 8 and 9 were being ordered, the operator merely typed 1-3 and 8-9 in an appropriate field on the order work from, and the system automatically "exploded" the record into five distinct records, one for each volume ordered.

One of the strongest features of the BALLOTS system was its search retrieval capabilities. Unlike most other technical processing systems. BALLOTS offered a wide complement of sear fields and allowed searching on truncated words, variant forms of entry, and keywords. A terminal operator could search the MARC file by Library of Congress card number, personal name, corporate or conference name, and title. The Catalogue Data File allowed for searching by all these elements, but also by Library of Congress subject headings, call number, and BALLOTS ID number. Searching of the In-Process and Reference files was more restricted than searching of the Catalogue Data File, but less restrictive than searching the MARC file.

As an automated technical processing system, BALLOTS was a landmark project far more sophisticated than earlier offline systems and more successful than its online contemporaries of the early 1970s. As might be expected, it had a tremendous impaction Stanford's operation, such as integrating technical processing functions more closely than before. The Acquisitions and Cataloguing departments,.

although remaining under separate supervision were physically consolidated. They had previously been located on different floors of the library. In addition, the number of staff was reduced. One-third of the staff positions in the Order Division were eliminated, as were several positions that previously had been responsible solely for typing unit entry cards, duplicating and typing headings on them, a sorting them into filing order: all functions that were computerized under BALLOTS.

Although serials control is an integral part of technical processing, development of automated systems for serials handling has usually been carried out somewhat independently of acquisitions and cataloguing. This had been the case with unit-record and offline batch processing systems and was equally typical of online development. Offline systems allowed libraries greater control in some aspects of the serials operation, particularly in claiming, and enabled holdings lists to be updated and printed much more frequently and with far less staff effort than in unit-record systems. A considerable amount of manual card and paper handling still was required, however, and the offline lists were a problem in that they tended to be generational, with periodic supplements to other periodic supplements to less frequent master cumulations. Online capabilities offered the potential of reducing the amount of handling and making available up-to-date records of holdings in one place.

In the early 1970s, and on perhaps a somewhat less dramatic scale, the system developed at the UCLA Biomedical Library was to serials what BALLOTS was to acquisitions and cataloguing and what the Ohio State University system was to circulation. Although not the first online serials control project to be implemented, the UCLA system was generally considered more sophisticated and flexible than its contemporaries. Design objectives included, among others, the elimination of all card handling and the generation of fewer hard copy lists. By 1972, there were records in the serials control database for about 12,000 titles, slightly more than half the library's current subscriptions. The format of the online records was similar to MARC, but with fewer fields. When an issue of a title was received, the operator retrieved the online record and updated it by keying a simple code. Other codes were defined for updating holdings when back or skipped issues were received.

In additional to the check-in operation, the system had automatic overdue detection and binding status monitoring. Keyword searching of the database could be performed, an especially crucial capability given the complexity and similarity of serials titles. The search component also allowed retrieval of titles by fixed field.

Online systems had many advantages over those based entirely on batch processing. The volume of paperwork and hard copy files was reduced, as well as the amount of staff time required for their maintenance. Although the "up-to-the-second information" characteristic of online was highly touted, many of the earlier systems only partially had this capability, as evidenced by some circulation functions that used minicomputers as front-end communications systems. Nevertheless, even those systems were able to store some of their more critical files in virtually current status.

One of the most important characteristics of online systems was search retrieval capability. Again, some of the early ones are very restricted in inquiry capability, but others were considerable sophisticated, such as at Ohio State University, Stanford, and the UCLA Biomedical Library described earlier. The design, implementation and continuing operation of the more sophisticated online systems were landmark achievements, but their costs were correspondingly high. In many instances, funding was aided throng grants or heavily subsidized by the host institution's general operating budget; the costs were far out of reach of the vast majority of libraries. It was estimated, for example, that the continuing production and development costs in operating BALLOTS doe a single month in 1974 were $34.225, and this figure pales in comparison to the design and development costs incurred before the system's implementation.

Bibliographic Utilities

Left with an alternative of in-house, single-library development projects, only the largest and most well endowed libraries could have used an online system for any technical support systems during the 1970s. As early as 1967, however, a second alternative was being formulated, and the outgrowth of this and similar efforts was the evolution of four system-OCLC, RLG, WLN, and UTLAS-whose use by the early 1980s, extended into several thousand libraries on the North American continent.

OCLC

Although some libraries continued to develop their own in-house systems for certain library functions, it was apparent by the mid- 1970s that automated cataloguing in particular was evolving in a different direction. The basis of this transformation was the Ohio College Library Center (OCLC), a system based on the simple premise that, recognizing minor local variations, cataloguing data for a given item were essentially similar from library to library. The Library of Congress MARC project had been as major breakthrough in the concept of shared cataloguing information in an automated environment, but the general pattern of sharing had been unidirectional and on an institution-by-institution basis. MARC tapes were sent from the Library of Congress to subscribing institutions, each of which then loaded the tapes and manipulated the data on its own computer. The idea that evolved for OCLC was a central file of cataloguing records that could be maintained on a single computer system and accessed through terminals sharing dedicated communications line connected to that computer. Not only would this enable libraries to share a MARC file, but it would centralize development costs of the system and virtually eliminated the need for each participating library to use the host institution's computer system.

Because the Library of Congress catalogued only portion of the universe of materials received by libraries, and since the MARC tapes included only the OCLC online system was the capability for allowing original input of records, using the MARC format, by the participating libraries themselves. The impact of this is seen by the fact that even by the end of the decade, less than one-fourth of the master bibliographic records in the OCLC database had been supplied by the Library of Congress.

OCLC was chartered in 1967 and Frederick G. Kilgour named as its executive director. System production first began with offline batch processing in 1970; 54 member academic libraries in Ohio submitted punched IBM cards with Library of Congress card numbers of items for which they wanted catalogue cards produced. The punched cards were searched against a file consisting of the Library of Congress MARC records, and when a match occurred, catalogue cards were generated and sent back to the requesting library within two weeks. In 1971, OCLC went online, installing terminals that allowed each library to search the growing OCLC On-Line Union Catalogue (OLUC), the bibliographic database of the system. The library could order catalogue cards merely depressing a couple of command keys on the keyboard attached to the CRT display terminal.

During the first several years of OCLC online operation, a number of far-reaching decisions were made that would enhance- and sometimes plague the cooperative effort. The display format revolved around the concept of a bibliographic "master record"; in theory there was to be only one'record in the database for any given bibliographic entity. When this master record for an item was retrieved by a library, any of the MARC fields could be modified to reflect local practices with respect to subject headings, forms of name entry, local call number, and so on; virtually any element in the record could be modified.

All local changes were reflected on the catalogue cards printed offline at OCLC and mailed to the library (and eventually on the library's magnetic tapes of its cataloguing activity when this service became available). These modifications, however, were not stored permanently online for the library. Therefore, when a library retrieved a record it had previously used for cataloguing, the bibliographic master record was displayed online, without the local modifications that the library had previously made.

The lack of capability to permanently store local information was probably justifiable in OCLC's initial stages. The amount of storage required to maintain this data for each cataloguing use of each record by each library would have been enormous, especially since most members of OCLC at that time had a low incidence of adding copies for titles they had already catalogued once. Nevertheless, it was not long after the system went online that some members began to express concern over the lack of a permanent online record containing local modifications for previously catalogued materials.

A characteristic of OCLC during the 1970s was a perpetual gap between announced plans and actual implementation, and the permanent storage and display of local cataloguing data-or at least of a scaled-down version of local holdings from selected fields-perhaps provides the most exemplary illustration. In early 1974 "Definition and Use of the 049 Holding Field," detailing a critical field used to record local data for card production and tape purposes, was published by OCLC partially in anticipation of an impending change, which would allow storage and display of modifications to master records. The actual change proved far less than imminent. Five years later, in 1979, OCLC's development schedule projected the capability of local holdings display for current cataloguing records to be available to members in January 1980, with access to local information for previously catalogued materials available sometime later. But less and less discussion of this capability emanated from corporate headquarters and the capability eventually disappeared from all development schedules.

The strategy initially used in creating the online file of bibliographic master records in OCLC revolved around the creation of as large a database as possible in as little time as possible. This may be over generalization, but there is little doubt that it was prevalent enough so that a great many of the permanent master records entered into the database by member libraries in the early years suffered in quality and completeness of information. Master records, particularly for retrospective cataloguing entered into the database, were frequently created from a description taken solely from the shelflist card of the first member library to convert the title. Thus quality and completeness depended in great part on any given library's past shelflisting practices, on the library's policy for input of new records into the database, and, beyond that, on the accuracy of the terminal operator. The philosophy of rapid creation of a database at the expense of detail and completeness of record could be seen in OCLC's approach in 1975 to providing records for serials titles, for which a specifically designed MARC format had only recently become available. To greatly increase the number of serials records in a short time, tapes of the Minnesota Union List of Serials (MULS) were loaded into the OCLC database. Although MULS contained accurate information as far as it went, it was primarily a locational tool and provided very abbreviated bibliographic data for cataloguing purposes.

Perhaps the greatest quality control complication in the long run was the extreme difficulty of upgrading master records when a mistake was detected or information found to be incomplete. Written forms had to be completed by a member library and mailed to OCLC; when received, the master record was examined by OCLC staff and modified according to the reported additions or changes. This process was time-consuming and cumbersome for member libraries, and not exactly a foremost staffing priority at OCLC. The result was that a library could easily retrieve a master record containing an obvious typographical error that presumably had been modified locally by any number of other libraries for their own card production, but that remained in the master record due to backlogs at OCLC in record upgrading. Owing to the prominent role of the OCLC database in the Conversion of Serials (CONSER) project, a limited number of libraries were given the capability of making permanent online modifications to OCLC serials master records from their own terminals, thus bypassing the manual error reporting procedure. This proved a tremendous success. The possibility of enabling a small number of libraries a similar online capability for records in other formats was a topic of discussion for several years, and was finally initiated in mid-1984. The approach used in creating its database and the difficulty in correcting errors in master records earned OCLC a reputation in some quarters as a "dirty database." To be certain, many early records in the database did suffer from lack of quality control. An often overlooked factor by critics, however, was that OCLC was an experiment without direct precedent and included among its membership a segment of the library community that had virtually no previous experience with any type of library automation. OCLC was not the first online system used for collective representation of cataloguing data from a number of independent libraries, but immediate predecessors were based on centralized input and thus centralized control. This was quite different from the structure of OCLC, in which any member library could input an original bibliographic master record for an item. Given this degree of autonomy and decentralization, combined with the lack of previous experience with library automation on the part of most of its members, and a lack of precedence to gauge the implication of shared databases, the early 1970s were an individual and cooperative learning experience for OCLC members which served to demonstrate both the strong points and the problem areas of cooperative ventures in library automation.

During its first year of online operation. OCLC remained a cooperative venture of Ohio academic libraries. During 1972, membership was extended to Ohio non-academic libraries, and in 1973 to libraries outside the state. Although the major computer facilities were to remain centralized at OCLC headquarters, a decentralized approach to the provision of general support services emerged by the mid-1970s. OCLC and various independent state and regional agencies entered into contracts for the broke ring of OCLC services and for provision of training and ongoing assistance. Some of these networks had predated OCLC; others were formed in direct response to the need for an agency to provide OCLC services in a particular area. Two exceptions to the general pattern of independent brokering were the formation of OCLC Western (referred to as PACNET-the OCLC Pacific Network), consisting of several branch offices on the Pacific Coast, and OCLC Europe, both being service agencies under the direct administration of OCLC. The independent affiliate networks, which have usually numbered about 20, have remained administratively separate from OCLC a relationship that has at times worked to the benefit of OCLC and at other times served as a source of conflict.

Within four years after OCLC's decision in 1973 to expand its base of participation beyond Ohio, the number of libraries using the system had increased to more than 800. Increasing numbers of public and special libraries were joining, but the majority of new members continued to be academic libraries. These included many members of the Association of Research Libraries as well as medium-sized university libraries, but an influx of new participants continued from among the ranks of four year colleges, a pattern that underscored OCLCs role in introducing automation into smaller institutions. A major factor in the opportunity for these smaller academic libraries to join OCLC during these years was the availability of implementation grants from the Kellogg Foundation.

RLIN

The concept of resource sharing was the basis for the formation of a number of formal cooperative ventures during the 1970s. One such, begun in 1974, was the Research Libraries Group (RLG), comprised of Harvard, Yale, Columbia, and the New York Public Library. Its board goals focused on the sharing of resources, collection development, and preservation and conservation of library materials. RLG felt that a common automated bibliographic system would enhance cooperative efforts among member libraries. By early 1978, the four systems under final consideration for adoption included OCLC, Standford's BALLOTS, the University of Chicago Library Data Management System, and the New York Public Library bibliographic control system.

In spring 1978, RLG announced agreement with Stanford for the use of BALLOTS as the group's automated bibliographic component. Although RLG may merely have chosen what it considered to be the best available system, the choice drew strong reactions from within, and outside the group. In June of the year, Harvard announced withdrawal from RLG, although Director of Libraries Douglas Bryant indicated that the choice of BALLOTS was not the motivating factor. A wide spectrum of emotions was expressed throughout the library community concerning RLG's decision not to go with OCLC, which many saw as the emerging national bibliographic network. In comparing the online features of BALLOTS and OCLC, there is no question that BALLOTS was the far more sophisticated and flexible technical processing system. Unlike OCLC, it also provided for online storage and display of an individual library's cataloguing data in a network environment, as well as other features such as searching by title keyword and subject, not available on OCLC. Although on a smaller scale than OCLC, BALLETS had also proved capable of serving as a shared system as early as 1975 when seven public libraries in California entered into a networking arrangement with Stanford, and the number of libraries using it has increased since then.

The greatest source of resentment among OCLC libraries about RLG's selection of BALLOTS was probably not so much the choice itself as it was the accompanying implicit, and sometimes explicit, attitude that OCLC and its "ditty database" were unacceptable, and that the needs of RLG members were somehow quite apart from those of the rest of the library community-including those of many prestigious research libraries that remained ardent supporters of OCLC. Equally crucial in the reaction, OCLC had come to be recognized by then as much more than a shared cataloguing database. Because of library identifier symbols attached to each bibliographic record, OCLC had grown into a tremendous tool for facilitating interlibrary lending and, to many, was the most current and reliable source of occasional information available in the United States. The selection of another system by RLG virtually cut off those libraries and their collections from this source of information and ejected a major obstacle to their participation in resource sharing on a broader scale. To many OCLC libraries and even to those using neither system, his detachment seemed a conscious and motivated effort to minimize the role of RLG members in the broader context of American library cooperation. The reaction to RLG did little at that time or later to discourage the image of elitism. Full membership in RLG, in essence, required a library to be a member of the Association of Research Libraries (ARL), and this restricted potential membership in RLG to a pool of early 100 libraries. RLG permitted other libraries to apply for participant status, meaning a library could use and contribute cataloguing data, but the feeling was that this did little to soften the image of elitism.

BALLOTS, which in the RLG environment became the Research Libraries Information Network (RLIN), may have been functionally superior to OCLC as a technical processing system, but not all of its distinctions were carried over into the new network. At Stanford, the system had been, and remained, a full technicals processing system, which traced an item and built on its online record from the initial point of ordering to its final point of cataloguing. Crucial in this progression was the In-process File (IPF), described earlier in this chapter. Although any RLIN member library had searching access to Stanford's IPF, there was no capability for other members to build a similar file for their own institutions. Thus, one of the strongest features of the original BALLOTS, which provided the continuity for its realization a more complete technical processing system, did not exist under RLIN in its earliest manifestation for any library other than Stanford.

WLN

During the 1970s, work was also being conducted at the Washington State Library on the design of an online bibliographic system. Supported by a $1.2 million startup grant from the state legislature, the system went online in 1978, the Washington Library Network (WLN) was being used in 12 public and 9 academic libraries in the state, along with 2 libraries in Alaska. Later that year, 3 libraries in Idaho and 1 in Oregon joined WLN.

From the start, it was apparent that WLN was a well-designed. and highly sophisticated system. It included retrieval of local information, subject access, and, not long thereafter, authority control. WLN took a cautious approach to building its bibliographic database. As in RUN and OCLC, Library of Congress MARC tapes were loaded, but unlike the other two utilities, WLN established a standing policy to centrally review all records input by member libraries.

In January 1979, the library press reported that the National Library of Australia had signed for membership in WLN had sold its system software to the National Library. The distinction was significant. All three of the major utilities OCLC, RLIN, and WLN-were based on a centralized computer system linked through telecommunications lines to terminals in member libraries; none of the utilities up until that time had attempted to transfer any part of its system for use in another computer.

In 1978, it was not entirely clear to American library community what role WLN would assume in national bibliographic networking. Although WLN was focusing on regional cooperation in the Pacific Northwest, OCLC had also been a geographically limited system at one time, and BALLOTS had been implemented in a single library. It seemed possible that a third nationally competing system may have been emerging in the form of WLN. In 1979, however, the network reaffirmed its regional emphasis, adopting a policy that expansion outside the Pacific Northwest would be restricted to sale of the WLN software in a manner similar to what had taken place with the National Library of Australia. In the years immediately following, a number of such transactions occurred, including sales to the Southeastern Library Network (SOLINET), the University of Illinois, and the University of Missouri. Membership in the WLN network in the Pacific Northwest had increased to 60 members by 1980 and, as OCLC had done slightly more than two years before, WLN modified its government structure to reflect the expansion of its membership base beyond a single state.

UTLAS

Although its impact in the United State has been limited, the University of Toronto library Automated System (UTLAS) was a fourth major online bibliographic networking system to have emerged on the North American continent during the 1970s. Implemented in an online networking mode during the mid-1970s, UTLAS had increased its membership to more than 200 libraries by the end of the decade.

UTLAS membership was limited primarily to Canadian libraries, with some important exceptions. In 1980, the network signed its first member in the United States, the Rochester, New York, Institute of Technology. The following year, UTLAS signed a million-dollar agreement with a Japanese firm to broker UTLAS in Japan. The system did not make concerted efforts to expand into the United States, but it is noteworthy that in 1981, in a comprehensive comparison of the four major utilities, the University of California at Berkeley ranked UTLAS first in overall technical capability. The University did not, however, opt for UTLAS. In 1984, UTLAS opened a U.S. branch office in New York, and it will be interesting to see what impact this will have on its position in the nation. Over the years, each of the four bibliographic utilities has strived to become more than simply a shared cataloguing database. Development efforts by one or more have gone into acquisitions subsystems, serials check-in capabilities, circulation systems, interlibrary loan communications, online union lists, provision of Computer Output Microform (COM) catalogues, and terminal compatibility for searching other databases.

WLN, OCLC, and RLIN made a tremendous impact on librarianship in the United States during the 1970s in terms of providing online cataloguing capabilities, but their impact in circulation control, acquisitions, and serials check-in was negligible. Some libraries continued to develop their own in-house systems to handle these functions. However, another alternative emerged, particularly in the area of online circulation, in the form of commercial vendors of automated library systems.

Commercial Online Systems

Commercial enterprise played a pivotal role in library automation long before the advent of online systems. Automation *via* unit-record equipment had been almost the exclusive domain of IBM. Remington Rand offered unit-record equipment comparable to IBMs, but its impact on the library market was negligible. IBM continued its domination into the early 1960s, when offline computer processing came into use in some libraries. As the decade progressed, however, computers manufactured by other firms began to appear in universities, corporations, and municipal facilities. By the end of the decade, IBM was still the predominant name in computers for library applications, but it no linger maintained the exclusively it had once enjoyed.

During its years of dominance, IBM had been responsible in devoting time and effort to assist in applying its equipment to the library environment. Libraries certainly did not receive an undue share of attention, but IBM representative were often assigned to help libraries with implementing applications, and the corporation published descriptions of and guides for use of its equipment in library applications. The company also sponsored seminars, the most notable being a symposium held in Endicott, New York, in 1964.

Although IBM and its new competitors expressed at least nominal interest in library applications during the 1960s, it was evident that this was an infinitesimal share of the total computer market. According to estimates in the early 1970s, less than one-tenth of one percent of the computers in the United States were being using by libraries in the way. To make these facilities still less conductive as a market, even those with computers were inevitably using equipment purchased by host institutions for a variety of applications, the foremost usually not being those of the library. Libraries had little control in either the selection of equipment or in the decision to replace one manufacturer or model with another. As long as large-scale, multipurpose mainframes were the only available computers, libraries were essentially at the mercy of their host institutions. Although some libraries established excellent relations with their computer centers and did play a role in automation decisions, procurement was an unpredictable and uncontrollable environment for many.

The advent of minicomputers radically altered the computer field for libraries, enabling at least the large ones to perhaps purchase their own equipment and create a more predictable environment. A number of libraries did purchase their own equipment and designed applications software in-house in the 1970s, but another alternative began to emerge in that decade-the library specific commercial vendor of automated library systems. In terms of the total computer market as viewed by larger corporations, libraries were too few to attract a great deal of attention, but the potential volume demonstrated a suitable market for smaller and specifically library-oriented commercial ventures.

CLSI and Circulation

One early commercial venture came from Computer Library Systems, Inc., later shortened to CL Systems. Inc., and later again simply to CLSI. The company's first automation efforts involved acquisitions systems, and one of its first installations, in 1972, was at the Cleveland Public Library, which had been using a batch processing system on IBM equipment for eight years. In a description of the CLSI system at Cleveland Public, Richard Palmer observed that, over a five-year period, the cost of the new online system was expected to be less than one-half the cost of the IBM batch processing system, had it been continued. In addition, the new system offered broader and more library-specific features.

CLSI soon turned its attention toward circulation control. Its LIBS 100 system and other vendor-supplied systems introduced subsequently come to be known as "turnkey," a reference to the premise that, upon delivery and installation, virtually all that was required to make the system work was to plug it in and turn it on. Although in practice this has not always exactly proved to be the case, the idea was essentially sound and formed the basis on which these systems would become cost-effective alternatives to in-house development. As so many libraries had learned in implementing their own online or even batch processing systems, the cost of design and development were considerable. With a mass-marketed system, such up-front development costs could be distributed among many customers and hence would be far less for each library then independent design and development. With a turnkey system, programming expertise was not required of the library staff or even at the host institution. Perhaps most importantly, the library's minicomputer could be operated and maintained within the library itself, and the software was marketed by vendors whose entire business was specifically library applications.

Other vendors joined CLSI in the online circulation control market during the early and mid-1970s, not for several years the field was fairly unstable. Various companies entered and left the market, were purchased by other companies, and radically redesigned their systems. By 1975, five commercial vendors were offering turnkey automated circulation systems with varying degrees of online and offline capacity. Two years later, three of them had cased marketing efforts in the United States and another had been sold and its system totally redesigned. CLSI provided the only continuity in this short span of time.

The year 1977 was pivotal, however, in that several new vendors of circulation control systems entered the market and would prove more stable than most of their predecessors. Among these were Data Phase, Geac, and Universal Library Systems. Entering the 1980s, CLSI was still the leading force in the commercial market, with 177 installations and more than 300 other libraries remotely accessing computers located at one of the installation sites. The fastest growing computer was Data Phase with 50 installations, followed by Geac with 22. Gaylord, active since 1978, had 11 installations by 1981. Although not actively marketing in the United State since about 1977, the Plessey online circulation system popular in Great Britain had 9 users in the United States and Canada.

Acquisitions, Serials Control, and Cataloguing

With the exception of early CLSI efforts, commercial activity in online acquisitions and serials control has lagged behind circulation control and did not really begin to make an impact until the late 1970s and early 1980s. The primary source of commercial developments also differed between the two areas. For the most part, vendor-supplied online circulation control systems have resulted from new commercial ventures into the library marketplace. In acquisitions and serials control, in contrast many of the earliest efforts came from long established library vendors; book jobbers for acquisitions and subscription agents in serials control.

Baker and Taylor's offline BATAB system was available to libraries since the 1960s, and by the late 1970s the system had been redesigned, enhanced, and offered online as LIBRIS. Around the same time, Brodart also announced availability of an online acquisitions system. By the early 1980s, book jobbers had been joined by other vendors, such as Ringgold and Innovative Interfaces, in offering online acquisitions, as well as by each of the four bibliographic utilities. In addition, several vendors of circulation systems were in the process of testing acquisitions modules, promising even more competition.

Commercially available online serials control systems have appeared comparatively recently. Two major subscription agencies, Ebsco and Faxon, each announced plans for an online system in 1981, capable not simply of ordering, but encompassing functions such as check-in and claiming, and not limited to titles ordered through the respective agency. Ebsco eventually abandoned development of its own on line check-in component, while Faxon did incorporate one into its online system. Also in 1981, the MetaMicro Corporation of San Antonio, Texas, announced a serials control software package for minicomputer application, although active marketing of this system eventually ceased. Activity in the not-for-profit sector also showed signs of life in the early 1980s, exemplified by marketing of the CHECKMATE serials control system by the California Library Authority for Systems and Services (CLASS) and by OCLC planning efforts to make its rather dormant serials check-in subsystem more attractive. Changes in the OCLC sub-system were made in 1983, but had a negligible impact in attracting new users.

Although the bibliographic utilities emerges during the 1970s as the clearly predominant supplier of automated cataloguing systems, there were a few commercial attempts to penetrate the cataloguing market. One of these was the BIBNET system, announced by Information Dynamics Corporation in 1974. BIBNET was to operate similarly to OCLC in a number of ways: it was principally intended to be a shared cataloguing database; it was to contain member input master records as well as LC MARC records; the master database was to be stored on centralized computers; and library identifier symbols were to be affixed to each bibliographic record as an aid to interlibrary loan.

Several features of BIBNET were plaunyed conspicuously different from DCLC and attempted to answer some of DCLCs more pressing problem areas. Keyword-in-title search capability was to be available, along with plans for the eventual introduction of subject searching of the database. BIBNET users would be encouraged to access the system though a mini-computer housed in the library to facilitate local production of offline products and to reduce telecommunications cost. By using a minicomputer, libraries could retrieve records from the master database, copy them onto a cassette tape, and then break the telecommunications link. Master records copied onto the cassette would then be displayed on a CRT terminal connected to the mini-computer, modifications made to the records, and the revised records copied into a second cassette. Catalogue cards and other offline products could be printed locally, based on the modified records on the second cassette. Although access to BIBNET could be gained through means other than a minicomputer, the front-end interface was strongly promoted as the most useful for allowing flexibility.

Information Dynamics had ambitious intentions for BIBNET. Not only was it to contain post-1968 LC MARC records, but there was a plan to centrally input access points into the online system for more than 3.5 million. Library of Congress manual cataloguing records created between 1953 and 1968. When a library retrieved such an index entry, it could notify Information Dynamics through the system that it would like a full record in the database for that title.

Information Dynamics would then create a record in MARC format for the title requested and load it into BIBNET within four days.

BIBNET'S entry into the marketplace coincided with the rapid and successful expansion of OCLC. The system simply never established a firm position. A more successful venture was launched several years later by Informatics, Inc., with the introduction of MINIMARC. It was mini-computer-based, but with no pretense as a networking system. The entire LC MARC database was supplied on floppy diskettes. The library retrieved these records locally on its mini-computer and modified them according to need. For titles not found on the LC MARC database, the library could create and input records into its own working file. Catalogue cards and other offline products could be locally produced.

Since a premise of MINIMARC was local processing, the system did not incur the telecommunications charges as did use of a bibliographic utility, and the overall cost were not as per-unit-dependent. On the other hand the initial investment could be as tenfold that of joining a bibliographic utility, and monthly maintenance and other costs were substantial enough to make participation in a utility more economical for smaller libraries. A limiting feature of MINIMARC was that, as a non-networking system, its core database was restricted to LC MARC records and was therefore smaller than those of the bibliographic utilities. Since its emphasis was so much on being a local system, it did not serve in any capacity as an interlibrary loan locational tool. In 1981, however, Informatics, RLG, and the California Library Authority for Systems and Services (CLASS) announced availability of 'an interface whereby MINIMARC users would be able to search the RLIN database through. their MINIMARC system equipment, an arrangement that would enhance MINIMARC as a local system with access to a broader utility. By 1981, more than 30 libraries had installed MINIMARC, and the number had increased steadily since then.

Another successful commercial venture into automated cataloguing was the Carrollton Press REMARC project. In 1980,

Carrollton announced a five-year project in which it would convert more than 5 million Library of Congress cataloguing records, not included on MARC, to machine-readable from. Libraries could submit brief data to Carrollton, in either machine-readable, or nonmachine-readable form, to match against both the LC MARC database and the REMARC database being created by Carrollton. For items for which a record could be found, Carrollton would supply machine-readable bibliographic records containing relatively complete LC cataloguing data.

In addition to MINIMARC and REMARC as alternatives to the bibliographic utilities, a number of commercial book jobbers and COM vendors were maintaining machine-readable cataloguing databases for their customers. These were really a quite different matter, since initially with these stored databases, a customer did not have direct online access to its own database. This circumstance has been changing, as some of these vendors now provide online access.

In the late 1960s, the only choice for libraries implementing an online system was to design and develop it in-house and use a large mainframe computer housed in central facilities at their host institution. During the 1970s, additional alternatives emerged: systems designed and developed be bibliographic utilities and commercial vendors; systems that could be operated on library-owned mini-computers and, more recently, on micro-computers. What was once a very restricted environment has broadened into a increasing range of options. As with unit-record equipment and batch processing computerized systems, the use of Online has been a learning experience for those libraries implementing their own systems, for the bibliographic utilities, and for the commercial vendors. Libraries implementing online systems in the late 1960s and throughout the 1970s provided a valuable basis of experience upon which other institutions could draw. This building on experience has helped to create a more solid foundation of general principles and specific tenets for automation of technical processing operations, but changes in technology and increasing competition in the marketplace certainly give assurances that the options available to a library are not likely to become stagnant or mundane.

Copy Cataloguing Procedures and Workflow

Overview Copy Cataloguing

Simply stated, the purpose of copy cataloguing is to provide bibliographic access to books and other library materials and to get those materials to the shelves and available for use in a timely fashion. The final product of the copy cataloguing process is a bibliographic record, the final form of which is either a catalogue process is a bibliographic record, produced through the adaptation of an existing catalogue record ("copy") to local standards. Access to existing records is made possible through computer terminal connected to a bibliographic utility. Records in these huge database may appear in various levels of completeness and are contributed through two primary source: *(1)* The Library of Congress ("LC copy"), and *(2)* individual libraries representing members of the bibliographic records through such utilities has made possible the practice of "shared cataloguing" and has made revolutionized cataloguing for an item is replaced with the more streamlined task if reviewing and modifying existing records.

While many variations exist, the typical copy cataloguing operation includes the following basic components.

(a) Staff: copy cataloguers, supervisors, and so forth.

(b) Terminals for access to a bibliographic utility.

(c) Agreed upon criteria for judging acceptable or usable copy; that is, which types of catalogue records can be accepted without review and which require a more through review to verify the accuracy and appropriateness of the various record components.

(d) Procedures for searching and identifying the various types of copy.

(e) Policies and procedures for the dispensation of materials for which usable copy cannot be found: for example, route material for original cataloguing, or store material in holding are for processing at a later date.

(f) Optional procedures for simply copy cataloguing (*e.g.*, procedures for editing and adapting LC contributed copy) and complex copy cataloguing (*e.g.*, procedures for editing and adapting member contributed copy).

(g) Cataloguing priorities: which types of material will receive priority attention and which can be deferred until a later date. For example, materials destined for a course reserve or reference location are often catalogued before other material.

(h) Cataloguing standards and others support documents: for example, Anglo American Cataloguing Rules-2nd edition (AACR2), international standard Book Description (ISBD), Library of Congress subject Heading (LCSH), Cataloguing service bulletin (CSB), training manuals. Local cataloguing practice manual, OCLC/LC MARC formats, Library of Congress (LC) class schedules, technical bulletins, and so forth.

(i) Materials to be catalogued: 1he copy cataloguing operation is supplied books and other materials from several source-new purchases, gift collections, temporary "holding areas" (materials awaiting the availability of catalogue copy), and backlogs.

Optional activities often associated with the copy cataloguing operation include: catalogue maintains; processing and final shelf preparation of materials *e.g.*, property stamping, call number labelling, etc.); and procedures for the processing of added copies, added. volumes, withdrawals, and transfers.

Typical Copy Cataloguing Work Flow

Detailed procedures for recorded editing and criteria for evaluating acceptable or usable copy vary local policy and practice (for an excellent treatment of specific cataloguing procedures, see Dowell [1976]). While local variations exist, a typical workflow sequence for the copy cataloguing of library materials is as follows:

(a) Conduct search for copy on bibliographic utility. This step can be done at the library's options either in the acquisitions department (per-order searching) or the copy cataloguing unit at one of several points in the cataloguing workflow.

(b) Distribute materials to appropriate units and staff. The routing of materials is often based on the nature and complexity of the available copy.

(c) Check local catalogue / shelflist, if necessary, to identify current holdings and to avoided call number duplication. (Checking for call number duplication is often not done when using LC copy; rather, bibliographic records are checked for duplicate numbers at the time of filing or during the loading of tapes in to the on-line catalogue.)

(d) Check local authority file, if necessary to verify headings and access points.

(e) Edit record on-line: verify and/or complete descriptive cataloguing, subject cataloguing and classification, assign, accession numbers (*e.g.*, OCRs barcodes), produce cards and/or machine readable records (distributed by the bibliographic utility).

(f) Route material to appropriate unit for physical processing and shelf preparation.

(g) Receive catalogue/shelf cards or machine-readable tapes from the bibliographic utility. Verify records against input records (*e.g.*, purchase order, work form, tag-sheet) and spot-check for errors while filing in the catalogue/shelflist. Verify machine-readable records as they are loaded in to the on-line catalogue (generally accomplished through a computer programme).

(h) Route material for which no usable record could be found to a temporary "holding area". Search one or more times, at predetermined intervals, for usable copy.

(i) If copy can still not be found after a predetermined interval, route the material on for original cataloguing.

Available Copy

On a procedural level identifying the type of copy becomes somewhat more complex. Examples of several basic type of catalogue copy include: LC/ AACR2,LC/PreAACR2, CIP (LC Cataloguing in publication), member contributed, UK-MARC, minimal versus full level cataloguing, and similar edition ("close copy"). Copy cataloguers must be trained to recognize these and other variant forms of catalogue copy. Procedures are designed to handle general classes of copy based on the relative complexity of the editing process and degree of expertise required on the part of the cataloguer.

Various criteria determine the acceptability of each type of copy and prescribe the procedures for adapting the record for local use. For example, UK-MARC often requires more extensive verification and augmentation of headings, LC/CIP requires the completion of several fields within the record, and pre-AACR2 copy may require updating to AACR2 form.

The criteria which define "acceptable" or "usable" copy vary among libraries and are depend on local cataloguing standards/ practice, on-line catalogue capabilities, and network regulations. Often, locally established criteria are a function of the library's perception of the relative quality (accuracy and completeness) reflected in records of different types and forms various sources. For example, full-Ievel/LC/ AACR2 records are often accepted virtually as is, while member-contributed copy is subjected to closer scrutiny. The final judgment as to what constitutes acceptable copy often boils down to how much "quality" the library can afford; verification and editing of records increases both the time and cost associated with cataloguing materials and getting them to the shelves.

While judgments concerning acceptable copy are often subjective, some libraries have taken a more empirical approach. For example, a list of likely source of copy is drawn up and a random sample of records from each source of copy is drawn up and a random sample both as to the type and number of cataloguing errors. Each source is then ranked in order or overall record quality. Thus, copy from the high-ranking "reliable" source can be processed with minimal verification and editing, while those prone to error can be subjected to closer scrutiny.

Although such statistical techniques offer useful objective data, the process of setting local policy continues to require considerable judgment and consideration of local needs and conditions. Particularly relevant are the capabilities of the local catalogue. Many on-line catalogues now offer a vast improvement in retrieval capabilities over the conventional card catalogue. With such powerful features, as keyword searching, Boolean searching, and the ability to search virtual all components of a bibliographic records, errors or omissions that would have rendered the record irretrievable to the patron using the card catalogue may be not at all critical in the on-line environment. Copy cataloguing policy should attempt to find the optimal balance among cataloguing efficiency, retrieval capabilities, and the usefulness of the information contained in the bibliographic record.

In addition to defending the criteria for usable copy, procedures must be implemented for handling materials for which no usable record can be found. A common practice is to hold materials until cataloguing copy (usually LC) becomes available. Among ARL libraries, holding periods of three to twelve months are typical. This is particularly true for non-English language material. The advantage of this practice is that expensive original cataloguing is avoided. The disadvantages are that the materials is not available for patron use until months later when it is eventually catalogued, and that material in holding areas must be balanced against the cost and the feasibility of performing original cataloguing.

Libraries may choose to shelve metrical for which copy can not be found by date of receipt and to retrieves such items from the holding areas upon patron request. This presumes that the patron has some way of determining that the library owns a particular item-perhaps through access to an automated acquisition system that identifies new receipts. Alternatively, brief bibliographic records can be keyed in to becomes available, a full-level record can be adapted and used to replace the interim record.

The practice of creating less than full-level bibliographic records is fairly controversial. Proponents argue that materials can be made available to the patron via on-line access to minimal level records until such time as these records can be upgraded, generally through a machine match and overlay process typically possible with on-line catalogues. Opponents and overlay process typically possible degradation of cataloguing quality and information retrievability.

Distribution of Materials

After materials are received from acquisitions and the search for usable copy has been performed, materials are distributed to the appropriate cataloguing units and staff. While the criteria for distribution vary among libraries, it is essentially the perceive level of cataloguing difficulty which determines the appropriate destination. The relative level of difficulty is often determined by the following;

1. Source of the cataloguing copy.
2. Language of the material,
3. Material type (*e.g.*, audio-visual, music, microform),
4. Presence of a usable call number,
5. Degree to which copy requires editing of descriptive cataloguing and,
6. Degree of subject analysis required.

Editing of Copv

The editing of copy varies widely with local practice and represents a process which can become quite complex. Dowell's

Cataloguing with Copy (1976) provides an indepth analysis of the process and can offer the reader complete coverage of this fine art. The basic steps in a typical copy editing process might be as follows. The item in hand is searched on a bibliographic utility (*e.g.*, OLC, RLIN) and a matching record displayed. This step may be simplified if the item has already been searched by acquisitions or a searching unit. In such cases, a numerical search key (LC card #, OCLC #) would have been recorded on any slips (*e.g.*, purchase order) accompanying the item. The record is examined carefully to verify that the records does indeed match the item in hand and to item the source and type of record. For example, a full-level/AACR2/LC record can be identified by verifying that the fixed field element "encoding level"= "blank", the "description"= "a," and the 020 field = DLC/DLC. Depending on the source and type of copy, and the local policies regarding such, a predetermined list of specific record fields and elements are examined for accuracy and completeness. For instance, if a full-level AACR2/LC record (not in series) is found, abbreviated procedures involving a minimum of checking can be followed. The copy cataloguer will quickly verify the fixed element "language code" and "date of publication" to ensure that they match the piece in hand.

Next, the cataloguer will check the 050 (LC call number) for accuracy of format and then scan the IXX field (author), 245 field (title), 250 field (edition statement), and 260 fields (place and data of publication) for typographical errors, accuracy, and completeness. Any discrepancy in edition is detected at this point. Finally, the 049 fields is edited to reflect local holding and, optionally, a 949 field added to provide item specific information such as OCR/barcodes number (accession number for circulation), branch location, media code, price, and so on. The cataloguer completes the process by invoking the "produce" function. Shelf/ catalogue cards and/ or machine-readable tapes containing the edited records are sent by the bibliographic utility to the library generally more within a week or two.

The process is generally more complex for member-contributed copy or less than full-level records.. For example, the 300 fields (physical description) must be completed for LC/CIP records; the subject heading fields (6XX) may need to be require additional attention, and so on.

A question often asked is how much of a bibliographic record can be accepted without checking? There is no single answer to this. The answer depends on the source and type of copy, the library's perception judgment as to the accuracy and completeness of the copy, the level of staffing and other resources the library can afford to devote to copy cataloguing, the patron population served and their particular information needs, the library's definition of the minimal acceptable level of service and access to information, the storage and retrieval capabilities of the local catalogue, and the "local culture" and its philosophy regarding the broader issue of bibliographic control.

The subject remains a hotly debated issue and has led many to rethink conventional wisdom regarding traditional access points and record content. Research is underway examimng the usefulness of the various access points and the Information content of the typical catalogue record.

Cataloguing Priorities

cataloguing priorities are established to determine the order in which different categories of materials will be catalogued. Such priorities are perhaps the major determinant of copy cataloguing workflow and are often influenced by interest external to those of the cataloguing department. Cataloguing priorities may be based on such considerations as the following.

(a) Imprint (*i.e.*, the timeliness of the publication). New; material is often given top priority. Material from backlogs may be done only after all other types of material have been catalogued.

(b) "Rush" materials, patron requests and "notifications", as well as cataloguing for a branch library or a reference location are often given special consideration.

(c) Relation of the item to the collection (*e.g.*, as determined by collection development subject specialists).

Whatever, the basis for the cataloguing priorities, they should be clear, will documented, and communicated to all interested individuals and departments that allows the copy cataloguers and other staff to easily recognize the treatment and priority that specific items should receive. This is typically achieved through the use of coloured 'flags" or specially designed forms that are clearly labelled as to the intended treatment and which include any additional information required to process the item accordingly.

A well documented and publicized policy regarding cataloguing priorities becomes critical when the volume of material exceeds the cataloguing capacity of the department. Under such conditions, the issues involved can become quite sensitive politically as various interest groups attempt to win priority attention for their materials; very few individuals want to see their new receipts relegated to a backlog. It becomes very important to negotiate mutually acceptable priorities which are perceived by all interest groups as being, if not ideal, at least rational and equitable.

While well formed cataloguing priorities are important, one must guard against policies that are exceedingly rigid. A certain amount of flexibility must be built in to the system in order to allow the copy cataloguing manager to adjust workflows around changing conditions. The inflow of materials will vary over time, not only in volume but in the relative composition of material type and the sources of cataloguing copy. For example, a recently received collection donated as a gift may include many items for which only member contributed or pre-AACR2 copy is available. In order to avoid flooding the unit responsible for this type of material, items from the collection may have to be fed gradually in to the workflow, while others remain in a temporary backlog. Last but not least, things should be kept simple. While it is tempting to try to accommodate all interests when negotiating priorities, too many exceptions and special treatments introduced in to the workflow can degrade the performance of the entire operation and , in the end, result in poor service for all parties involved. In summary, priorities, while being flexible, should be designed to minimize exceptions and help achieve an optimal turnaround time for all materials.

Staffing and Training

Level of Staff Required

Copy cataloguing is done by the full range of staffing levels ranging from student assistants and clerical staff to para professional and professional staff. As with other aspects of copy cataloguing, the level of staff deemed appropriate for a given level of cataloguing complexity varies among libraries. Generally, clerical staff and beginning level paraprofessionals are thought by most to be well equipped to handle abbreviated copy cataloguing procedures, such as those used in adapting LC copy. Intermediate and higher levels of paraprofessional staff are thought more appropriate for working with member contributed copy and with more complex problems of yet higher complexity, such as those associated with classification or the establishment of subject headings ate often reserved for professionals or the highest level paraprofessional staff. In a typical arrangement, the copy cataloguing department is headed by a professional, with individual units supervised by high level para-professionals.

Because the definition of staffing levels oil essentially an arbitrary local distinction, perhaps the more relevant issue concerns the level of knowledge and expertise required. Depending on the relative complexity of the cataloguing task at hand, staff require varying leave's of familiarity with such codes and standard as AACR2 (as-well-as earlier codes), International Standards Book De cription (ISBD), LC/MARC formats, library of Congress Subjects Headings. (LCSH), and LC classification schedules. At the simplest levels, staff with little exposure to the full breadth of these codes may be able to do an acceptable job of copy cataloguing if provides with clear and simple decision rule-based instructions. These instructions allow minimal latitude for judgment on the part of the cataloguers and limits their actions to those prescribed by specific "if-then" rules. Any situations that fall outside of the prescribed decision-rules are referred to staff members of higher expertise. As the level of cataloguing complexity increases, so too do the requirements for expertise and familiarity with the various code and standards.

The managements challenge then is to match knowledge requirements with specific levels of task complexity. Dowell's Cataloguing with Copy (1976) includes a chart and checklist relating just such specific knowledge requirements with the various tasks associated with copy cataloguing. The first chapter identifies the following task components of cataloguing: filing; filing to catch discrepancies; preliminary checking of entry points given on outside cataloguing matching description between item and outside copy; making simple corrections on outside copy or completing CIP; making major changes on outside copy; adding notes concerning contents and relation to other publications; making cross-reference for names, series, or local use; making additional added entries; adapting suggested classification numbers to local use; performing original descriptive cataloguing; assigning original subject heading and assigning original call numbers. Using the task components and suggested knowledge requirements as a guide, the manager must go on to fine-tune the training of copy cataloguers and adjust staffing levels to reflect local needs, quality standards, and cataloguing policy.

Number of Staff Required

Both the level and number of staff should be matched to local cataloguing volume and workflow patterns. Variables to consider include the relative frequency of various material types (*e.g.*, books, microfilms, serials), the ratio of acceptable copy to adaptable copy (*e.g.*, the percent of materials with full-level LC copy versus member contributed copy); the language of the material, the presence of any backlogs, the total volume of material to be catalogued, and the degree of fluctuation in the receipt of materials. For example, a department with a separate unit for cataloguing with LC copy and another for member-based cataloguing, will want to adjust staffing so that the capacity of each unit marches the relative proportions of LIC and inember copy associated with incoming materials. If such coordination is not made, one unit is in danger of being overwhelmed while the other units is searching for materials to catalogue.

Of course, the problem here is that non of these variables remain static-equation budgets fluctuate, spending on new receipts is generally heavier at the beginning of the fiscal year than at the end, backlogs shrink or are eliminated, unexpected gift collection may be donated, changes in approval plan profiles are made, a change in collection development emphasis may change the proportions of English and non-English receipts, and so forth. Such uncontrollable variables underscore the importance of building flexibility in to the organization of the copy cataloguing department, the training of staff, and the design of workflow.

Staff Training

Most libraries employ a one-one training programme that moves from simple to more complex copy cataloguing over a period which varies from three to twelve months. Usually under the tutelage of a high-level paraprofessional or professional, the trainee is first taught the basics of searching the bibliographic utility (*e.g.*, OCLC, RLIN). After mastering the art of moving about in the database, the trainee is then taught to recognize the various types and sources of cataloguing copy-first and foremost, to recognize full-level/AACR2/ LC copy. The next step is to begin to learn the steps in editing simple LC copy and saving the results in a "save" queue for review by the instructor at a later date (usually the end of the day). This process, known as "revision" continues until the instructor is confident that the. trainee has mastered the concepts and procedures involved. A similar process of training, practice, and revision is then followed for more complex cataloguing such as CIP, preAACR2 LC, and member-contributed copy.

Such training is quite time consuming. Following periods of heavy staff turnover, the cataloguing instructors may find themselves doing nothing but training new staff, with little or no time to perform their own cataloguing. A few libraries have developed accelerated programmes for training a large number of new staff for such occasion or during the start-up of a new department. Pennsylvania state University Library, for example, has developed a training programme that is based on a combination of classroom course, computer assisted exercises, hands-on experience, and small group instruction. The developers claim that this programme can have new ready to produce within Several weeks.

Organizing the Copy Cataloguing Operation

Organizational Options

Several basis choices are available for organizing a copy cataloguing department or unit. Among ARL libraries, the following are the most common dimensions by which organizational structure vary.

(a) Centralization or decentralization of cataloguing operations.

(b) Organization by either "form" (*e.g.*, separate units for monographs and serials) or by "function" (*e.g.*, acquisitions, cataloguing).

(c) Separate or integrated cataloguing operations. Original cataloguing and copy cataloguing can be combined into one department or organized separately.

(d) Separate or integrated procedures for variant types and sources of copy. Simple (*e.g.*, LC copy) and complex (*e.g.*, member copy) cataloguing can be integrated it, to one unit with each cataloguers performing both levels as required, or separate units can be established.

(e) Interface with other departments such as acquisitions, processing, original cataloguing, catalogue maintains. (Interdepartmental communication is important. For example, policies need to be coordinated with the circulation department regarding procedures such as catalogue before or after the binding process).

(f) Procedures for finding usable copy. For example, pre-order or post-receipt searching can be then be "flagged" to identity the matching record before reaching the copy cataloguing department, separate search and distribution units can be set up specifically for verifying the availability and identifying the nature of cataloguing copy.

A major that governs the choice regarding the letter dimension is to avoid duplication of effort in having to search and re-search the same item at multiple stages in the cataloguing of an item. A related workflow variable concerns the disposition of materials for which no usable copy can be found. A common practice is to send lower priority material to a backlog and routinely re-search them at periodic intervals. Such practice have involved out of the need to reduce the volume of material requiring original cataloguing.

(a) Authority work may be integrated in to normal copy cataloguing routines or handled by separate units (*e.g.*, original cataloguing, catalogue maintenance, or an authority control unit).

(b) Input and edit. Some libraries prefer to separate the intellectual function of reviewing and adapting a catalogue record from the actual inputting and outline editing. Copy cataloguers will adapt usable copy and record the necessary changes on a workform which can then be passed on to clerical staff for input in to the database. Other libraries seek to avoid the redundancy inherent in this practice by having the record called up only once and edited immediately by the cataloguer.

Variables Affecting Organizational Design

The choice of organizational options discussed above will differ from library to library and is influenced by a variety of local needs, resources, and considerations. First among these variables is the library's definition of "copy". While variables such as library size, number of branches, number of volumes, staff size, and budget are often cited as bases for overall organizational design of cataloguing operations, the organization workflows and individual processing units is influenced most by how a library defines the various types of copy and the relate complexity involved in adapting each type of copy to local standards.

Typically, a distinction is made between LC and member contributed copy. Either separate procedures, or in some cases separate units are then designed to process each type of cataloguing one for processing LC-based copy, the other for adapting member contributed copy. Establishing separate units has the advantage of allowing the less complex cataloguing to be done without delay; that is, materials for which LC copy is available is not held up by the more the time-consuming member-based cataloguing. This is consistent with the traditional production-line maxim the asserts that "the entire process can go only as the slowest step "By eliminating the bottlenecks created by the more time-consuming cataloguing, materials for which readily usable coy available can be catalogued and sent to the shelves with minimal delay.

An additional advantage of establishing separate is that different staffing levels can be employed. For example, entry level paraprofessionals may be trained to perform the LC-based cataloguing, while the more highly paid intermediate and upper level paraprofessionals are reserved for more complex cataloguing. Staffing costs, as well as training time, can be minimized.

Such a separation of units, however, is not without certain drawbacks. The efficiency of this arrangement hold up as long as materials representing both types of copy (LC and member) are readily available and the cap of each unit is well matched to the existing workflow. (The existence of a large backlogs is ideal for this arrangement. As fluctuations in new recipes result in shortage of LC copy, the backlogs can be tapped to keep the units adequately supplied). If either class of copy (usually LC) falls off, the result will be excess capacity and idle staff in one of the units. A single integrated unit, with each cataloguers doing all classes of copy, has the advantage of greater flexibility in adapting to fluctuations in the number and nature of incoming material. Thus, if separate units are employed, it is important to build flexibility in to the procedures and to identify alternative activities for staff during such fluctuations.

Other variables that come in to play when considering alternative organizational designs, staffing needs, and required resource include the following.

Format of Material. Will the copy cataloguing department process only book-format monographs? Or, Online Technical Support Systems will the workflow include music. Audio-visual materials, microform, and so on?

Library Collections. What special interest must be served? Will cataloguing be done for departments such as special collections, reference, or branch libraries? What special needs and turnaround times are involved?

Language or Alphabet of Material. Are non-English language or non-Roman aplhated materials catalogued or sent on to other special units? What priority do these materials receive?

Other Produces. Will the copy cataloguing department have to perform transfers, withdraws, added-copy or added-volume routines?

Subject of Materials. Should separate units or staff designated to handle different subject areas such as Humanities, Science, or Literature?

All of these variables must be considered in light of the availability of staff—staff with the background or training to work with foreign languages, specific areas, and the various MARC formats.

Copy Cataloguing Organizational Models

While the organization of the copy cataloguing operation varies among libraries, the general components and principles involved can be seen in several variations on a common theme. (For detailed descriptions of thirteen ARL libraries' copy cataloguing operations and organization, see Clerk 1987). Components of a typical organizational model appear below.

Search and Distribution Unit. Searches bibliographic utility for copy, identifies nature of copy (*e.g.*, LC/ AACR2,CIP, member), and routes material to appropriate processing unit based on locally establishing criteria.

Copy Cataloguing Unite(s). Many libraries have their abbreviated procedures or separate units for cataloguing materials for which full level, AACR2 LC copy is available (typically called "fast" or" rapid" cataloguing).

Maintenance/Bibliographic Support. Performs support functions for the units such as typing and filling in the public catalogue, shelflist, and authority file; maintains the local catalogues and files (both on-line and manual) through the addition, deletion, and correction of bibliographic and authority records.

Added Copy/Added Volume, Withdrawals, Transfers. Often performed either in the catalogue maintains unit or the copy cataloguing units.

Marketing and Physical Processing. Often part of or closely associated with the copy cataloguing units. (Error in call numbers are often detected during the marking process; this step may serve as an additional quality control mechanism for the copy cataloguing units).

As with all organizational decisions, there is no one best structure. The choice of structure depends on many interrelated variables including the personnel and expertise available.

Productivity and Performance Standards

Production Statistics

Automation offers the potential for improved statistical reporting function for better management decisions and control. Whether manually or through the local automated system, data should be collected and analysed as a means of providing the manager with relevant feedback on the efficiency of various operations. Data typically collected includes the total number of titles/ volumes catalogued by each cataloguers, unit, department, and so forth. The record count might also include a breakdown of materials catalogued by class number (*e.g.*, for collection development use).

On-line capabilities may also include a management report utility capable of generating a variety of statistical summaries and analyses. In addition to raw counts of performance data, the report may include various numerical analyse (*e.g.*, the ratio or percentage of LC to member copy, average titles catalogued per full-time equivalent staff, average titles catalogued per hour, etc.).

If the local on-line system cannot provide such management reports, data can be recorded on specially designed forms and later input in to a microcomputerbased speradsheet (*e.g.*, Lotus 1-2-3, Super Calc). Typically, individuals cataloguers record their production statistic at the end of each month. The cataloguing data are then keyed in to the spreadsheet programme for summary and analysis.

Productivity Standards

A 1984 survey of 27 libraries (participants in meeting of the RTSD/CCS copy Cataloguing Discussion Group) found that of the 13,000 to 96,000 titles catalogued annually, copy cataloguing (22,000 to 72,000 titles) accounted for approximately 64 percent of these totals (Hudson 1986). The survey also reports a range of 769 to 6,000 titles produced per copy cataloguer (FTE) per year.

It is difficult to make any general statements concerning average productivity levels. The actual productivity of individual cataloguers depends, among other things, on the level of cataloguing complexity.

Production statistics gathered between 1986 and 1988 at Arizona State University Library, for example, show that cataloguers adapting LC copy can produce 500-700 titles per month (with five, four-hour cataloguing sessions at the terminal per week), whereas cataloguers working with member copy average about 300 titles per month (based on five, three-hour terminal sessions per week). These levels, however, will vary greatly with local practice, the number and length of terminal sessions, and the organizational structure of the copy cataloguing operation.

Quality Control

Performance is not measured only in terms of total titles catalogued. The accuracy and completeness ("quality") of the bibliographic record should also be of significant concern to the copy cataloguing manager. Finding and maintaining the optimal balance between cataloguing productivity and cataloguing quality is one of the more challenges aspects of maintaining the cataloguing operation.

The means of monitoring cataloguing quality very among libraries. A typical methods is to match each newly produced shelflist card against the record of original input (*e.g.*, purchase order, workform) and to revise (make corrections) during the filing of cards in the shelflist or catalogue. In an automated environment, records can be reviewed on-line and on "error reports" produced during the loading of each new tape of catalogue records. These methods tend to be rather informal and focus primarily on catching highly noticeable errors.

Libraries may also purse a more systematic approach to quality control. For example, libraries may require cataloguers to revise the filing in the public catalogue on a periodic basis (*e.g.*, weekly). Other approaches involve taking periodic random sampling of the catalogues/ shelflists or of the records produced by individual cataloguers. The sampled records are then thoroughly reviewed for accuracy and completeness. These more systematic approach require a significant investment of time and expense. The costs involved should be weighed against the marginal increase in cataloguing quality.

Systems Analysis and Design

The copy cataloguing operation can be quite complex, making it difficult for the manager to identify ways in which procedures or workflows can be improved. While improvements can be made through a more intuitive approach, formal system analysis techniques can help identify bottlenecks radiance that might otherwise go undetected.

Among these techniques, flowcharting is perhaps the most popular and useful. Through the flowcharting process, each individual action (task) and decision is identified and placed in precise sequence to other steps in the process. The flowchart's graphic depiction of the steps in the cataloguing process make it easier for the manager to spot weakness in the workflow design.

Systems analysis techniques such as flowcharting also offer an excellent way to document the copy cataloguing operation and should be included with any textual material such as procedure manuals. Training of new personnel can be enhanced through the clear picture of the cataloguing process that the flowchart provides.

In addition to the finished product, the flowcharting process itself can be an invaluable exercise in that to forces one to thoroughly examine and understand each step in a process. Flowcharting enthusiasts, in fact, are found of claiming that "if you can't flowchart it, you don't understand it". The flowcharting process should be repeated at regular intervals or whenever a major changes is made in the workflow. Often, seemingly insignificant changes in a procedure can be revealed to have an impact on other points in the process once seem from the enchanced perspective of a flowchart.

The Impact of Automation/Emerging Trends

Shared Cataloguing and Networks

The availability of thousands of bibliographic records through the large database of the bibliographic utilities that made copy cataloguing possible. The impact on library operations has been tremendous and has wrought many changes in local procedures and practices.

Among the more significant effects of large-scale shared cataloguing has been the impact on staffing levels. For many libraries, the availability of adaptable cataloguing copy has reduced the volume of materials requiring cataloguing. The streamlined procedures used for copy cataloguing do not require the extensive expertise needed to do original cataloguing. Thus the least decade has seen a shift in support of copy cataloguing operations.

Ironically, while bibliographic utilities were created initially to provide printed catalogue/shelflist cards, the availability of machine readable records and outline catalogues has led to a reduction in the number of card files maintained by modern libraries. This, in turn, has greatly reduced traditional library activities such as card typing and card filing. Staff are now being reassigned to tasks such as reviewing and maintaining records on-line or reviewing printouts (error reports) produced following the periodic loading of bibliographic records in to local on-line databases.

Not all aspects of shared cataloguing have led to time or cost savings. Along with the benefits of having access to the catalogue records of the bibliographic utilities comes the responsibility for maintaining the integrity of the database. Records contributed to the database are not the exclusive property of any individual library and, therefore, must adhere to agreed upon standards for accuracy and completeness. In this sense, a library's cataloguing becomes more closcly scrutinized and subject to even greater, and more time consuming, quality control measures. Libraries must also make sure to consider the various legal restrictions (*e.g.*, copyright) which may be imposed by the bibliographic utilities on the use of catalogue records.

On-line Catalogues

Along with the development of shared cataloguing the increasing implementation of the on-line catalogue has had a major impact on library operation practices. Library scholar and practitioners are by no means agreed on the implications of the new technologies for the future of bibliographic control.

The debate stems from the powerful indexing and retrieval capabilities of the newly developed on-line catalogues. At one end of the spectrum are those who argue that traditional access points and cross-references are less critical given the on-line catalogue's ability to perform searches based on keyword, boolean operators, would proximity, and search key truncation. Other, more conservative opinions, argue that the extremely literal manner in which the on-line catalogue performs indexing and searching makes to more, not less, important to ensure that access points, records tags and indicators, and filing characters be closely examined for accuracy. Thus, it appears as though the new technologies and retrieval capabilities are at this point a mixed blessing, rendering some aspects of bibliographic controls less critical while increasing the importance of others.

On-line catalogues have also impacted the nature of bibliographic record maintenance. With the capability to access local catalogue records on-line, separate maintenapce operations can be established to enter records and record modifications directly in to the local on-line database. This is particularly true for such procedures as added copy at these would have precisely been done through the capabilities of the bibliographic utility, which changes to the records appearing only when the library loaded the next tape of the on-line catalogue, these operations can be performed immediately and in real-time.

The extreme precision with which the on-line catalogue performs searching and indexing has introduced new problems in to the maintains operation. As catalogue records new are loaded in to the catalogue *via* tape, or on-line via direct transmission, the system performs a number of checks on the validity of the content and format of the incoming field tag, subfield, and indicator against a stored table of valid values: any discrepancy is noted (usually in the form of a printout identifying the records and the source of the problem). Due to the literal character-by-character can result in a rejected record and a maintains transaction that must be reviewed manually. The manager of the copy cataloguing operation, therefore, face a trade-off. As copy cataloguing procedures becomes more streamlined, and the review of individual record elements less through, the likelihood of generating a future maintenance problem increases. Thus, the efficiencies and economies realized through the abbreviated copy cataloguing produces can be partially offset by an increase in maintains transactions. The management challenges is to find a balance of cataloguing and maintenance procedures that makes optimal use of staff time, ensures adequate record quality, and minimizes total processing costs.

Recognition of the workflow trade-offs described above, along with other similar phenomenon, have led to the claim that the staff time-saving promised with on-line catalogues is largely a fallacy. While libraries have experienced any reduction in total staffing requirements. When comparing the costs of maintaining manual versus automated library systems, however, it is important to recognize that we are in a sense comparing apples and oranges. The on-line catalogue has opened up a whole new range of capabilities and represents a quantum leap in terms of improved library services. Although staffing requirements remain the same, or have increased somewhat, the level of service and potential for further improvements has been greatly enchanced.

Post-processing of Catalogue Records

Among the more powerful features of the on-line catalogue is the capability to perform a systematic machine-based matching process by which large numbers of bibliographic records can be quickly reviewed element by element. A familiar example of this process is the "global" search and replacement feature often associated with on-line authority control systems.

Such machine-based operation not only facilitate the catalogue maintenance function but also offer the possibility of performing certain aspects of the cataloguing process after the bibliographic record has been created. For example, by integrating the LC name and subject authority files in to the on-line catalogue, it becomes possible to perform a verification process as bibliographic records are loaded in to the database. Headings associated with incoming catalogue records can be checked against heading in the stored authority file. Should an incoming heading match a cross-reference, the system can substitute the authorized from of the heading before allowing the bibliographic records to pass in to the database.

Some aspects of catalogue records creation and maintenance lend themselves to such machine processing operations while others do not. The computer is a relentlessly literal device that can operate only according to precisely defined decision rules. Only those operations that can be reduced to a finite series of logical steps and lend themselves to well-formed machine algorithms are appropriate for such processing. In such, the highly labour-intensive process of manually reviewing a particular record element during the adaptation of catalogue copy can be replaced by a post-processing machine operation that is quicker, cheaper, more efficient, and more accurate.

These new post-processing capabilities suggest a trend and catalogue maintenance function. Cataloguing procedures must be reviewed and possibly resigned to take advantage of these post-processing opportunities and to increase the efficiency of the manual review process. By relieving the copy cataloguers of those tasks that can be done more efficiently through machine-based processing, the manual review process can concentrate more effectively on those elements of the catalogue record which have a more critical impact on record retrievability. Thus, the management challenge becomes one of finding the optimal balance of manual review and post-processing maintenance.

Other Trends

The rate at which new technology is developed makes it difficult to anticipate the direction of future library operations and procedures. Certainly, an increasing number of libraries will implement on-line catalogues and other automated systems. These systems will also continue to be improved with new, more powerful retrieval capabilities. These developments will further fuel the discussion over the nature and content of catalogue records. The improved capabilities of the online catalogue do not necessarily mean an easier time for library operations. The improved retrieval capabilities, more readable screen (record) formats information access, but make more conspicuous the errors and imperfections in the catalogue records. Much of what may have gone unnotices in the card catalogue may become glaring errors in the automated environment.

Expert systems represent another technology on the horizon with the potential to dramatically affect the copy cataloguing operation. These systems, originally developed to facilitate medical dances, may prove ideally adaptable to the highly codified, rule-based structure of the cataloguing process. While most researchers are agreed that such systems can never replace cataloguers, both original and copy cataloguing may be greatly facilitated through the assistance of such systems.

The precursor to such systems can already be found in the increasing use of microcomputer-based workstations such as the "smart" terminals developed by the bibliographic utilities (*e.g.*, OCLC's M310 Workstation). These workstations have already taken advantage of prepackage software that allows records to be downloaded, edited off-line, and updated in batch model. Some libraries have taken this basic concept a step further and have developed local microcomputer programmes to allow them to perform increasingly sophisticated record maintenance operations, including, for example, the processing of non-Roman character sets and diacritics. Libraries are also making increasing use of outside vendors. Commercial vendors, library networks, and bibliographic utilities are offering an increasing variety of database "clean-up" service. For example, machine-readable (*e.g.*, magnetic tape) copies of a library's database can be run against a vendor's own authonty file and the catalogue records updated. The completed file of updated records can then be returned to the library for recording in to the on-line catalogue database.

New technologies and system capabilities have also influenced thinking on the entire organizational strutcture of the libraries to access the complete holding of the library's catalogue *via* remote terminal. The possibility of decentralizing operations may now be reconsidered.

□

8

Functions Automated Acquisitions

The term acquisition commonly denotes procurement of library materials which are published on nonrecurring basis including books, technical reports, government publications, and audio-visual materials. The acquisition of journals, magazines and other periodicals literature is considered a facet of serials control. A separate chapter is therefore devoted to study automated serials control.

Libraries in the United States had introduced automated acquisitions as early as 1959 using for book ordering systems like keypunch equipment, card sorters, and tabulating machine. In the early 1960s, batch-processing, computer-based acquisitions systems were developed by a number of academic libraries. In the late 1960s and early 1970s, several academic libraries in U.S. implemented online acquisitions systems—the most widely known being the Book Order and Selection System (BOSS). Despite these promising initiatives automated acquisitions systems failed to attract the widespread library and vendor interest. However interest in automated acquisition increased steadily since the late 1970s. In the 1980s, there are in U.S. a variety of organizations such as cooperative systems, booksellers, as well as integrated software packages and turnkey system which are used to assist acquisition work. Automated acquisition is immensely significant for the libraries. It provides a base to computerize other library activities without much labour. It contributes to the development of integrated libraries systems in which a single bibliographic data base serves the various information processing requirements of technical services, references and administrative. applications. Bibliographic data held in machine readable form can later be increased or modified to support circulation, cataloguing or other library activities eliminating duplication of work routines.

Functions of Acquisition Section

A good ordering and acquisition system may comprise the following activities:

1. Receiving records of items for acquisitions.
2. Ascertaining whether those items are already in the library or in the order procedure. If items are in the library, how many additional copies are to be ordered. If previous editions are there, what are the identities of new editions recommended for the order.
3. Checking of invoices or bills, if supplied.
4. Accounting under fund heads and sending bills for payment.
5. Making input of the order in the specified format.
6. Checking whether orders are overdue and, if so, chasing the supplier and sending reminders.
7. Maintaining record files for items on order.
8. Accessioning of items received.
9. Updating the whole record to ensure the latest position from time to time.
10. Maintaining the master file of orders and acquisitions. (Mahapatra)
11. Maintaining the accounts.
12. Keeping statistics.

BOOK ORDER FORMAT IN AUTOMATED SYSTEM

A format of the book order complising basic information is given below:

Order Number and Date

ISBN
Author
Title and edition
Publisher and date of publication
Price
Fund head
Number of copies
Bookseller or vendor
Stipulated date within which supply should be made.

The data field of the International Standard Book Number (ISBN) is a fixed one. Data fields of other information may vary in length from item to item. Therefore, the record structure for the order system must be specific and this can be determined by the strings of bits.

The accuracy of bibliographical details is most essential in an automated acquisition system. ISBN can help in this respect. While the items have been received and acquisition made, a batch of printouts may be used for various record purposes, such as cataloguing records, book cards for the circulation section etc.

Books are also received through gift or exchange. In these cases, certain computer operations are not required. The ordering function, the chasing function, the accounts and billing functions are eliminated. But these items have to be recorded on receipt and accessioned accordingly. Statistics should be kept as these are vital part of the library holdings.

INPUT

Whether selection of material and varification of bibliographic data, etc., is carried out manually or by automated methods, it is essential that ordering and related bibliographic information is converted to machine-readable form for entry into a computer-maintained master acquisition file. The following data is generally input to the computer to perform the above mentioned functions in local library setup.

1. Data regarding new orders. (Bibliographic detail)
2. Revisions or amendments to orders placed.
3. Position, whether received or not.
4. Records of acquisitions.
5. Records of accounts.
6. Whether reminders have been sent, if not received?
7. Records of received books.

OUTPUT

The output data of the computer for ordering and acquisition functions include the following:

1. Printouts of the items ordered, to be sent to the booksellers directly.
2. Printouts of items ordered, but not received.
3. Printed reminders to booksellers.
4. Bibliographic records used for catalogue records.
5. Accession records.
6. Book cards for the circulation section.
7. Processing slips.
8. Statistics of various natures.
9. Printout lists of recently acquired items.
10. Accounts under fund heads for budget control as well as current state of different budget heads.
11. Processed data of any kind relating to ordering, acquisitions and the analysis of data for decision making.
12. Any data required for the integrated computer system. (Mahapatra)

FINANCIAL CONTROL FUNCTIONS

The library manager and the accounts section greatly benefit from the improved accounting control over library activities through computer. By maintaining fund file the benefits accrued are as follow.

1. The computer automatically conveys information to accounts department about payments made or to be made.
2. The computer prints an exception message if placing a particular order exceeds the appropriation or budget for an account or project.
3. The computer keeps accurate and current accounting records including amounts spent by divisions or departments of the budget, dates spent, balance available, and totals as needed.
4. The computer system keeps up-to-date records of budget allocations by department, branch library, section, project, type of material or any other accounting breakdowns.
5. The computer keeps accurate and current records of the balance of deposits where advance payments have been made.

In most libraries, the format of the accounting data files are governed by the requirements of the accounting department or section. It is the duty of the systems analyst to design library information system in line with the requirements of the accounting department. Generally, at the time of order, the computer should transfer to the accounting department the amount of money to be paid on prepaid orders and to be paid after delivery. This enables accounting department to keep up-to-date records of uncommitted budget.

OTHER AUTOMATED FUNCTIONS

1. The computer can be used to identify and print followup reminders for incomplete processes, unpaid invoices,

overdue orders, violations of processing rule and other control checks.

2. Computer can monitor processing work. It can record items that have been received but not catalogued. If the computer prints out listings of such items at frequent intervals, they can serve multipurpose for the staff and the users of the collection.

3. If desired, computer can prepare lists of all orders placed each day and register all items received each day. It can be an essential tool in maintaining control of the acquisitions process.

4. The computer may be used to keep accurate records of the number of orders and receipts processed, by whom, to what vendors, etc. These records .provide library management with complete information on the acquisitions department workload. On the basis of this, reports can be prepared weekly, monthly, or as needed to count and summarize the types and number of documents, transactions, etc., processed.

5. As previously indicated most automated acquisition systems have the ability to print claiming and cancellation notices to vendors at predetermined intervals and also arrival notices to the requesters when items are received in the library.

RELATIONSHIP TO CATALOGUING ACTIVITIES

After the acquisition function has been automated, much of the data needed for cataloguing the item, is available to the computer in machine-readable form. Title, author, publisher, date of publication, corporate authors, technical report numbers, etc. have all been Keyed in either at the point of ordering or at the point of receipt. The computer can prepare a cataloguing worksheet for the professional cataloguer containing all the information entered up to the point of cataloguing. In order to complete cataloguing process, the professional librarian provides subject headings, assigns a call number, and reviews the work done by acquisition section. The cataloguer may also modify or correct any item of information from cataloguing viewpoint. A well-designed computer system should have the ordering/receiving data feed automatically into the cataloguing subsystem, thereby relieving the cataloguer from labour duplication.

Data Files

A computer based acquisition system warrants at least three different files as detailed below:

1. **Main Order File.** It is usually arranged by the order number. Here the order number is the key for access to any record kept in the computer. This file should be kept updated with the changes either in the bibliographical record, or in the price record, or in the actual cost record, or in any other respect immediately.

2. **Vendor File.** This file contains the name and addresses of the vendors (booksellers) used by the library. The purpose is to save labour. Vendor code can be used on the order record. The vendor file with the assigned codes generally contains the following data elements:

   1. Vendor code number.
   2. Vendor's name and address.
   3. Telephone number.
   4. Telex number.
   5. Cable/Gram.
   6. Currency accepted.

3. **Requester File.** This file is essential because, the requester number is to be recorded in the order file. Whenever the document is received in the library, intimation is sent to the requester. The requester file generally consists of the following data elements:

   1. Requester Number
   2. User's Name

3. User's address
4. Telephone number, etc.

Outstanding purchase orders file is also maintained by certain libraries. It contains all items ordered but not yet received.

Whenever books are received, the computer held order record is amended immediately. The receipt of books is recorded in the acquisition part and the order records for such books is closed. The reported delay in supply of books may be added to the record in the coded form indicating that the order remains outstanding for certain reasons.

It is better to make additions, deletion, amendments or corrections to the order file in batch-processing and to monitor progress of work done and financial situation at intervals of short duration. Obviously, the whole work design and operations depend on the capability of the computer, computer hardware and software.

BIBLIOGRAPHIC UTILITY SYSTEMS

All the four of the major North American Utilities such as OCLC, RLIN, WLN, and UTLAS, offer online acquisition systems to member libraries. They have the large databases of bibliographic record on which a library can draw upon. They offer acquisitions components that are tied in with their bibliographic databases, allowing for the transfer of certain types of information from existing bibliographic records directly onto the order records being created by individual libraries. All the four online acquisition systems are discussed here briefly.

(1) OCLC (Online Computer Library Centre). OCLC "Acquisition Subsystem" provides access to the Online Union Catalogue from which orders may be generated. There is an online in-process file, automatic transfer of constant data (*i.e.* bibliographic information) to other online files, fund accounting and report generation, as well as receipt and claiming. As of 1984, orders were mailed to the vendor since no direct transmission of orders to vendor was available. But now the ACQ 350 Acquisitions System of OCLC can communicate with the OCLC online union catalogue for the bibliographic verification and electronic order transmission (Saffady).

(2) RLIN (Research Libraries Information Network). RLIN II (the acquisition module) is available to libraries through California Library Authority for Systems and Services (CLASS). It is a comprehensive system from verification to receipt of item and direct accessions etc. Fiscal aspect is not covered. Verification is done online. It allows access to member library not only to its own holding records but also the holdings of the Library of Congress and the 200 member libraries. Through RLIN's system, a member library can maintain, in the acquisition system, not only a record of titles ordered, but also titles considered and rejected. Orders are still mailed to the appropriate vendor/jobber by the library. Direct electronic order placement with a vendor is not possible at this time.

(3) WLN (Washington Library Networks). "Acquisition Subsystem" consists of four files in-process, standing orders, name and address, and account status. These files, combined with cataloguing files, allow the library to operate and maintain acquisitions records for an item from selection to "on the shelf status". It handles both individual and standing order transactions. An order is created by entering the order command and a purchase order number, after finding the appropriate bibliographic record in the data base. This automatically links the orders to the "Bibliographic File" and causes a formatted order screen to be displayed. It is also possible to create an order record which is not linked to the Biblographic File. Once the necessary order information has been added to the "In-process File" record, a purchase order can be printed, or the order can be routed directly to any vendor using the WLN On-line Transmission of Orders facility. Purchase orders, are printed or routed automatically to vendors three times a week. But Saffady reports that, at present, the system provides overnight electronic transmission to several dozen booksellers. The record can be updated online using individual commands and formatted screens. Bibliographic information can be added, deleted, or altered in "In-process File" records without affecting the "Bibliographic File."

(4) UTLAS (The University of Toronto Library Automation System). In Canada this is a regional library network. The UTLAS system (Online Acquisitions control System) is similar to the other bibliographic utilities in that the basic functions are covered-verification to payment. What is special about this system and WLN is that, unlike RLIN, it is possible to place many orders electronically: "speedier service through electronic communication with vendors holding UTLAS vendor accounts." Another unique feature of UTLAS is its international scope; the bibliographic data base for verification covers much more than American publishers' output and publication in the English language.

Book Jobber Services

A large number of booksellers and library suppliers are now offering online access to their databases. These organizations typically started to use computer systems to run their own ordering and supplying processes during the 1970s, usually beginning with a file of stock titles only but now have built large MARC-based bibliographic records. Most of these services are accessible using teletype-compatible terminals which might also be used for carrying out online searches on DIALOG etc.

Baker & Taylor and Brodart in United States are the largest book jobbers-which maintain a large bibliographic database, although not as large as do the Utilities. They have several automated acquisition systems available: LffiRIS II is a system tied into the Baker & Taylor mainframe computer system and several variations under Bata SYSTEMS are designed to allow libraries to use their own computer systems. LIBRIS II allows searching a data base of 350,000 titles created by Baker & Taylor. The database is updated weekly. Orders can be generated online and electronic order placement to Baker & Taylor is possible. The system allows for fund accounting and is capable of retaining both the current and previous years' budgets for reconciliation purposes. A warning system is incorporated to protect overspending. The system can be used to print orders for other vendors.

Brodart's OLAS system is accessed on a time-sharing basis through terminals located in subscribing libraries. It requires minimal capital investment in equipment. OLAS users may pay a monthly or annual subscription fee for unlimited connect time or incur connect time charges based on actual usage. Brodart maintains a substantial database which can be searched online for bibliographic verification. The user has the ability to transmit orders electronically to vendor.

Teleordering

Tedd records another development seen in UK which links the publishing and bookselling trades in Tele-ordering. Intelligent terminals in bookshops are used to record details of orders, using their ISBN s. This information is sent *via* the telephone to the Tele-ordering computer system where the ISBNs are checked against Whitaker's British Books in Print database and the full author/title details are retrieved and order to the publishers are despatched. The advantages include cost savings, less errors, improved reporting and speedier distribution, all of which affect the acquisitions system in a library.

Bibliographic Databases

Quite a number of machine-readable databases are found in the market. Books in Print database is available through several online search services. It is a machine-readable counterpart of several printed trade bibliographies. Bowker has introduced a CD-ROM implementation of BOOKS IN PRINT PLUS and BOOK REVIEWS PLUS.

In U.S. the Library Corporation has introduced the Book Indentification and Ordering System which is a microcomputerbased CD-ROM system designed for bibliographic verification and book ordering. It features the ANY-BOOK data base of English-Language titles available from over 22000 publishers. Menu-driven software permits searches by author, title, ISBN, or LC card number. Retrieved records are displayed as orderform images containing bibliographic and ordering information. When the operator enters additional ordering information, the system automatically calculates prices, checks for items already on order, and prints order forms. It can also transmit orders electronically to designated publishers or jobbers. (Saffady).

❐

9

Automated Cataloguing

As with the computerized circulation control, the Librarians have been interested in automating cataloguing systems. Unit Record Equipment were the first used as mechanized methods for cataloguing purpose in 1940s. The catalogue data were Keypunched and the punched cards were filed in relevant sequences. Many punched-card catalogues were produced and printed in 1950s. Saffady reports that precomputer equipment such as card sorters and paper-tape typewriters were in use in 1940s in United States. The computers were first applied in early 1960s to produce catalogue cards and book catalogue. Hence typewriters became redundant around mid 1960s.

It is obvious that during 1960s computers were used in cataloguing but in batch processing system. In batch processing, catalogue data were punched in cards and then transformed in the paper tape or magnetic tape. In some machine, however data were directly input in the punched paper tape or recorded on the magnetic tape. Gradually, programmings were made on the magnetic tape or discs. which could be manipulated automatically. But in this period different libraries used different types of computers and there was no uniformity in the catalogue card format. The individual libraries had to spend a large sum on the custom-developed computer system in order to attain speed in work. This situation warranted the necessity for standardization of catalogue data and shared cataloguing. Thus the two aspects of cataloguing system developed during 1960s, became the most vital for computerized cataloguing. These are the standardization of the catalogue entry with the standard bibliographic description having unique identification mark for each document with the International Standard Book Number (ISBN) and shared cataloguing under a computerized library system using MARC format. Different ISBDs have been prepared by IFLA to attain uniformity through computer.

Automated cataloguing is possible by adopting anyone of the following systems.

1. Participating in a bibliographic utilities, such as OCLC, WLN, etc.
2. Using commercially available systems such as Mini or Micro MARC or software package used primarily for cataloguing.
3. Applying integrated system which is also used for acquisition and or circulation purpose.
4. Utilizing book jobber or COM vendor services.
5. Adopting simple local input from the acquisition system.

What Is MARC?

MARC is an acronym derived from Machine-Readable Cataloguing. Within the United States, the terms MARC, LC MARC and USMARC are interchangeable. The term do have slightly different meanings such as follow:

1. MARC is a generic term applied to the universe of MARC formats, including UKMARC, CANMARC, InterMARC, and so on;
2. LC MARC refers to the set of options and content designation called "MARC II";
3. USMARC is a new name of LC MARC, introduced in the Underlying Principles document in 1983. There is no sharp distinction in content between LC MARC and USMARC. The term USMARC or MARC are also applied to MARC extensions, formats such as OCLC MARC and RLIN MARC that include data in addition to USMARC data.

MARC I

MARC I pilot project began in April, 1966 in which sixteen libraries participated. By the year 1968, the Library of Congress had distributed over fifty thousand English language monographs records. The purpose of MARC I was the automation of cataloguing, indexing, searching and retrieval functions. The participating libraries made better use of the MARC tapes distributed by L.C., in a variety of ways in producing catalogue cards, book form of union catalogues, specialized lists of materials under subjects, lists for acquisition on purposes and the like. The LC MARC database-the accumulation of Library of Congress cataloguing data in machine-readable form-now contains more than 2.5 million records.

MARC II

The MARC I format was based entirely on the structure of the L.C. catalogue cards and covered monographs only. Encouraged by the success of MARC I, staff of the L.C. started redesigning the procedures and programmes to cover material in other forms, and developed character set to include all the major Roman alphabet language as well as Romanized forms. Meanwhile the British National Bibliography (BNB) showed interest in the UK MARC Pilot Project. Similarly interest was also shown by many foreign libraries to design a standard communication format suitable for interchanging bibliographic data not only from one source organization, the L.C., to many participating libraries, but also for exchanging information on cooperative basis among libraries at the international level. The US, the UK and other countries wanted a machine-readable catalogue format that would be a common one for international exchange of cataloguing and bibliographic data. Such an interchangeable record format was designed and was called MARC II.

It was a one-format structure on the machine-readable medium capable of containing bibliographic data of all forms of library materials, such as books, monographs, serials, maps, music etc., and related records. The structure or the physical representation of the machine-readable medium; the content designators, such as tags, indicators, and subfields codes used to identify the data elements; and the content or the data itself such as author, title and bibliographic descriptions are the three components of the LC MARC format.

MARC II officially began in March, 1968. Distribution began for all English Language material providing a weekly magnetic tape of zonal 1000 records. Thereafter, other documentation begain to be issued, including formats for other materials over the period 1970-73. In 1972 films records were distributed, by 1973 records for serials, maps and French books, by 1975 German Spanish and Portuguese materials.

MARC II is a subscription service. By subscribing to this service a library can acquire, in machine readable form cataloguing data for American and other foreign publications as described above. In fact the Library of Congress catalogues the documents *i.e.*, books and non-book materials, records the data on magnetic tape and supplies copies of the tapes to various interested libraries. The libraries which get the copy of magnetic tape, can then produce printed catalogues of their collections entries on cards and various kinds of bibliographies (author or subject etc.) by using a computer. Most libraries obtain access to MARC data through products and services developed by publishers computer system developers, time-sharing services and other intermediaries. MARCFICHE is the earliest of MARC-derivate products. At present a growing number of vendor supply the MARC database on CD-ROM disks or digital optical videodiscs accompanied by software which supports the retrieval of specific cataloguing records and the printing of card sets. Example include the BIBLIOFILE.

Uses of MARC

MARC tapes are being used for various purposes. Following are some of their important uses:

1. A centrally prepared catalogue can be distributed to the receiving libraries in a machine-readable form.

2. In spite of increasing acquisitions, the catalogue can be kept up-to-date without employing additional staff.

3. The MARC tapes can be utilized for acquisition functions *i.e.*, selecting, ordering and claiming unsupplied books without any additional cost. They can be used to produced spine labels, book pockets etc.

4. The MARC tapes can be used for producing conventional card catalogue by the subscribing libraries, as demonstrated by the University of Toronto.

5. The production cost of card catalogue on the computer (MARC System) is lesser than that of purchasing the Library of Congress catalogue cards.

6. The MARC data can also be used for producing book catalogues as demonstrated by the Washington State Library.

7. It automatically performs resource-sharing functions.

8. The MARC tapes can be used for computerised SDI service.

Mini or Microcomputer-based MARC is commercially based cataloguing system. Practically a microcomputer is housed in the Library and a set of floppy disks is provided which contains the entire MARC database. It is then quickly retrieved and edited as needed. (J. Rice).

Limitations

George Piternick points out the following few limitations of the Machine-Readable catalogue systems:

1. The MARC record for any title is almost similar to the conventional bibliographic record, as such it inherits all its limitations.

2. The MARC format will be limited, at least for the next few years, to the English language books because the MARC character set is severally limited in respect of special characters and diacritical marks.

3. Expenditure on account of machine time by the participating libraries will go on increasing in view of the weekly shipment of about 1,200 records or about 62,000 records annually requiring 15,000 feet of magnetic tape.

4. The time gap between the creation of MARC record and a catalogue record copy by the participating library, which is inherent at present in the existing card production methods of the Library of Congress, will not be removed until and unless both the cards and tapes are prepared from the same machine-readable record.

MARC records are no longer created only. by L.C. but also by many other agencies, and are available through bibliographic utilities and from commercial services.

Retrospective Conversion (RECON) In MARC

The MARC Distribution Service was enlarged and proved to be efficient in making conversion of all current intake into the machine-readable catalogue. But all these were for the current holdings of libraries only. Librarians were interested to the preparation of machine-readable catalogue of their older holdings and to replace their card catalogues with machine readable catalogues. But it was realized that uncoordinated activities by individual libraries would entail expensive repetition of work in converting the existing catalogue into the machine-readable form. Personalised efforts would also be devoid of uniformity in headings and forms.

RECON Pilot Project was initiated in August 1969. It continued for two years and approximately 58000 records were converte. The most significant technical achievement of this project was the development and implementation of the format recognition process.

The British. Library is also converting to machine-readable form all records printed in the British National Bibliography and they include all books published in Britain since 1950. The retrospective catalogue conversion made by the British Library is held in the BNB/ LASER file which keeps more than 700,000 MARC records from 1950 onwards.

UNI MARC

The implementation of US MARC, UK MARC and ISBD, the increasing number of national MARC formats etc. created an environment for international cooperation in interchanging bibliographic data. The IFLA Working group discussed some of the problems encountered in the area of universal standardization and agreement on content designators in machine-readable format. The concept of SUPER MARC as an international system for exchange of information was agreed upon in principle.

A draft of the international MARC format was made in 1975 for universal use. Finally, for international exchange of MARC records, a new machine-readable format was designed and is known as UNI MARC. It has been envisaged that the national organizations producing MARC records will produce them in the national standards for use within the country and will reformat them according to the UNI MARC format for international exchange. The international and universal MARC has become a reality.

Online Catalogues

The growth and development of MARC for machine-readable cataloguing of current materials and the retrospective conversion of manual catalogues to computerised ones represent the history of the offine computer system in library cataloguing.

The process of creating and editing the records in the batch system through the offine computer was however labour intensive and time-consuming. The capabilities of the online computer system for random access and operation in "real time was realized by the library administrators. The libraries planned to use the online system for cataloguing. During the early 1970s, the online system was used in its early phase. In the online system, the machine-readable files, either MARC or local were transferred from the magnetic tape to the magnetic disc or drum where random access was possible. Visual display units (VDU) or computer terminals were used for input and output operations, and these terminals were fitted with the line printers for the hard copy output.

Defining The Online Catalogue

What exactly constitutes an online catalogue is difficult to explain satisfactorily. A few important definitions are recorded hereunder. Library of Congress defined it as follows:

> "An online catalogue is an access tool and resource guide to the collections of a library or libraries, which contains interrelated sets of bibliographic data in machine-readable form and which can be searched interactively on a terminal by users".

National Library of Medicine gave a compact definition:

> "[An online catalogue provides] online access to the complete bibliographic record of all the library's holdings with minimal access points being the same as these available in a card catalogue".

Research Library Group (US) gave a characterized definition of online catalogue as follows:

An online Catalogue:

1. Provides the public with direct access to a library's bibliographic data base through the use of a terminal.
2. Is searchable through a variety of access points greater than those available through card form catalogue.
3. Retrieves information from a local library file, and if not successful locally, retrieves information from other libraries files.
4. Is searchable with a common command language which may be transferred when the public moves from one library to another.
5. Provides instructional help.
6. May be accessed remote from the Library's location.
7. Displays such results in readily understandable form.

8. Provides links to card form catalogues, reference help, circulation files, etc.

These definitions were written in 1980, but as of 1983, there was still little consensus as to what an online catalogue really is. James Rice attempts to feature online catalogue as under:

"An online catalogue is a fully interactive catalogue of holdings that has the potential of being accessible in any number of ways. It is by far the most dynamic form of catalogue because the user does not need to adapt to any physical limitations (*e.g.*, dictionary listing, divided catalogue, or book pages). Users simply input a query such as an author's name, subject headings, or keyword from the title, and the computer responds with an answer that allows for further communications".

In sum, an online catalogue is an organized, machin-ereadable accumulation of bibliographic records which are maintained on disks or other direct-access computer storage media for retrieval by library users and staff members working at interactive terminals or appropriately configured microcomputer workstations. In addition to saving space and automating file maintenance, online catalogue permit remote access by authorized persons equipped with compatible terminals, and they can support information retrieval operations such as keyword searching of titles and series names. (Saffady).

Online catalogue may be custom-developed (inhouse) for specific library use or purchased as prewritten software packages or turnkey systems. Examples of custom-developed online catalogues include the L.C. computerized catalogue, the MELVYL system at the University of California, the Library Computer System (LCS) at Ohio State University. Prewritten software packages suitable for online catalogue implementations include BRS/SEARCH from BRS Information Technologies, a powerful information retrieval programme that is available in mainframe, minicomputer, and microcomputer versions. Besides this several vendors in U.S. and elsewhere offer turnkey information storage and retrieval systems which include preconfigured combinations of hardware and software components suitable for online catalogue implementations, STAR system is an example.

Since the mid 1980s online catalogue practice has been dominated by integrated library systems which cdmbine database management and catalogue access capabilities with circulation control, acquisitions, serial control, and other operations. Such systems may be implemented as complete turnkey systems or as prewritten software packages designed to operate" on a library-owned mainframe, mini-computer, or microcomputer.

Most recently for online catalogue implementation, large number of vendors in U.S. offer public access catalogue systems which employ CD-ROM storage technology. Examples include the IMPACT system from Autographics, THE INTELLIGENT CATALOG from the Library Corporation, and the LEPAC system from Brodart. In such implementations the library provides a machine-readable version of its catalogue typically consisting of MARC format records on magnetic tapes obtained from bibliographic utilities or other sources, to a CD-ROM system vendor who indexes and otherwise prepares it for onversion to one or more CD-ROM disks. CD-ROM catalogues are now increasingly mentioned as an alternative to COM for union catalogues and similar implementations.

BIBLIOGRAPFFIC UTILITIES

Most libraries in the United States, Canada and elsewhere, instead of developing their own inhouse systems prefer to obtain access to machine-readable cataloguing record through one of the bibliographic utilities, *i.e.*, organizations which maintain large databases of cataloguing records and offer online access and other services to subscribing libraries only. Examples include the Online Union Catalogue implemented by the Online Computer Library Center (OCLC), the Research Libraries Information Group (RLG), the cataloguing support service operated by the Western Library Network (WLN), the Cataloguing Support System (CATSS) offered by Utlas International, Canada, the LIONS system operated by the New York Public Library and so on. The British Library Automated Information Service (BLAISE) is also now one of the world's largest commercial services. Its catalogue production is made through LOCAS (Local Catalogue Service) which is an integral part of BLAISE.

While these organizations differ in database size and composition, the number and nature of their subscribers and the specific capabilities they support, each maintain a database of L.C. MARC records, supplemented by original MARC-format cataloguing contributed by subscribing libraries. Working at local terminals, participating libraries can retrieve cataloguing copy, modify it to meet local needs, and order printed card sets, machine-readable cataloguing records on magnetic tape, and other bibliographic products. Supporting thousands of online terminals, accessing millions of machine-readable records, the Bibliographic Utilities are among the world's largest and most intensively utilized computer-based information services.

Online Cataloguing With Bibliographic Utilities

Any library which is a member of centrally located database like OCLC or RLIN etc., is given facility for online processing of cataloguing records. By having access to a central database, an individual library can make use of the existing records in the most efficient and effective manner for a number of purposes. Following is a brief review of some of the key processes involved in online cataloguing.

Terminal

On-line cataloguing is performed on a terminal installed in member library. This terminal is connected to a central database subscribed by the Library.

The terminal generally consists of two parts-a CRT (cathoderay tube) terminal, which looks like a television receiver, and an attached keyboard similar to that of a typewriter except that it contains special functions keys for system use and speci library characters. Many terminals are accompanied by line printers.

Searching

The main purpose of searching is to ascertain whether a particular record is in the database.

Searching is generally performed by means of search keys. The search keys may consists of alphabetic characters, numeric characters, or both. The most commonly-used search keys are derived from the following elements in a record: name-title, name, title, subject entry, LC card number, ISBN, ISSN, and a special control number in the data base.

Frequently, a particular search key may call up more than one record, because the computer will respond with all the records containing the same search key. In such a case, a list of the items containing only brief information will be displayed and the searcher then decides which particular record in the list is to be displayed in full.

If the inhouse terminal reports that the record for the item in hand is already in the data base, it can then be used for any purpose. From cataloguing standpoint, the cataloguer compares the item being catalogued with the record held in data base. If there is no variation, the record then can be processed for cataloguing purposes *i.e.*, card can be printed from the record; and the record can be added to the library's own tape for producing COM catalogues if required. However if the record varies in certain details from the item being catalogued, it can be modified or edited to suit individual purposes. If the item in hand is not held in data base, the cataloguer on his terminal keyboard, catalogues the item in accordance with the standardized entry format and then it is automatically added into the central data base.

One great advantage of on-line cataloguing is the instant feedback. In editing, the modification made to the information displayed on the screen, and the modified or edited record is shown instantly to ensure that all necessary modification have been correctly processed.

Inputting Cataloguing Records

The inputting process is used to store cataloguing data in machine-readable form in a data base. After the cataloguing information has been identified and organized according to cataloguing rules, the subject headings and call number have been assigned, and the individual elements have been encoded or tagged according to the MARC format, the record is then ready to be input into the computerized data base.

The inputting process can also be performed in an online mode through the terminal. Results of input can be displayed immediately for proof reading and any necessary correction.

COM

COM (Computer Output Microfilm) catalogue developed as an outgrowth of book catalogue. COM recorder is a type of nonimpact computer printer which converts machine-readable data to microfilm or microfiche without creating an intervening paper copy. The process begins by first converting the catalogue into machine-readable form. The database is then stored on magnetic tape or disk or some other secondary storage medium. The microform output is usually on 105 x 148 mm. microfiche or 16 mm. microfilm. The COM format is getting popularity. Special Readers are required for the magnified display of COM generated images. Reader/printers can be used to create paper copies. In US and UK several book jobbers and vendors have developed software capable of producing COM catalogue from library supplied, machine-readable bibliographic data. It eliminates the need for an in house COM recorder. Also several of the bibliographic utilities themselves offer COM catalogues as an output alternative. Firms such as Brodart, Blackwell North America etc. are active in this market.

COM catalogues offer several advantages. Some are outlined hereunder:

1. It is inexpensive to reproduce and can be placed in many locations inside and outside of a library.

2. There can be separate films for author entries, title entries, and subject entries.

3. Several records can be viewed at one time.
4. Entries can be easily copied if a microform reader/printer is available.
5. Equipment is relatively inexpensive.

Some disadvantages of COM are:

1. Microforms are often not very readable compared to print.
2. It is not easily updated.
3. Updating is by supplements which may confuse the catalogue user.
4. The microfiche format may lead to interfiling of a base catalogue with supplements.
5. Deleted materials remain in the file until the next update.
6. Special microform reader/printers are expensive.

As COM catalogues gained popularity in the United States and elsewhere, several vendors attempted to introduce special readers for library applications. These readers can store upto 1200 feet of 16 mm. microfilm-the equivalent to twelve ordinary rolls on an internal reel. In most cases, the library's online COM catalogue can be contained in this reel which remains inside the reader and need not be handled by the user.

OPAC

Library automation has finally introduced online public access catalogue (OPAC). James Rice reports that at present more than 50 libraries in the United States are using this form of catalogue. Although most of these are in large libraries, a few are in medium-sized or even small libraries. Many more libraries are also trying to adopt OPAC. Such catalogues allow any member of the library community to search the catalogue data base in order to see if the library holds specific title of document to be informed of its location in the library, and if the catalogue system is linked to the circulation system, the enquirer be intimated whether the item is readily available or is on loan to other etc. It is stated that the availability of turnkey circulation systems have contributed to the development of OPACs and Geac turnkey system is getting much popularity in the libraries of UK and US.

IN-HOUSE AUTOMATED CATALOGUING

Library automated systems were first developed at local level in the United States. In fact some of the automated systems identified with vendors or bibliographic utilities were actually based on systems that first existed in individual libraries. Where in-house system is introduced, the libraries usually maintain a main file of catalogue records of the library's holdings. It is regularly updated and generally printed at periodic intervals. When in a library computerization starts, there is every need to convert retrospective catalogue into machine readable form and add it to the main file to make it complete.

Following are the main processes involved in a cataloguing systems:

1. Preparing worksheet.
2. Generating machine-readable records.
3. Verification of the records and generation catalogue.
4. Generation of added entries.
5. Generation of indexes and cross-reference.
6. Printing the records.

The output depends on the physical form of the catalogue chosen by the library. The chief forms are:

1. Line printer paper catalogue
2. Phototypeset catalogue
3. Microform, and
4. Card catalogue.

MARC FIELDS (ACCESS POINTS)

Before computer-based cataloguing starts, the library has to resolve many problems such as the actual and potential use of the library by the staff, students and other users; the length of data entry for various other usage within or without the institution etc.

Tedd referring to a research made at Bath University says that the following MARC fields can satisfy over 97 percent of readers requirements:

TAG DEFINITION

CONTROL FIELDS

001 Record Control number

050 LC call number

082 Dewey Decimal classification number

MAIN ENTRY HEADING FIELDS

100 Personal name main entry heading

110 Corporate name main entry heading

111 Conference, congress, meeting etc., name entry heading

TITLE FIELDS

240 Uniform-title—excluding collective-title

245 Title and statement of responsibility area.

248 Second level and subsequent level title and statement of responsibility.

EDITION FIELD

250 Edition area

IMPRINT FIELD

260 Publication, distribution, date, etc.

NOTES FIELD

503 Edition and history note

SUBJECT HEADING ETC. FIELDS

600 Personal name subject heading

610 Corporate name subject heading

611 Conference, congress, meeting etc. subject heading

ADDED ENTRY HEADING FIELDS

700 Personal name added entry heading

710 Corporate name added entry heading

711 Conference, congress, meetings, etc. name added entry heading

745 Title added entry heading-excluding uniform title

800 Series added entry (personal name-title)

840 Series added entry (title)

Automated Cataloguing Procedure

For designing in-house computerized cataloguing, the Librarian and the programmer should keep in view the length of information that could be expected from the catalogue. But it is not essential for local libraries in Pakistan to provide all the fields given in MARC record. The following fields can be sufficient in a medium-sized library:

1. Classification number
2. Main entry (personal or corporate)
3. Title
4. Imprint and collation
5. Series statement

6. Subject headings
7. Keyword entries
8. ISBN/ISSN/LC Card number

Coding Structure

To evolve coding structure for codifying the fields (type of entry) is technically a part of system designing. A logical coding is required for developing inhouse software which is based on: *(1)* Overall system designed *(2)* type of computer language to be used for development of computerized system. However in some latest computer free format, pattern comprising all the parameters, has been developed. Cataloguer can use and skip any field (access points) at one time depending upon the length of cataloguing data required without changing the entry codes every time.

Swihart and Hefley illustrate type of entry codes which is reproduced in the following table. This code identifies to the computer the type of data a record contains.

Type of Entry	*Method 1 short Mnemonic*	*Method 2 Longer Mnemonic*	*Method 3 Numeric*
1	*2*	*3*	*4*
Computer index number	CI	CINDEX	01
Security restriction code	SR	SECUR	02
Corporate agency author	CA	AUTC	12
Personal author	PA	AUTP	14
Title	TI	TITL	22
Report number	RN	REPNO	31
Contract number	CN	CONNO	33
Grant number	GN	GRANO	35

1	*2*	*3*	*4*
Number of pages	PA	PAGES	51
Number of illustrations	IL	ILLUS	52
Number of figures	FI	FIGS	53
Date of publication	DP	DAPUB	54
Place of publication	PP	PLPUB	55
Abstract	AB	ABSTR	61
Subject heading	SU	SUBJ	71
Keyword	KE	KEYWD	73

Type-of-entry codes.

The above table is illustrative only. It is not applicable to anyone library. If the practicing library is not using a standardized software, it can develop its own type-of-entry-code on such patterns.

DATA INPUT

Records may be entered 'off-line' or 'on-line'. With the offline an input form is normally completed by the cataloguer which is then passed to a punch or other operator for 'translation' into a machine-readable form, *e.g.,* punched cards for inputting to the computer. With the on-line, records are entered direct into the computer via an on-line terminal keyboard.

1. Computer Index Number. The computer index number is consecutive (accession) number which has no intrinsic value. This number is assigned to every title in the library.

2. Main Entry. It is established according to AACR2 or name authority file for oriental names etc. Cataloguer using name entry code, types the name of the author on the keyboard of the computer. It appears on the screen. If the name of the author already exists in computer held record, it is skipped. Traditionally the author entry has been considered the "main entry". But with a computer system, there is no main entry in that sense. Author or title entries have no more importance as such. All entries in automated system stand equal.

3. Title Entry. Titles are entered into the record in the exact format and spacing in which they should appear in the printed catalogue cards. Subtitle is entered in subfield. If software allows title can be permuted to offer more approaches to the important words in the title. Stop words are ignored.

4. Imprint and Collation. Imprint implies the place of publication, publisher and date. Publishers are entered under place, followed by publisher name. It follows title entry and then collation is recorded.

5. Series Entry. A name/title series entry is given if desired. Both name and title series are stored in name and title files respectively.

6. Subject Headings. L.C. or Sears' List of subject headings can be used for alphabetical subject access. Thesauri are used in specialized subject fields. Subject headings can be entered as required either in plain alphabetical language form or as a numerical subject entry code as are given in thesaurus etc. Subordinate subject headings can also be used if the system programme allows.

7. Keyword Entries. Keyword entries can be provided by permuting titles. This increases access points and strengthens subject approach in the catalogue.

8. ISBN/ISSN and LC Cards Number. The ISBN/ISSN access point file contains International Standard Book Numbers and International Standard Serial Number that may be used as access points when searching cataloguing database. Pakistan ISBN serves the same purpose. They all provide unique identification of an item and are convenient search keys. The LC Card number APF contains LC card numbers assigned by the Library of Congress. They may be from LC MARC cataloguing reçord or from the item in hand.

ADVANTAGES OF AUTOMATED CATALOGUING

Innumerable benefits are accrued from automated cataloguing practice. There is no time-lag between accessioning and cataloguing.

Routine and repetitive jobs are done efficiently. Besides the catalogues, a variety of records is produced as byproducts. These are the catalogue cards or machine-readable records that serves as a basis for the production of COM or book catalogue, various printed records, book plates, book pockets, book cards, spine labels etc. It is also possible to use COM for the production of Union Catalogues, bibliographies, Reference tools. The computerized catalogue can be integrated into a total information system particularly in academic and special libraries. It encourages cooperative cataloguing and centralized cataloguing.

In the on-line system direct input can be made through the terminals. It is also possible to correct, revise or amend the data on the existing record format required for new editions of the same titles. The authority files can be kept. Sorting and filing sequences can be rearranged according to requirements.

Catalogue entries and catalogue data can be arranged by specified criteria and in various sequences, such as the number of books on a subject or by an author, list of books on a specific subject, list of books written by a particular author, list of authors on a particular subject, and the like.

❐

10

Multimedia Catalogue

A basic problem in special cataloguing, is whether or not to incorporate entries for various special material in a general catalogue of a library. This issue can be considered under three main headings: *(a)* the compilation of a separate catalogue for each individual form whether each is book or nonbook; *(b)* the compilation of a special multi-media catalogue incorporatipg all non-book materials; and *(c)* the compilation of a single catalogue to include entries for all materials in library whether book or nonbook.

A precedent is set by various agencies which issue single-medium lists and catalogues. Some of these agencies are firms and other organisations which deal with specific medium and so of course these examples cannot be said to advocate separation in retrieval systems in libraries. A well known example is the British national film catalogue, recording the stock of one organisation. However, we should mention that the Library of Congress, which receives all materials under copyright deposit, issues separate catalogues for such forms as films and filmstrips; and phonorecords; and in the past it issued one for maps and atlases. We should also mention that BNB issues a separate publication of scores and works about music in the British catalogue of music, even repeating the entries for works about music as compared with BNB itself, although classified according to the BCM's own scheme. Notwithstanding, we recommend the principle of integrating, as far as possible, entries for all forms. The chief reason for this is that information enquiries do not necessarily cite a particular form, and even if they do they may not cite yet other relevant physical forms. This may happen because of ignorance on the part of the enquirer, who may be, say, book-oriented, and may not know of other forms. Current awareness services might include, under certain subject headings, not only bookform materials but any form of presentation of a subject. Such a facility would, we suggest, be of direct value mainly in teaching institutions, at all levels.

A further factor in favour of integrated catalogues is the increasing use of various forms in conjunction with each other. This situation is no novelty. The fact of accompanying material' has been long known and catered for in codes. A very common example is that of a recording, which will perhaps be on disc, with accompanying letterpress material, such as one of Chaucer's Canterbury tales together with a copy of the printed text. In the past, the accompanying material has usually be regarded as subsidiary, even though in fact it may have been necessary for the full exploitation of a document, *e.g.*, a film strip intended for instructional purposes with accompanying teacher's lecture notes, or records. Contrary to current emphasis on the audio-visual 'kit' as a new phenomenon, we suggest, then, that this form has been with us for it is difficult to decide which is the predominant medium, *e.g.*, as to whether a sound recording 'accompanies' a text, or the text' accompanies' a sound recording. For this reason, as well as to ensure that all materials are exploited as fully as possible, we suggest that a so-called multi-media catalogue is needed. However, since accompanying materials is often in textual form, it seems reasonable to reach the logical 'the media' and conventional textual material in the same catalogue. For similar reasons it is theoretically justifiable to include any 'special' textual material such as serials in the integrated catalogue.

Nevertheless, there will still exist the need for a physical form approach, mainly, we feel, for the librarian's benefit for stock record and housekeeping purposes, but also in some cases for the immediate use of the library's clientele. The latter may happen, when, say, a teacher is making up a film or record programme for general use, or when a new piece of equipment has been acquired and the teacher particularly wishes to experiment with it. The librarian's need may arise from the need for a stock record for such purposes as stockchecking, statistics, accounting, and calling up of items not received. Strictly speaking, these last are not catalogue uses, the basic object of a catalogue being the exploitation of stock by users, whether directly or indirectly. However, as we know, much of the data for housekeeping purposes is the same as that used for exploitation. Inevitably, with the use of a basic set of data for various purposes, there arises the concept of an integrated systems approach, with the use of a computer for selecting from a comprehensive store, and manipulating the data to specific ends. From the user's or librarian's housekeeping point of view, entries for documents in a particular form could be selected, manipulated and printed out in whatever order was required for the purpose. An essential need is to be able to list all materials in a particular form, *e.g.*, filmstrip. In turn, this means that each physical form must not only be represented, as in standard, eg AACR, cataloguing practice, but also it must be a field on its own, and with a tag to facilitate its use as an access term. Nowadays AACR is justifiably regarded as working basis for much full bibliographic cataloguing, and its structure is usually assumed in MARC formats, whether for book or for nonbook materials. AACR does include provision for spelling out some physical forms a potential tags.

Phonodisc could reasonably be made a field, with its own tag. Similar provisions apply for other physical forms starting with the stem 'phono...', such as phonotape and phonowire. It should be possible to enable a search to be made on the stem 'phono' to facilitate retrieval of all sound recordings, whatever their physical form. "Incidentally, in the example given above, the full stop (period) has been omitted at the end of the author heading, and following 'Phonodisc', despite its being, inconsistently, included in the code. However, by accident, the code may have provided a means whereby nonbook, as differentiated from book, forms of material might be retrieved by computer, the full stop acting as a searching and retrieval device for most 'special' materials as opposed to conventional materials. According to AACR, other special forms are not so conveniently indicated by a potential field attached to a uniform title.

A problem exists for music scores, which are not designated as such in headings or uniform titles, although in some instances the word 'score' occurs in the collation. Yet another problem occurs even when a potential field is suggested in AACR; this is when there is a possible difference of opinion over a term to be used. This would not pose much of a problem for locally generated data, but it could cause some degree of difficulty at least it locally generated entries using the 'British English' term had to be merged with, say, LC generated entries, which naturally would use 'American English'.

Similar types of problem are manifested by the many other forms of document, when it comes to computerised manipulation and retrieval of selected forms, as well as of subjects. And, as we feel we can assume, computerisation is the only feasible hope of achieving a multiple-access approach to both information as such and special forms of presentation. We wish to sum up, at this point, that not only a multi-media catalogue may be needed, but also that a generously multi-approach catalogue is needed. There should be approaches along the lines of a principle which we feel Cutter would have approved. Potentially, in one sequence, one could approach or trace information according to, not only author-type and title headings, but also subject headings and physical form headings; subject headings could consistently be subdivided according to form of presentation. As we have said, such a complex manipulation of data and approaches can be realised only through the use of the computer.

Some libraries are already computerising, or planning to computerise, their bibliographic data on special materials. In some cases, systems are being, or have been, introduced for certain individual forms, depending on local need, eg the Library of the Western Australian Institute of Technology has a multiple-approach computer-printed catalogue for slides. At the time of writing other media have not been planned for in this particular instance. Despite some academics' pipe dreams of an integrated systems approach, there is a lot to be said for experiment with a single medium. Problems relating to programming, computer storage, and access can be identified and solved comparatively inexpensively. However, we suggest that such achievements should be regarded as research and development projects rather than as ends in themselves. A most important aspect of such an experimental project is actual use of the resultant catalogue or index. In a comparatively 'closed' situation, as in the library of an educational institution, potential users of such a system can be canvassed and their comments recorded and analysed.

When libraries reach the point of finally appreciating that so-called 'special' materials are not so special that they may be rejected as 'normal' stock, or if actually acquired hidden away and largely avoided, it should be possible for multi-library catalogue use studies to be made. From these could emerge an idea of what library clienteles really need in relation to special materials. Judging by one experiment, in Pearl River Public Library, New York, when a multi-media catalogue and even stock-integration-policy is implemented, the users readily respond to such facilities: 'Users do like to find related materials on a given subject on one place'. Admittedly, as the article says, 'one situation does not connote a trend'; but we suggest that this situation is at least a symptom of the, as yet, unrealised potential of once 'special' library materials.

Just as normal monographic materials are being recorded on centrally produced computer tapes, as it happens MARC tapes, so there is more and more talk of doing the same for special materials. Also, as is commonly known, there are central computer stores, regional, national, occasionally international, of bibliographic data relating to articles, reports, etc. in certain subject fields. These can be searched on demand for specific subject requests. At the moment, MARC tapes for monographic materials are sold to interested libraries to use as they think best or apparently, at present, to be merely accumulated with a view to future use. Also, as one useful by-product, MARC tapes are used centrally as a basis for the computer output microfilm production of the 'micro-microform' Books in English by BNB. There is not as yet a convenient facility for libraries to draw upon a national, let alone an international, central computer store for only the data which they require, either for documents which they have in stock or for searches on demand from users. However, there is a proposal, and presumably a hope, for setting up such a central, national, store, in Britain, to be tapped on demand for certain special materials.

The Gilbert Report is confined in scope to audio-visual materials used in education. However, education and modern teaching techniques are probably the main stimulant to the increase in use and acceptance of at least the large audio-visual sector of special materials likely or even unlikely to be encountered by most librarians. Further, the report interprets 'education' in a broad sense, and some documents which might formally be dubbed 'recreational' are likely to be embraced by its proposals. This interpretation does not affect the variety of physical forms, but it could affect the size of any central store established, and this in turn could mean that any local library's stock of nonbook materials may stand a reasonable chance of being as well comprehended by the central store as, say, a general library's book stock might be covered by MARC tapes.

The physical forms contemplated are listed as follows:

SOUND OR AUDIO RECORDING

Gramophone record: a recording of sound on disc.

Sound or audio tape: a recording of sound on magnetic tape carried on an open reel.

Audio cassette or cartridge: a sound tape contained in a cassette or cartridge.

Visual images: still

Slide: a small unit of transparent material containing an image, mounted in rigid format, usually 2" x 2", and designed for use in a slide viewer or projector.

Filmstrip: a roll of film containing a succession of images designed to be viewed one at a time.

Transparency: a sheet, or combined set of sheets, of transparent material, carrying information, designed for use with an overhead projector.

Wallchart: a large sheet of information arranged in tabular or diagrammatic order, designed for public display.

Flipchart: an integrated graphic presentation on separate sheets hinged together in easel format.

Flash card: a card having words, numerals,. or pictures, designed for rapid identification, with or without an integrated sound track.

Print: a picture with accompanying text which makes the print significant for study purposes.

Art Print: a printed reproduction of a work of art-eg painting, drawing, sculpture, etc.

Picture or Drawing: a two dimensional drawing, painting, portrait, photograph, or a print of any of these, produced on opaque backing.

Visual images: moving

Film: film, bearing a sequence of images which create the illusion of motion when projected, and carried on an open reel.

Film loop: an endless loop of motion picture film usually contained in a cassette.

Film cartridge: a length of motion picture film contained in a cartridge.

Videotape: magnetic or other tape, carrying a series of TV images recorded magnetically, electronically or holographically. (Any of these may bear an integral sound track.)

Visual Images with Sound

A recording of moving visual images may carry an integral sound track (*e.g.* Sound Film).

A set of slides, or a filmstrip, may be accompanied by an associated sound recording on a gramophone record or, more usually; tape (commonly referred to as Tape-Slide).

Programmed Materials

Carried on transparent, opaque or magnetic substrates and designed for viewing directly or by projection, or for use with a computer; may have the physical form of a book.

Artefacts and Realia

Map: a flat representation of part or all of either the earth or the heavens.

Globe: a sphere with a representation or a map of the earth or of the heavens.

Chart: a sheet of geographic or other information arranged in tabular or diagrammatic order.

Relief model: a three-dimensional geographical map other than a globe.

Model: a three-dimensional representation of an object, either exact or to scale.

Diorama: a scene reproduced in three dimension by placing objects, figures, etc. in front of a representational background.

Realia: actual objects or specimens.

Microforms

(Microreproduction: a miniature reproduction of printed or other graphic matter which cannot be utilised without magnification.)

Microfiche: a microreproduction on a flat sheet of film.

Microfilm: a microreproduction on a roll of film.

Micro-opaque: a microreproduction on opaque material.

Aperture card: a card with an opening or openings within which micro-reproduction on film is mounted.

Combinations

Kit: a combination of items in two or more media designed to be used as a unit.

Game: a boxed set of materials designed for educational play.

It is envisaged that any records of documents would include commercial;, 'semi-commercial' (from, say, professional bodies), and even some locally produced items. Incorporated in fact the core of such a data base-would be entries from large national collections in Britain such as the National Film Archive and the British Institute of Recorded Sound.

We might note at this point that in 1972 a proposal was made from another source that there should be a 'British national discography' along the lines of the British catalogue of music and of course BNB itself; if such a work were realised its contribution to the type of database contemplated could be substantial. Also here we might recall that the Library of Congress has a potential which has progressed beyond this stage: its catalogue coverage already embraced audiovisual materials thanks to US legal deposit, which appears to be automatically comprehensive of all physical forms of documents.

To return to the Gilbert Report, with its attempts at cumulating such data as is at present available in Britain, we have to appreciate that, at the moment, a large variety and types of records would have to be drawn upon to realise the hope of a comprehensive collection of bibliographic data on nonbook materials. It is anticipated that such information could be reconciled, and incorporated consistently into a central store, without the central cataloguers having to sight the actual documents. This situation may, at first sight, seem to be analogous to that of compiling union catalogues of, say, books, or serials. However, in such cases, it is usually expected, or at least hoped, that entries have been compiled by professional cataloguers and, at least to some extent, according to a standard recognised code. We feel that Gilbert possibly minimises the technical difficulties in such a process. However, we feel that such a process. However, we feel that such a project is possible, and that bibliographic niceties so dear to some dare we say, conservative—cataloguers must give way to the immediate need of producing data of use to many libraries. To digress, but with a purpose, we might recall that some BM cataloguers seem to have wanted to delay indefinitely the photo-printed BM catalogue while they indulged their penchant for bibliographic perfection on the bibliographic information needed all over the world. We had the privilege of meeting Sir Frank Francis, then BM's director, in the early 1960's and he commented that, in effect, he had to get his cataloguers to eschew academic bibliographic niceties and to get on with producing a catalogue for real live use. Librarians must have in mind not colleague-cataloguers' academic criticism, but the ultimate use of their product in document and information retrieval. In short, if any minor errors emerge hard luck. The main concern should be use of the data to enable documents to be identified and exploited by users of libraries all over the country or even the world. In sum, then, we support the layman's proposition of integrating data from whatever source so that it can be drawn upon in real live situations. It is better to have some however inconsistent sort of information about nonbook materials, and soon, than wait for the millennium when all material is catalogued perfectly down to the last punctuation mark. We do not apologise for this apparent tirade: there are still far too many cataloguers who derive more satisfaction from the use of a square bracket than from the knowledge that they are serving users' needs for information today, not in three months' time when they finally have finished their games and pass on their toys to a vague depersonalised public whom through unfortunate library management-they never meet.

So, then, we keenly recommend the concept of the centrally accumulated data base hoped for in GILBERT, and we further hope that people can be found to do the accumulating, assimilating, and production for use of such information.

However, to realise such a hope, two needs must be borne in mind: *(a)* an overall organisation; and *(b)* a detailed organisation for the manipulation and output of bibliographic data according to the needs of requesting centres, assumed to be libraries which receive and formulate enquiries.

An overall organisation is worked towards by a system as reproduced from GILBERT. This includes four components: *(a)* the actual producers of documents; *(b)* central cataloguing agencies; *(c)* a computer store; and *(d)* printers for producing usable hard copy as required. It is technologically possible for *(c)* and *(d)* to be parts of the same apparatus: a lot depends on the physical type of product expected in reply to an enquiry, and the type of physical presentation acceptable by users. A single enquiry might be satisfied with a 'one off' computer printout, but a resource centre's own complete catalogue may demand a more sophisticated physical presentation.

An overall organisation is further enhanced by the system reproduced from GILBERT. The essential advances of this system on the previous diagram is that it introduces the real users of nonbook materials, and it shows how they are integrated into an information retrieval system ranging from producers, via a central store and enquiry coordinating service, through catalogue agencies, and back to enquirers.

A major component of this system is the Central Bibliographic Service, linking libraries and similar information service centres with a computer store and with cataloguing agencies, and, ultimately, with users of nonbook materials the final objective of the exercise.

So far, we could envisage the service as providing computer-printed lists for individual enquiries. However, this concept would, in effect, put the cart before the horse. Before individual searches are initiated, it is reasonable to expect general lists to be searched, in much the same way that Index medicus may be searched manually before a MEDLARS search is initiated by computer. The report, then, envisages a printed bibliographic service, which corresponds to the records of normal books covered by BNB or—in the film world—works covered by the British national film catalogue.

A noteworthy quotation from GILBERT is that 'no significant problems were encountered, and that there is every reason to suppose that the MARC system can be used for the cataloguing of NBM. The inference is that all nonbook materials could conveniently be catered for in the MARC format, and presumably entries for all forms could be integrated into once catalogue.

The sample catalogue entries would be part of a so called HELP IS system: Higher Education learning Programmes Information Service, as an adjunct to LERMISTOR: Learning Materials Information Store. But, confirming what we said earlier, the range of types of materials and of actual documents prepared for the system make it seem likely that the actual store of bibliographic data, and the spadework which would go into programming in the broadest sense, would encompass a lot of the work of all sorts needed to make the hole system operative.

It may be useful at this point to try to consolidate the main components of creating the type of integrated system envisaged in the report as a whole, and as demonstrated micro-economically by its sample Catalogue of materials available for exchange produced in March 1971 and including a variety of audiovisual materials.

First the documents have to be made, and, as with printed monographic media, they come from a great variety of organisations, and may range from commercial materials for national or even international distribution, to perhaps items locally produced for use in just on equcational institution. An example of the latter-local products which comes to mind, though in fact Australian, is a series of video-taped lectures made in the Princess Margaret Hospital, Perth, for the education of nurses. A decision must be made somehow and somewhere as to which documents are to be recorded in the central system. A sort of parallel situation in letterpress materials might be the locally printed or typewritten-reports on research, *e.g.*, higher degree these, produced by the thousand in colleges and universities.

We then come to the need for all such worthy documents to be catalogued, adequately and according to a generally accepted method. An obvious need is that documents on one subject but in varying physical forms and from a diversity of origins must finish up with a uniform subject heading, whether verbal or codified. This operation would call for the recognition of a uniform subject approach if it were to cater ultimately for a wholly consistent integrated record at the projected central store.

Then comes the need for items' entries to be selected and to be notified to the central store. Approaches and description need to be either consistently expressed or given fully enough in whatever form for consistent records to be brought together accurately at the catalogue compilation centre. The problem of integrating dissimilar entries for similar documents is as old as the compilation of union catalogues, and goes back to at least medieval England when a union catalogue of the manuscripts in monastery libraries was compiled. The problem is vastly intensified nowadays because of the fantastic increase in the quantity of documents, and in the present context it is inevitably exacerbated by the variety of physical forms. A J Wells has stated 'The largest single problem in system terms arises at this point since there is no unique identifier for each item which would provide a ready means of eliminating duplicate standard descriptor fields from the file. This is a major problem since the same item may be input into the data bank from any or all of the agencies. Inevitably here we must bring up the fact of standard book numbers, and further, international standard book numbers. There is an obvious need for some form of unique identifying tag for nonbook materials, just as there has developed a system for normal books in several countries, eg Britain and the USA. To plan and execute such a system would involve a lot of planning, and in fact we find it hard to envisage it being carried through. Presumably a prefix for each form would be required, as well as a unique number for each document. A unique identifying system does already exist for sound recordings in disc form, even though the notation used, assigned by manufacturers (ie publishers), is often complex. It is conceivable that at least commercially produced documents could be subjected to the same type of routine to which publishers of books seem to have responded so well in those countries, not using standard book numbers. It would appear that cooperating publishers of books have readily appreciated the value of such a system.

The next stage is the assembling and editing of bibliographic data at the relevant centre and its feeding into the store, say in computer disc form of facilitate the random access envisaged. This stage necessitates the allocation of tags and fields in a uniform way: this is why we have inferred that initial compilation of data should be made if at all 'possible, according to an accepted code for author/title and description and according to a standard system for the subject approach. UDC is the most widely accepted system-whatever faults it may have at present. An advantage of UDC is that it has built in symbols for various types of physical form, which can be represented either through the use of the colon for linking 'main' notations, or through the addition of symbols, to represent physical forms. We suggest that in a central store the use of 'main' notations would represent the type of flexibility required for access according to physical form, as well as the obvious requirement for access according to the subject of a document. Further, experiments have demonstrated that UDC-despite its occasionally awkward facet indicators can be computerised. The inputting of bibliographic data might, we feel, be the most difficult part of the operation possibly even more difficult than locating information in the first place. However, experiments with MARC-based formats seem to indicate that the project is viable. Input would embrace the functions of both bibliographic-oriented and retrieval-oriented catalogues, as we call them. This means that bibliographic detail in description and approaches would have to be as detailed, minute, and varied as might be needed by any user of such, a system. If, for example, the system were to be completely acceptable and useful, it would have to embrace' depth indexing' as well as the more conventionally expected approaches and detail.

We now come to the ultimate objective of the system: use. It is envisaged that the data base would be drawn upon in four main ways:

(a) Machine-readable data, in the form of magnetic tape, could be obtained as required by user-libraries and resource centres, preferably using 'Standard Nonbook Numbers' for access, but the system should cater for other approaches such as conventional author/title headings as commonly cited and as arrived at by the application of, say, AACR. We reiterate here that work is in progress on a new comprehensive nonbook code in Britain, but at the time of writing this had not been produced.

(b) The central store could be used for printouts resulting from searches initiated by local libraries, etc. in response to requests for comprehensive information according to any approach: subject, physical form, author, collaborator and so on. Such a function would be similar to that performed by various data banks in selected subject fields at the moment.

(a) and *(b)* could overlap in that a local centre may acquire magnetic tapes to use in local specific subject and/or form searches.

(c) A more sophisticated application approaches the limit of accessibility to data stores usually envisaged, in that a local centre could possibly be on line to the central store. We know that mainly, according to our observation, on-line systems seem to be operated by industrial and commercial organisations. So, it is 'technologically feasible that a similar system could be used for objective information retrieval via a local community-oriented service.

(d) Finally, comes the vital factor of location of required documents. In this respect, the central store would serve as a union catalogue.

Despite the lists produced in the US by NICEM (National Information Center for Educational Media), there is not in progress any system attempting to do all that needs to be done. We feel keenly that the time will come when either such a system has to be realised or we shall lose contact with nonbook-based information and its sources.

□

11

Cataloguing Department

This is an important department. Primairly the cataloguing department is organised as a unit of Preparation Department or Technical Department. But in big libraries like National libraries, this department is organised as a separate department.

Library work/functions are divided in two parts:

(1) Work behind the screen

(2) Work on the screen.

The first work is called the inner organisational stages of work like, book selection, ordering, Accessioning, cataloguing, classifying and transcriling of library holdings. Cataloguing is a work done behind the screen. It has no concern with the library service Departments.

Catalogue Division prepares and maintains the records which reveals the holdings of the library. The operations involved in the preparation of records consists of descriptive cataloguing, subject Cataloguing.

In some libraries the acquisition and cataloguing work has been brought together in a single department. In the very large organisation, operating in a spacious building, this scheme whereby all the technical processes are placed under the single head proves advantageous by promoting more effective coordination and integration of these operations, by helping to hold to a minimum the duplication of certain library records and by limiting the span of administrative control.

Cataloguing department is organised with indirect purposes. It is given special emphasis because of its specific character. Cataloguing department is a department which needs special attention while organising. Any carelessness or misplanning may effect the library service badly.

POSITION OF CATALOGUING DEPARTMENT

(University and Public libraries)

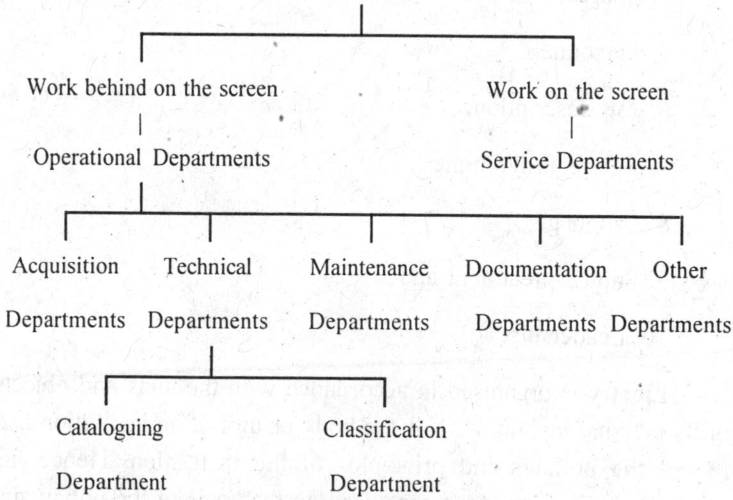

NATIONAL LIBRARY

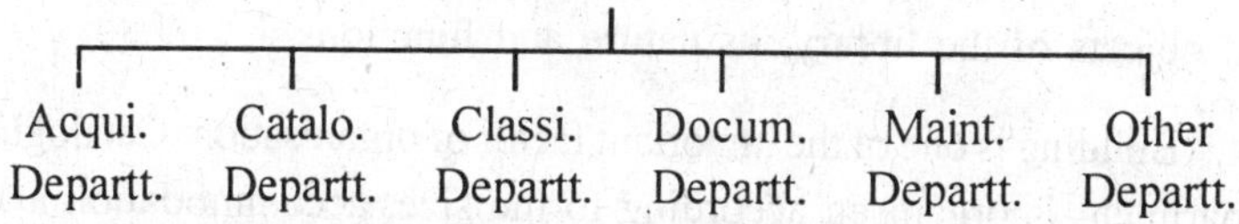

Location. Cataloguing Department is organised adjacent to classificition and Acquisition Department as it cannot work without cooperation of other two departments. Sometimes all these three departments are organised in a separate wing and in a separate position of the building which is fully aloof from all service departements and situated at a peaceful place. It has its separate enterence other than the service departments.

Organisational Structure

The organisation of cataloguing department differes from library to library as its size and nature depends on:

1. Aims and objects,
2. Building,
3. Type of material,
4. Budget,
5. Personnels,
6. Job description,
7. Future programmes,
8. Language,
9. Subject treatment and
10. Leadership.

Library is organised in accordance with the aims and objects of its peternal institution. It is the body or unit of an institution and follow the policies and principles of the institution. Hence, its cataloguing Department is organised on the basis of the policy and principles. In other words cataloguing Department fulfils the aims and objects of the library, its nature and functions.

Building is one of the important factor of organisation. Catalogue department is organised according to the size, accommodation and space provided to this department in the planning of a library building. Attention should be paid to lighting, ventilation, furniture and work space.

There are various types of libraries of specialised material National Reference library, Public library, Map library, Microfilm library, film library, manuscript library etc. etc. Cataloguing department take into consideration all such type of material, when it is organised.

Budget is the main factor effecting the organisation of Cataloguing department. Became the cataloguing department requires a fairly large part of the budget of the library, it is necessary to analyse carefully the budgetary needs of the unit. Generally budget of the department is distributed in the following catagories:

1. Salaries of the professional staff.
2. Salaries of the semi-professional staff.
3. Printed cards purchased.
4. Catalogue cards used in the work.
5. Equipment of various kinds.
6. Stationary.
7. Typewriter.
8. Duplicating machine,
9. Catalogue card produce machine.
10. Card cabinets,
11. Book trucks,
12. Microfilm reader.
13. Pasture chairs for cataloguers.

Salary of cataloguers vary from library to library and state to state. There has been some standardisation in the salaries of cataloguer. It is always higher then the other personnels of other departments other than technical section. Salary is catagorised in three grades:

1. Junior cataloguer's grade.
2. Senior cataloguer's grade.
3. Selection grade for cataloguers.

Cataloguing department utilise services of various types of personnels:

1. Professionals for cataloguing.
2. Semi-professionals for filing and arrangement of cards.

3. Non-professionals for listing, arranging the books, transcribing work and other work entrusted by the professionals.

In some of the more efficient libraries, the distinction between professional tasks in the department and the clerical activities is direct and definite. The professional person is concerned with the establishment of entries, the making of unit card, and the assigning of subject headings. It also takes decision on technical points. Semi-professional persons are engaged in searching and for priliminary cataloguing.

There should be a proper and standardised job description among the personnels of cataloguing department. It should be qualitative as well as quantitative. Division of work should be done on various lines:

1. Differences in training,
2. Experience of personnels,
3. Process,
4. Arranging the cards,
5. Filing of cards,
6. Typing of cards,
7. Reproducing cards,
8. Language,
9. Type of material: serials, rare books, maps, musical scores, and microfilms,
10. Subjects.

The extent to which the work of the catalogue department can be divided depends chiefly on the size of the staff. Obviously, the problem is simple when the cataloguing is done by one cataloguer with the assistance of partime or temporary assistants. Problem of organisation and work-division is inevitably become more complex when the number of staff is increases.

Planning is the foundation of organisation. Proper planning of a cataloguing department may lead to economy and work efficiency. Hence, while organising a cataloguing department, a thorough planning should be made and in many stages. What will be the future programme, should be foresighted by the head of the library.

Language is also a factor involved in job-description. National libraries and otber libraries receive reading material on various local and foreign languages. Cataloguing department engage cataloguers specialised in various languages for maintaining efficiency in the work.

Organisation on the basis of subject and language common in the large libraries. The ability to work with books in foreign language is important.

Special technique involves in the processing of various of reading material-serials, audio-visual material, microfilms. All these material require a degree of specialised knowledge for which work division on the basis of types of material is indicated.

1. Cataloguing units:

(i) Sorting and dating of order slips,

(ii) Searching of new titles,

(iii) Cataloguing of type of material,

 (a) Serial cataloguing

 (b) Book cataloguing

 (c) Other material

(iv) Revision work,

(v) Typing work,

(vi) Reproducing work.

2. Maintenance unit:

(i) Books with jackets,

(ii) Books without jackets,

(iii) Paper back books,

(iv) Inserting of book-pockets,

(v) labeling.

Organisational Work

Cataloguer—cataloguer is the main person to organise the department. It is the cataloguer, who can establish or run the cataloguing department. A cataloguer should possess the following qualities:

1. It is not everyone who is cut out to be a cataloguer,
2. Scholarly knowledge,
3. Knowledge of many more languages other than his local language,
4. Broad mindedness,
5. Foresighted,
6. Good organisor,
7. Knowledge of literature,
8. Book-lover,
9. Good reading habits,
10. Patient worker,
11. Tactful in dealing,
12. Good memory,
13. Capable of cooperating with others,

14. Knowledge of library techniques.
15. Good knowledge of catalogue codes,
16. Ability of leadership,
17. law-temperament,
18. Flair for accuracy,
19. Good personality.
20. Good handwriting,
21. Knowledge of the attitude, demand and approach of the readers.
22. Aware with the working of other departments of the library.

Cataloguer in charge of the department should be of clearmind, sound knowledge of subjects, language, library techniques and the approach of the readers, He should have working knowledge and good experience of supervision of a technical section. He should not be man who may be misled by others. He should be decision maker while establishing the entry. A cataloguer is supposed to be one of the guides to researchers. Though the cataloguer is not directly related to readers, but he may guide by applying various entries of all possible aspects of the subject. Cataloguer should be a professional man who can justify the bibliographical operations.

Catalogue Codes

Choice of catalogue: while planning a catalogue department, a serious thinking should be the type of catalogue:

1. Dictionary catalogue, or Classified catalogue.
2. Printed catalogue, or card catalogue.

There are difference of opinion on this choice. European Countries are following subject-alphabetic catalogue, a mid way of dictionary and classified catalogue. U.S.A. and its allied countries are following printed catalogue. India is following handwritten catalogue. But so far dictionary or classified catalogue is concerned, Indian cataloguers are divided. Most of the libraries of India are following dictionary catalogue. Classified catalogue has, also been the choice of some libraries like B.H.U. and Madras University libraries.

Choice of Catalogue Code

There are few important catalogue codes:

1. AACR (British and American text)
2. Classified catalogue code (Dr. S.R. Ranganathan).

Efficiency of cataloguing department depends on the catalogue code used in the library. It is a primary question to be delt in advance before the organisation of cataloguing department. There should be serious thought on the choice of catalogue code. Catalogue code to be choose should be based on:

(a) Logical thinking,

(b) Scientific terminology,

(c) Detailed rules and regulations,

(d) Simple in language,

(e) Followed easily,

(f) Maintain accuracy, consistency, and simplicity,

(g) Suitability to the needs of the readers,

(h) Performance to satisfy the different approaches of the readers.

There are rural libraries adopted local cataloguing, which is harmful as after a long-period, it will not be possIble to continued or revise the cataloguing rules in accordance with standard catalogue code. Temporary cataloguing should be avoided.

The library catalogue in bookform is found commonly in European libraries as:

(a) It is convenient to use.

(b) It can be carried easily from one place to another.

(c) Copies may be placed for use in every room.

But on the other band, entries can neither be added nor withdrawn. It is out dated as soon as it is printed or compiled.

The library catalogue is widely used in medium size libraries in Europe and all libraries in India, Pakistan, Sri Lanka, Bangladesh, and all other developing and under-developed countries. Card catalogue is simple in arrangement, convenient in withdrawal.

While making choice of a suitable catalogue code, the system of arrangement of filing catalogue entries should also be decided. There are many important systems-cutter filing rules, ALA rules for filing catalogue cards, and, Rules for filing of classified catalogue by Dr. S. R. Ranganathan. the arrangement by letter is suitable for small and medium size library, word-by-word arrangement for reference libraries, and Mixed or Midway system of Ranganathan to specialised libraries.

There is a close relation between classification and subject heading work. It is a cataloguing process. The official record of the subject headings used in the library and the standard publisher lists are the essential tools for assigning subject headings and making subject reference cards.

Card Duplication. When the cataloguer has completed his copy slip or master card for each title of a group of new book, often in combination with light pencil marks underlying appropriate information which the typist can copy direct from the title page, a clerical assistant can perform most remaining operations. There are many methods adopted for card duplication process-memeograph, multigraph, xerox, stencil, metel plates, typewriter and tape activated electric typewriter and the IBM or Remington Rand punched card machines.

Each typed card must be examined by the cataloguer for possible errors. When a larger number of card is required, it is necessary to adopt the unit card method.

Cataloguer's Tools. Cataloguing department is equipped with so many essential tools used in day to day cataloguing process for references:

1. Subject bibliographies,
2. Union catalogues,
3. Cummulative index,
4. Authority file,
5. Catalogue codes,
6. Standard Lists of subject headings,
7. International dictionary of language and subjects,
8. Terminology index,
9. Biographies,
10. Catalogue cards,
11. Guide cards.
12. Classification scheme,
13. Cataloguing problem file,

Revision Work. No doubt cataloguers are technical hands and' have thorough knowledge of cataloguing procedures adopted in library. Even than a final checking of cataloguer's work is made as to maintain consistency and accuracy. It is a routine work. The work of revision requires competence in all phases of cataloguing work and familiarity with the cataloguing and classification policies of the particular library.

While making judgement and descretion the Jeviser needs the following considerations:

1. Time divoted,
2. Capacity of the cataloguer,
3. Correctness of entries,
4. Availability of cataloguing tools,
5. Correctness of subject headings,
6. Bibliographical description.
7. Examination of transcription,

Revision work is made by the chief cataloguer or head of cataloguing department. Revision should be done carefully and in details continuously. Checking work may be discontinued after the cataloguer enjoy full confidence in him about the knowledge of library policies, accuracy and ability. No card should be filed until unless it is properly checked by the reviser and scruitiny mode.

Shelf List. Shelf list is an important card prepared by cataloguer. In some libraries, order card is used as shelf-card. Shelf list is prepared in two types:

(a) Shelf list as a copy list or unit card.

(b) Shelf list as a shelf slip.

It is prepared in two sizes:

(a) Size of the catalogue card. 5" × 3"

(b) Catalogue card. 5" × 2"

It is a permanent record and kept under safe custody of the chief cataloguer or the responsible person of the library. Shelf list is an important property of the cataloguing department. It is checked, revised and handed over to the custodian. It is properly recorded. Shelf listing work is done by the custodian or the person of his belief.

Filing. Filing work is an important work. All cards, whether, author, title or subject are filed by a competent person of the cataloguing department. It demands closed supervision until the filer is thoroughly families with filing rules and has attained such a degree of accuracy as to make further supervision unnecessary.

Filing work is generally accomplished in two stages;

1. All cards to be filed in to the catalogue are arranged according to the filing rules and filed in to the catalogue.

2. After the cards are arranged, they are filed in to a file supplementary to the card catalogue proper. Following precautions are taken while filing cards:

(a) Scruitiny be made,

(b) Cards should be distributed and arranged first,

(c) System should be decided before hand,

(d) Filing work should be done daily or weekly,

(e) Shelflist should be counted and filed separately,

(f) Filing work should not be given to raw hand,

(g) Author, title and subject cards should not be filed on one day or by one man.

In small and medium size libraries at least, card should be arranged in as nearly a straight alphabetical sequence as possible, ignoring punctuation and differing types of entry. Simplified cataloguing rules enables usually make it possible for card filing to be done by intelligent, interested non-professional assistants. Neither the classified catalogue nor the dictionary catalogue is of practical value in public libraries, but some attempts are being made in arranging entries under a given subject by date of publication so old material can be passed over.

Book Preparation. The process of book preparation is usually performed by the non-professional person of the library. While all possible cards are produced orre-produced, the books are made ready for circulation *i.e.* preparation work includes:

(a) pasting of slips or labeling,

(b) marking of numbers or lettering,

(c) Jacketing,

(d) counting,

(e) cutting pages of books with incut edges,

(f) Adding marks of ownership by means of bookplates and by ink embossing or perforating stamps,

(g) Making and inserting of book cards.

The process of above a, d, e, f are completed before the books are distributed to the cataloguers. Lebelling is, of course, not necessary if the call number is lettered directly on the building, which, in libraries, is accomplished by means of an electric styles and special transfer tape. In small libraries marking is done by hand. An accesion number is used large enough to have numerous copies of a book, to distinguish the copies, so this is needed on the book pocket, book cards, and at one place in the book as well as on the shelfirst or official catalogue cards. If each worker visualises the reader waiting the book, things will more faster and his day's work will be more interesting.

Reports and Statistics. A Annual report is prepared by the chief cataloguer or the Incharge Assistant Librarian of the cataloguing department and submitted to the Librarian or the Head of the library. The main purpose of this report is to:

(a) transmit facts respecting the department,

(b) inform the performance of the work,

(c) highlight the administrative problems,

(d) suggest the future planning,

(e) recommend the improved methods to increase the efficiency of the department.

The report consists a written survey accompanied by statistics. The report should be concise, and call attention to problems and suggestions regarding personnel, methods and equipments etc.

Book statistics is prepared in the cataloguing department. Larger libraries record their book statistics just before the book leave the catalogue department when all processes are finished and books and cards are together. Withdrawals are to be recorded also. Each type of books received in exchange, donation or gift are recorded with their source. A simple monthly statistics nimeographed, with a crossline per day. Statistics includes:

(a) Accessions.

(b) Book records.

(c) Card records.

(d) Record of kind of material books, serials, maps etc.)

Some cataloguing departments maintain elaborate statistics which are time consuming for the individual catalogue or other assistant to complete. It should be reduced by making spot studies by the librarian over short period of time to determine the effectiveness of the operations.

Cost Economics. Study of cost cataloguing is necessary to have full knowledge to determine which units are functioning effectively and expenditure involved in operation. The main purpose of preparing cost economics is to:

(a) determine the cost of cataloguing work.

(b) limit the departmental budget.

(c) evaluate the function of the department in relation to its cost.

(d) value the service cost.

(e) do the work more economically without lowering stan dard.

(f) satisfy the administrators about the functioning of the department.

(g) compare the cost of cataloguing department with other departments.

(h) take precautions to minimise the wastage in operation.

(i) evaluate accuracy for economy.

(j) make future planning.

Cataloguing department enjoy the highest of the library which has attracted the attention of the librarians although no one has devised as yet a way determining how much cataloguing should cost. There is a opinion that it is consuming a large portion of the library's budget. Miller made an important contribution toward this goal in his analysis of acquisition and cataloguing costs in a University library.

Cataloguing cost is influenced by many factors: Needs of the library users, the standards of service, the size, and the character of book collection, physical arrangement of the library, Administration and Organisation of cataloguing, and the efficiency of the staff.

Cataloguing cost may be minimised by taking following steps:

(a) Certain processes for which professional training is not necessary, clerical help may be more economical.

(b) The needs of readers should be studied and all phases of work should be analysed with a view towards satisfying those needs efficiently and economically.

(c) Gain should be real not imaginary. To reduce expenditure at any cost is not the solution.

(f) Changes should be avoided which causes excessive in convenience to the readers.

(g) Economics should logically start with the larger things and proceed down to the smaller details.

(i) Professional processes should be carefully defined and separated as far as practicable.

(j) Full advantages of equipments should be exploited.

(k) Cataloguer should decide that library records are actually needed with a view to eliminate all unnecessary duplication.

(1) Selective cataloguing should be applied.

(m) Detailed cataloguing should be limited to rare books.

(n) Simplified cataloguing method should be applied.

(o) All rules and practices which result in time consuming should be eliminated.

(p) Number of entries per title may be reduced.

There are two avanues to reduce cotaloguing cost-cooperation, and centralisation. Such agencies are minimising the cost of cataloguing.

❐

12

Role of Computers

The Computer can either purchased right away or in easy instalments or can be hired. No doubt, various computer manufacturing companies allure the prospective purchasers by stressing that the total cost of the computer can be realised in the form of savings and the cost of service for which additional staff has to be pressed into service. However, in view of the fast-changing computer technology and the increasing manufacture of sophisticated computers during last few decades many computers will become obsolete thereby putting the libraries to irreparable loss, it is but advisable that not only big computers are taken on hire basis but minicomputers and other turnkey devices should be made use of for performing specific jobs so that the risk-remains with the manufactures or it is *minimal* and the library is assured of latest Computer to be taken into account in the respect include the following.

1. Main-frame Computers VS. Mini-computers.
2. Capabilities of various Computers, especially in relation to library applications.
3. Reliability and Service of various makes of different manufacturing companies.
4. Hardware and Software.
5. Specifications and Accountability of various makes of computers.
6. Amenability to national and international standards.
7. Easy servicing and availability of spare parts.

8. Warranty & Safeguards.

9. Free training for hard ware & soft ware.

Kinds of Computers

Computers are of two kinds *i.e.*, *(i)* Analogue and *(ii)* Digital. The former is useful for scientific work as it helps in calculating the accepted information according to a pre-determined pattern which may be mechanical, electro-mechanical or electronic. In other Words, it helps in processing the information in a physical from *i.e.* in terms of weight, volume or electric current. For example, it can translate temperature, flow, speed, attitude, voltage an other physical variables into related electrical quantities and for this purpose it uses electrical equivalent circuits. The latter type of computer *i.e.* Digital Computer is a general purpose computer as it helps in calculating and processing the accepted data in digital form.

In other words, it makes use of conventional letters, symbols and numbers for the purpose and is, therefore, suitable for processing of information in general and for various other commercial business. and office applications. It is this type of computer which is used in libraries. The digital Computer can be further divided into two types *i.e.*, batch processor and Real-time Processor. It processes the data accumulated into batches or groups over a period of time. It consists of the following four component units:

(i) The hardware *i.e.* the machinery which is designed to carry out instructions necessary to perform the assigned jobs.

(ii) The Inputs Units help in converting the data passed on to them into a standard from acceptable to the Central Processor.

(iii) The Central processor of the heart of the computer consists of the storage unit, the control unit and the arithmetic unit.

The data in the store section of the computer is governed by the software the programme *i.e.,* a series. of instructions which are devised by the computer manufacturer or by the computer users or their agents. The capacity of the central processor is measured in thousands of units which may consist of one character of a byte or a computer word.

Real Time Processor

The Real Time Processor is designed to process a large volume of data. In this system, the units called terminals have a direct connection or on-line connection with the computer in such a way that data can be fed to the processor directly. Generally, the terminal is an electric type-writer through which the operator keys in information or interrogatories. In this system, there is no need of presenting this information on machine-readable media i.e. magnetic tape punched cards or paper tape because in it the programme can directly control the processing of data received from a terminal *i.e.*, an electric typewriter besides adding it to the files on backing store or sending back to the terminal the data already available on file and that is why is called real-time processor because quick service even though the data is received from many terminals.

As such, these two processors differ from each other on the basis of input and output units used by them. The main advantage of a digital computer is its speed of processing the data. It carrier out the instructions of the programme in a fraction of a second. The speed of the peripherals expressed its one thousandth of a second or one millisecond while that of the central processor is indicated as one thousand millionth of a second or nanosecond. It is evident that the speed of the former is slower than that of the latter, the reason for it being than in the former electro-mechanical devices are used while in the latter electronic devices are made use of. It is claimed that computers can serve as a panacea for all the existing ills libraries since these can be made use of for performing efficiently all sorts of jobs from the procurement of the reading materials to their organisation and use. In another words, these include the acquisition, classification and cataloguing and the circulation and use of the reading materials besides making provision for information and retrieval systems.

The Computer-based book order System of the Michigan University library started with the use of 1401 Tape Computer and the present type of 360/40 computer. The system consists of the following processes:

1. The name and address of the book-sellers or suppliers are stored in a disk file and each one of them is assigned a number.
2. The book orders for the books to be procured are key-punched and each of the book-sellers is identified by the number alloted to him as stated in *(i)* above.
3. Out of the ten copies of the order forms, two copies are mailed to the book supplier and the third copy is field in the order by the order number, while the remaining seven copies are field in a separate file to be used for classification and cataloguing work.
4. The orders are batched and sent to the data processing Centre on the campus twice a weak. On the following days, ten copies of the order forms are received by the library alongwith pre-punched cards in triplicate for each order and a list of orders according to each book budget a location besides an undated cumulative supplementary list representing all new orders placed in the library system and all transactions done against the orders placed earlier.
5. The pre-punched cards serve various purposes, namely to indicate receipt of the book the need to pay the bill, to count the books added to the stock and to remove the order card from the order file in case the book is classified and catalogued.
6. The cumulative supplemental outstanding order file is passed against the budget allocation and statistics files every fortnight which helps in printing the up-to-date position of funds so as to help the Order Section Incharge to control

new orders. In this way, two supplementary order tapes are printed every month for bringing up to date the master outstanding order file, indicating the position of each order at that time.

7. Letters for the unsupplied items are issued.
8. An Expenditure Statement is prepared monthly.. It indicates the amount already spent up-to-date and the amount which is still unspent.

Advantages

1. Many repetitive jobs are performed at one and the same time, thereby reducing the number of staff members for the Order section.
2. An accurate, up-to-date-and automatic information is made available about the latest position of each book order placed there by helping to avoid unnecessary duplicate ordering.
3. An accurate up-to-date and automatic information is made available about the best position of each head of the book fund *i.e.*, how much amount has already been spent and how much is in balance thereby either to limit future orders or to accelerate the pace of orders so as to utilise the funds in time.

The Yale University Library System

This system provides for all the processes through which a book..has to pass through the moment it is selected for purchase and is made available for use by the readers.

The Cornell University Library System

In the second system, an order-search from is used for placing a book order which remains there alongwith the L.C. cards up to the time of receipt of the book. In case, L.C. card is not available machine generated orders for L.C. cards are produced automatically.

On-line Systems

Besides in three other University libraries the On-Line Systems are in use. These include the "LOLA Library OnLine Acquisitions Sub-System Washington University Library "Rice University's On-Line Acquisition System and "The University of California at Irvine's On-Line Acquisition System".

Washington University Library System

The fires system has been designed to perform all technical services and processes consisting of various separate sub-stems of which one is the Acquisitions subsystem performs the following seven functions:

1. Preparing an entry indicating request for purchase.
2. Preparing a book selection entry and its checking.
3. Preparing a book order and its processing.
4. Preparing a standing order Plan.
5. Receiving the book.
6. Processing Bills,
7. Preparing a report of the books received.

The Rice University Library Sysem

The second system at the Rice University in based on MARC II tapes and holdings at eighteen libraries of the Gulf Coast which are cooperating in the project. In this system, when a suggestion for the purchase of a book is received, the above record is first checked up to know whether the book in question is already in one of the libraries.

If it is there, a report to this effect is generated but if the book is not available in any of the libraries but if the information is available in the file, the order for the book is added to database. Simultaneously, a multiple crder from and receipt card in order to update the record are generated and the cost of the book is debited to book fund. In case the order relates to multiple volumes a card for each volume is produced.

If the information about the book is not available in the file i.e. data, the details of the order are included in the holdings and the non-order file. On receipt of the ordered book, a cataloguer work sheet is produced which is used to correct, and update the existing record before catalogue cards for the book are prepared. In this system, a teletypewriter, called CONTROLMATIC Model 37, is used to supply to the cooperating libraries the current information received from the Library of Congress besides the preparation of classified extracts and the card listing to be used by Book Selection as a book selection tool.

The University of California System at Irvine

The third system at the university of California at Irvine makes use of IBM 360/50 along with a central core memory of 512 K. It consists of two sub-systems *i.e.* book found accounting and purchase order writing. The first sub-system is to record, process and make available financial information regarding the book fund. The second sub-system besides writing purchase orders is to debit automatically the cost of book ordered besides conversion of the foreign currencies.

Computer-based Periodicals Acquisition, Processing and Control Systems

The acquisition, processing and control of periodicals have been eluding a permanent solution due to their idiocyncrasies. In many cases, the periodicals have been controlling the librarian instead of the librarian controlling the periodicals. The latest method to bring them under control takes the help of the computer, which is considered by many a panacea for various ills of library jobs including those of processing and controlling of periodicals and serials.

Though efforts to develop a computerized system were started in the 1940's yet the first important system was designed and developed as late as 1962 only which was fully put into operation in

1964. The earlier systems were using computers for keeping parallel records on manually-run systems, whereas the latter system discontinued their use.

The periodical's work involves the following main jobs:

1. Ordering and Bill Passing.

2. Receiving supply.

3. Claiming the unsupplied periodicals.

4. Preparing lists of Holdings and Union lists.

5. Administrative Control.

6. Completing the volumes and sending them for binding.

7. Classification and cataloguing.

To perform these functions efficiently, various computer-based systems have been brought into use. In India also, computer is being used for the acquisition, processing and controlling of periodicals. Most of these systems have the following components of records, inputs and outputs, with, however, minor variations besides converting the existing manual file onto a magnetic tape.

Inputs

(i) Location Mark.

(ii) Call number.

(iii) Title.

(iv) Periodicals holdings information with years and volumes.

(v) Month and year of the latest issue received in the library.

(vi) Supplier and his code number.

(vii) Source of supply *i.e.,* either by purchase, gift or exchange.

(viii) Fund Allocation.

(ix) Period of subscription.

(x) Unique Identification number for each periodical title in the file.

(xi) The existing position of a periodical i.e. whether it is active or not.

(xii) Binding Code Numbers and other Binding Instructions.

(xiii) Frequency of publication i.e. number of issues per volume and number of issues per year.

(xiv) Expected dates of publication and receipt in the library.

(xv) Expected dates of the receipt of TCI, *i.e.* Title Contents and Index pages.

A Mnemonic Title, *i.e.* Abbreviated Title is used for the purpose of checking the receipt of a periodical issue.

Outputs

In most of the systems referred to above, the outputs consist of the following:

(i) Master File List which is an alphabetical list of periodicals, by Main Entry, received in the library indicating details of periodicals holdings of the library, is meant for staff use.

(ii) Public Holdings Printout, also an alphabetical list of periodicals by title or main entry which is meant for public use and consists of daily, weekly and monthly lists. These lists are very simple and contain only such information as is relevant to the users.

(iii) Supplement printouts which include daily receipts to be cumulated weekly.

(iv) Non-receipt And Claim List for all the overdue issues of periodicals.

(v) Titles List indicating the list of periodicals received in the library and their location but without the information regarding the total number of volumes held by a library.

(vi) Subject List for public use *i.e.* subject-wise list of periodicals.

(vii) Shelf List *i.e.* A classified list of periodicals with information about holdings.

(viii) Duplicate Lists *i.e.* lists of all periodicals of which more than one copy are received in the library.

(ix) Inactive Titles List.

(x) On Order List.

(xi) Cross-References List

(xii) Subscription Agent List.

(xiii) Active Titles List.

Advantages

1. A Computer-based periodicals System enables a better access to the periodicals records to the staff.
2. It provides better service to the users.
3. It provides more accurate records.

Disadvantages

It involves huge expenditure for the conversion of the existing manually operated periodicals file onto the magnetic tape. Development costs of a computer system are exorbitant which are lost over a period of time. The cost of continuing operation of computer-based periodical system is not less than that of the manual system. Rather, in some cases, it may be even double of the latter, although final estimates are not available. In the computer-based system the time taken for checking a title is not less than in the manual system.

However the following few recent developments in the computer application to periodical systems which are under way may be helpful in improving situation:

L.C. MARC Serial Format

The library of Congress MARC Serials Format will serve as a communication format for periodicals between a reporting library and a receiving library in respect of the following:

(i) The national Union catalogue symbol for a reporting library.

(ii) Periodicals Holdings information.

(iii) The period of periodicals available.

(iv) Retention information.

Standard Serial Numbers

The second development is the use of an International Standard periodicals Number, officially called the American Standard identification Number, for serial publications which is specifically useful for periodicals checking work. This number is to consist of seven decimal digits besides an eighth check digit.

Computer Based Cataloguing Systems

MARC projectThe use of computer in cataloguing *e.g.* MARC I Pilot project was started in November, 1965 by the Library of Congress. The main aim of this project was to distribute Library of Congress cataloguing in a machine-readable from to various libraries for the reading materials received by them so as to facilitate them to meet the explosion of knowledge and the increasing demand for easy and quick provision of required information.

Working of The System

The MARC II was completed in 1967 with the development of a new format capable of transferring bibliographical data to the receiving libraries. The system consists of the following stages:

1. It presupposes the existence, of a centralized or cooperative classification and cataloguing system on the pattern of that of the Library of Congress.

2. It also requires that the participating libraries of the programme should install computers and appoint programmers in their respective libraries.

3. The Computer-Based MARC Cataloguing System consists of the following main sections or programmes:

    (i) MARC Maintenance Programme for keeping the MARC file up-to-date- by means of the weekly tapes received from the Library of Congress.

    (ii) MARC Selection Programme for selecting entries from the MARC tapes, converting character codes, preparing a record in a format suited to an individual library and for printing two proof copies to be used by cataloguers of the library.

(3) MARC Correction Programme for editing the selected entries preparing the proof copy of the edited list, punching cards for using in converting to paper tapes and for typing book cards and spine labels in case a Flexowriter is used.

(4) MARC Card Print Programme for printing catalogue cards for the selected items may be presorted and alphabetized filing purposes.

(5) Update-Generate Programme for updating the Master file and generating the entries and changing for print files.

(6) The Weekly Print Programme for printing the weekly supplements for the printed catalogues and the list of new books by call number.

(7) The Monthly Pint Programme for bringing up-to-date the print files of the catalogues, and printing monthly supplements and a list of new books. These monthly supplements' are cumulated to print the full catalogue.

Advantages of The System

1. A centrally prepared catalogue can be distributed to the receiving libraries in a machine-readable form.

2. In spite of increasing acquisitions the catalogue can be kept-up-to-date without employing additional staff .

3. The production cost of card catalogue on the computer is lesser than that of purchasing the Library of Congress catalogues cards.

4. The MARC tapes can be utilized for acquisition functions *i.e.* selecting and ordering and claiming unsupplied books without any additional cost.

5. The MARC tapes can be used for producing conventional card catalogue by the subscribing libraries as demonstrated by the University of Toronto.

6. The MARC data can also be used for producing book catalogues as demonstrated by the Washington State Library.

Limitations of The System

George Piternick points out the following few limitations of the Machine-Readable catalogue system:

1. The MARC record for any title is almost similar to the conventional bibliographic record, as such it inherits all its limitations.

2. The MARC format will be limited, at least for the next few, years, to the English language books because the MARC character set is severally limited in respect of special characters and diacritical marks.

3. The time gap between the creation of MARC record and a catalogue record copy by the participating library which is inherent at present in the existing card production methods

of the Library Congress, will not be removed until and unless both the cards and tapes are prepared from the same machine-readable record.

4. Expending on account of machine time by the participating libraries will go on increasing in view of the weekly shipment of about 1,200 records or about 62,000 records annually requiring 15,000 feet of magnetic tape.

Latest Developments in The System

The COMARC project has been taken up by the library of Congress with the financial help from the Council of Library Resources. Under this project, the Library of Congress receives records based on Library of Congress Cataloguing representing those of selected libraries which have converted their catalogues into MARC format. These records are to be checked with the Official Catalogue of the Library of Congress for updating and redistribution through the MARC distribution system.

Computer Output Microfilm

The Computer Output Microfilm (COM) was developed in the U.S.A. by Stromberg Carlson Company. It used the Charactron tube for projecting the computer output onto an unexposed film at high speed. The Charactron cathode ray tube was invented in the early 1950's which was responsible for displaying the results of computer processing on the phosphor-coated face of a television screen. Later on, a microfilm was attached to the screen of a television so that the information given by a computer was recorded.

This device was responsible for the invention of Computer On Microfilm. The latest types of computers which were capable of recording more than 100,000 characters per second were responsible for the replacement of electra-mechanical line-printers were, in their turn capable of printing 1,200 lines per minute each line having a width of 132 characters.

Further a COM is capable of recording photographically a full page at a time as compared to a line only printed by a line-printer.

Moreover, a microfilm has another advantage over the paper in the sense that the microfilm has the capacity of storing more information in a particular amount of space as compared to that of hiș paper equivalent as the microfilm of 105 mm x 148.75 mm size can store 225 pages of text with the reduction ratio of 42:1 into this computer, microfilms having 16mm or 105 mm width are fied. The former are wound in spools or cartridges while the latter are cut into microfiche.

The end product of a Computer Output microfilm is a magnetic tape which contains the requisite bibliographic information besides the concerned printing and format control codes provided for the final images. This magnetic tape afterwards enters the said computer machine thus exposing a master micro-negative through which a microfilm master is developed and duplicate copies are prepared from the negative.

Pre-requisites for Maximum Output

In the following situations, the computer Output Microfilm can be helpful in ensuring optimum output:

(i) There is data file in a machine readable form.

(ii) The facility of a computer is available.

(iii) The data is of such nature which requires frequent sorting and reorganisation.

(iv) The data is to be printed out in cumulated from for mass distribution.

(v) The readers are ready to use the material in microfilm form.

Advantage of COM

If the library catalogue is to be produced in microfilm from instead of a book form, the following may be major advantages of using a COM:

(i) **Easy to Handle.** As compared to computer print-out the microfilm or micro-fiche are less bulky and thus are easy to handle.

(ii) **Compact Storage.** Because of their lesser bulk, the microfiches & microfilms take lesser space as compared to card catalogue or printed book form catalogue.

(iii) **Less Expensive.** Storage & duplication Because of their lesser bulk, th microfilm or microfiche catalogues are lesser expensive so far as their storages is concerned. Similarly, duplication of microfiche is much less expensive than their master copies once the negative are available i.e. their cost ranges between one tenth to one-hundredth of their master copies.

(iv) **Cumulations are Less Costly.** As the catalogues are to be kept uptodate, so frequent cumulations are essential. In case of printed book form catalogue the cumulations take much time and are quite costly & still remain out-of-date, whereas the microfilm editions produced by computer are less costly.

(v) **Requires no Binding.** The microfilm edition of catalogues being self-contained require no binding and hence lot of money is saved on that count.

(vi) **Takes Lesser Time.** As compared to conventional printed book form of catalogues the production of up-to-date COM microfilm catalogues which are capable being used immediately takes much less time *i.e.* it takes between 24 hours to 48 hours only.

(vii) **Less Production and Distribution.** Costs Not only the microfilms are lesser costly than paper but their distribution is also much cheaper than a book because these can be sent by air mail at lesser cost as their weight is light than that of the book.

(viii) Easy Availability of Microfilm. The microfilms are much more easily available as compared to paper.

Limitation of COM

The following are few limitations of COM when used for library catalogue applications:

1. Needs Costly Apparatus. Not only the COM equipment is costly and is out of the reach of each library but it also requires costly microfilm readers at various and places.

2. Limited Supply of COM Apparatus. Very few libraries in the world have COM service bureaus. Hence they have very little utility for majority of the libraries. Moreover, their rentals are so high that majority of the libraries can afford to avail of their services.

3. Limited Number of Type Founts & Styles. Similarly, very few stylised type-founts are available which restrict their use throughout the world. For example, except for few Japanese character sets, most of the COM machines use the Roman alphabet. As such, in the countries using other than Roman alphabet, the utility of COM machines is very much limited.

4. Preparation of Paper Copies is Difficult. In case paper copies of microfilmed matter are required it will cost much because the equipment for enlarging paper copies from film negative needs special equipment which is not only available at each point of service but is very expensive also.

However, these limitations of COM can be overcome. The COM machines are being used by various libraries for other library purposes also which include the maintenance of circulation records in process ordering information for acquisition and feeding cumulation and publication of catalogues directories and yearbooks etc. The OCLC started in August 1970 is a non-profit Corporation which was originally planned to be a network of academic libraries but now it has more than 700 user libraries with 1200 terminal including types of libraries including one national library *i.e.* the national Agricultural Library.

Major portion of its budget is composed of fees received from non-Ohio Libraries *i.e.,* in 1974-75, more than 62% or 1,213,330 out of a total budget of 1,956, 981 came from non-Ohio Libraries.

It is an line system. Its data base consists of the LC MARC records, catalogue entries contributed by its member user libraries. It is a shared cataloguing system in the real system. Its data base is more than 2.3 million out of which one-third is from LC MARC data.

Advantages

1. The system is very effective as the response time for title searches was 25-30 seconds.
2. Since it has adapted the battelle System the OCLC enables its users at remote places to search the central catalogue by author, title and subject approaches.
3. Its common products include computer line-printed catalogue cards besides spine & book labels accession lists & OCLC catalogue tapes for the purpose of producing COM catalogues.

The new systems which will provide genuine on-line cataloguing include the following.

(i) Washington Library network.

(ii) The university of Chicago Library System.

(iii) The New York public Library System.

Computer-based On-line Real-time Library Circulation Systems

Many computer-Based On-Line real-Time. Circulation Systems have been devised during 1960's beside many other data collection and batch systems. These include the following.

(a) The State University of New York at Buffalo's Real-Time Library Circulation system.

(b) The Illinois State Library On-Line Circulation control System.

(c) The on-line Circulation Control System at Midwestern University.

(d) The Bell laboratories Library Real-Time Circulation System.

In the first system an IBM 2741 typewriter terminal and the CDC 6400 computer are used. It needs borrower's Identification card but does not require any book card. To issue a book the borrower's identification card number and the call number of the book to be issued are passed into the computer by means of the typewriter and the typed matter is inserted in the book.

Thus completing the charging of the book. This transaction needs 20 seconds. This system handles more than 300,000 per annum at the State university Library of new York at Buffalo. It has the capacity of hooking into the system of the branch Libraries circulation work. In this system the computer can be asked through the terminal of find out the position of any item. Moreover, overdue notice and circulation statistics can be processed automatically. In this system the master circulation file consists of charged books only instead of the shelf list or other record of complete holdings of a library.

The Illinois State Library System

The second system which came into operation at the Illinois State Library operates on an IBM 1710 system using IBM 1031 terminals as inputs. It needs punched book cards and borrower's card. For issuing a book, the borrower's card and the book and card are inserted in the badge section of the terminal. To find out whether the borrower is a valid borrower, the programme calls for the master file of borrowers.

In case the borrower is a valid user, his number and the information about the book are transmitted to the computer for final editing. After final editing, the information is put on the daily transaction pack in consecutive order to facilitate its further processing after few hours later on. Thus the issue work of a book is complete and the book is handed over to the borrower after due date slip is inserted in the book. At the time of return of a book its call number and cutter number are checked from the book card and the reserve list and the returned cards are arranged in consecutive order with daily returns pack. If a book being returned is already reserved by a borrower the computer sends the information to the 1033 printer terminal which provides the call number, Cutter number, borrower's number and the date of reservation of the book.

After, it, the returned book is handed over to the Reservation Assistant for further action. In the evening the computer lists and punches one cards for each transaction of the day besides sorting them into Dewey Cutter and serial number orders. After this, a programme for updating the record is called in the computer for merging the sorted transaction with the master circulation record.

This programme called CIRCUP takes up the transactions one by one for necessary action. In case of a discharge of a book it removes it from the master file but if it is a case of an issue of a book, it adds the information to the master file. The programme called DUE NOT prepares a new master file whenever it is updated besides printing the daily statistical information in the classified order by Dewey Decimal Classification. This system is not only capable of printing the overdue notice for borrowers alongwith their mailing addresses, but also provides monthly statistics about the use of library.

In this system, the book ID cards are generated from the shelf list kept on punched cards but it has not been made to serve as a basic record for circulation purposes. It is claimed that in this system the average cost per transaction comes to about 32 percent besides cutting down the number of staff members employed in the circulation section from twenty-two to nine only. Further this system works on a time sharing basis. In other words an interrupt feature controlled by 1026 controller, allows the central processing unit to work only when the information to be handled is fed into it.

The On-line Circulation Control System at Midwestern University

In this system, an IBM 1401, an IBM 1031 data collection system and 1033 printer are used, it needs book cards and borrower's cards badges. The IBM 1401 is shared by other departments of the University. For issuing a book the book card and borrower's card/ badge are inserted into IBM 1031 data collection system. Before the issue of the book, the processing of the computer is interrupted for finding out whether the borrower is a valid borrower which takes about second of CPU time.

If valid the printer 1033 prints a book slip to be inserted in the issued book. Thus the book is issued. The total time taken in charging a book is about 10 seconds of returning a book, the information about its reservation if any is passed on to the circulation. Assistant automatically because of the on-line updating of the circulation file.

Advantages of The System

This system automatically provides to the circulation desk information about the reserved book borrowers membership validity due date of return of the books fines due and other statistical data besides printing a daily circulation file. Like the Illinois State Library's circulation system, this system also does not use the shelf list as the basic record for circulation purpose. The real Time circulation control system invented by the Bell Laboratories called BELLREL is one of the latest in the series. It uses 360/40 computer to which are linked by Dataphone the terminals kept in three different libraries.

Each of the three libraries keeps two terminal with keyboard, printer and card read facilities. In the system, a Union list of all three libraries is maintained which can help in finding out the position of every book stocked in the libraries of the system *i.e.* indicating whether a book is available in a library and can be got issued. Similarly, Direct Access Files maintained in the system provide information about the total book collection of a library *i.e.* shelf list and the position of the books issued and reserved.

The system can perform 22 transitions related to issuing, returning and reservation of books besides other queries about them. The system batch processes daily issue lists, pre-due and over due notices, lists of books in great demand and other related statistical information.

It is claimed that the system can handle more than 300,000 transaction annually. However, in charging it takes about 23 seconds which is more than that taken by the three other systems described above and many of the manual systems.

A Computer-based classification system is being experimented at the Documentation Research and Training centre, Bangalore. It is based on Colon Classification Schedules. The following procedure is followed for the purpose:

1. The schedules of Colon Classification are transferred on tape which include the schedules of Basic Classes Special Isolates and Common Isolates.

   For this purpose a punched card with 80 columns is used which provides the above-mentioned information a follows:

   (a) Basic Classes 1-8 columns

   (b) Basic Subject Terms 9-40 columns

   (c) Number of reels of tapes locating special isolates schedule 41-48 columns

   (d) Indication for card sequence 49-80 columns

2. The Kernal term of the document to be classified are fed into the computer.

3. In the synthesis procedure the compotents of a required class number are picked in the sequence in which they should be synthesized manually according to the set principle and postulates.

4. The computer assigns automatically the appropriate class number to the document in question.

□

13

Electronic Media in Library

Computer is a device used by many people all over the world for different purposes. Its use is increasing in our daily life. It is used in laboratories, hospitals, schools, colleges, houses, offices, industries, etc. Its use is multifunctional. It is used for computing, communication, designing, learning, etc. It helps to get things done at a faster rate with accurate results. Hqwever, the accuracy depends upon the programme or software used. Computer receives the data, processes and provides information as required by the user. To transform the data into information, a computer and a set of instructions are required. Use of computer means using physical device or hardware and a set of instructions or software.

French defined these terms as follows:

(a) **Computer.** is a device that works under the control of stored programme, automatically accepting and processing data to produce information that is the result of that processing.

(b) **Hardware.** is a physical device found in the computer system.

(c) **Software.** is a programme or a set of instructions used on a computer system for data processing.

(d) **Types of Computers.** Quantity of the data to be handled by the computer and processing depends upon the size/ capacity of hardware and the programme.

Computers are categorised into three types on the basis of hardware. The types are:

1. **Mainframes.** These are large general purpose computers with extensive processing, storage, and input/output facilities.

2. **Mini Computers.** These are physically smaller computers compared with the main frames.

3. **Micro Computers.** These are maintained and run with the help of a single integrated circuit known as chip. Large systems use main frames and large software system to handle the data as well as to provide the information.

Software

Software plays an important and decisive role in use of hardware. Computer access is controlled by the software. The same hardware can be used for different purposes by changing the software. The function of hardware changes on the basis of software. Additional facilities can be provided with the help of software system. It can be divided into two categories.

— Operating system (as);

— Application programme.

Operating System. Operating system is a programme used as a means of instructing computers to carry out operational tasks. It controls and facilitates other programmes to use the hardware in a safe and controlled way. It monitors and controls hardware use. It also aids and monitors application programme. French defines OS as a suite of programmes that takes over the operation of the computer to the extent of being to allow a number of programmes to be run on the computer without human intervention by an operator. Operating system is a system software.

Application Programme. Application programmes are developed to perform a specific job or application. They are developed in any language. They are also developed in sets, to be used in conjunction with one another. These programmes vary in size depending upon the job. These are either written by user himself or by a software specialist. The programmes are either general or specific in purpose. The general purpose programmes are useful to any user and specific purpose programmes are useful to specific users.

Large Software System (LSS): LSS uses computers to process large and complex data. Processing should result in production of information in different formats as required by the system managers. To deal with the complexity of problems, there is need for a LSS. Development of a LSS is difficult because of:

— continuous change;

— difficulties to predict;

— not distinct;

— difficulties to test and evaluate.

To alleviate the problem of a LSS, Rammurthy *et al*, suggested the support of automation, graphic aids, metrics and knowledge based system.

Development of a programme is a big task and it can be divided into stages. French had recognized the following six stages.

— Understanding the problem;

— Planning the method of solution,;

— Developing the methods using suitable aids;

— Typing the instructions into the computer using a programming language; Testing the programme; and

— Documenting all the work.

Development of the software can be broadly divided into four stages. They are:

— Understanding the requirements;

— Design;

— Implementation; and

— Maintenance.

The two stages, namely, understanding the requirements and design are the major activities. It may be difficult for a single individual to develop a LSS. Several programmers, managers and designers have to be involved in the development process. During the development process programme files, documents and test cases are produced. Rammurthy *cl al* stressed the need for resource and activity management to avoid inconsistencies due to high level concurrency in activities and to keep track of the project.

Programme Languages. To write the programme, programme languages have to be used. The languages used can be categorised into two types:

— Low level languages; and

— High level languages.

Low Level Languages. French defines low level languages as machine oriented languages in which each instruction corresponds to or resembles a machine instruction.

High Level Languages. These are machine independent and problem oriented. They reflect the type of problem solved rather than the features of the machine. They can run on different machines. The programme can be changed to another computer. Users can store or exchange programmes. They are portable and can be altered to meet the changes in technology. These languages are also used to develop the large software systems.

French listed the following general features of these languages:

— They have extensive vocabalary of words, symbols and sentences;

— The programme statements are translated into machine in instructions. The translation is done by compiler.

— The programmer can work independent to that of machine.

— The rules must be obeyed while writing the programmes.

— Instructions in high level languages are known as statements.

French divides the languages into five types:

— Commercial;

— Scientific;

— Special Purpose;

— Command; and

— Multipurpose.

Gilbert categorized languages into four types on the basis of broad application areas. They are:

— Numeric/Scientific calculations (*e.g.*, ALGOL, BASI FORTRAN);

— Business data processing (*e.g.*, COBOL, PL/1);

— Military data processing (*e.g.*, JOVIAL, PL/l); and

— Computer science research in symbol manipulation and artificial intelligence (*e.g.*, LISP, SNOBO).

Language has to be selected to suit the application. The suitability can be determined by:

— Notational characteristics;

— Compilation characteristics, and

— Operational characteristics.

The programme style should direct the computer to execute the algorithm and should also convey the design and techniques to other programmers, who may want to change the programme. Relevant programme language is chosen to write the programme and there are certain other considerations such as qualities of programme, methods and IPSE.

Qualities of Programme. Yourden'listed the, qualities of a good programme as follows. A good programme:

— works.

— works according to specification.

— is flexible.

— is ready on time.

— or atleast can fix.

— has no bugs.

— is well documented.

— executes quickly.

— makes efficient use of memory.

Gilbert gave the aspects of quality as follows:

— correctness,

— robustness,

— performance,

— utility,

— reliability,

— ease of use,

— work capacity,

— response time,

— portability.

The programme should have as many qualities mentioned above as possible.

IPSE. IPSE means Integrated Project Support Environment IPSE and software engineering environment are synonymous. What is environment in this context? According to Sommerville, environment is used to encompass all the automated facilities (such as electronic mail, documentation support, etc.) that are available to the software engineer as an aid in the task of software development. Environment is divided into three classes. They are,

Langauge Oriented Environment. This environment supports programming in one particular programming language.

Educational Environment. This environment helps in learning the programmes by beginners.

Software Engineers Environment. This environment helps to develop the large software system, *e.g.*, ISTAR, ENCOMPASS. These are developed to support software process. The support is from feasibility study to operation and maintenance.

Methods of Programme. Different methods (main) used to develop programmes are:

— Modular programming (MP);

— Structural programming (SP); and

— Object oriented programming (COP)

Modular Programming. Yourdon defines the module as similar to that of programme, that is, it is a collection of instructions sufficient to accomplish some logical programme. It is considered synonymous to subroutines and sometimes defined in terms of physical constraints.

Encyclopaedia of computer science and engineering defines modular programming as a logically self-contained and discrete part of a larger system. A complete programme is a collection of modules.

While using this method, the programme is broken into smaller and simpler subtasks. These sub-tasks facilitate to write correct programmes. It is. comparatively easy to design, write and test each subroutine of a programme, which is equivalent to module. According to IBM users, the size of a module is 4096 (Max) bytes of memory. Every module accepts input, which is well defined set of processing actions and produces output that is well defined as to content and structure. Every module will have only one entry and only one exit point. After executing programme of the module, it always returns to the statement.

In this type, each module is independent of other. This method also facilitates to change any module without changing the rest of the programme and is useful when combined with others. Modular programme is easy to control, debug, write, maintain and change. It may need more memory space and also require a great deal of extra work.

Yourdon listed the following techniques to achieve the modular programme.

— Break programmes into small independent sub routines;

— Use decision tables;

— Use of symbolic parameters;

— Separate input and output functions; and

— Do not share temporary storage location.

This programming is ideal for large software systems as it can be divided into manageable pieces/modules. Each module can be distributed among the people and all the work done by them independently.

Structured Programming. Structured programming is a new approach in programming. It provides improvement over other methods of programming.

Yourdon defines it as a philosophy of writing programmes according to a set of rigid rules in order to decrease testing problems, increase productivity and increase the readability of the resulting programmes. Its technique is to eliminate GO-TO statement. It also includes concept of top-down programme design and programme restructure and conventions. Encyclopaedia of computer Science and Engineering defines SP as a methodological style whereby a computer programme constructed by concatenating or coherently nesting logical subunits which either are themselves structured programmes or else are of the form of one or another of a small number of particularly well understood control structures. SP is developed in a top down or layered fashion. The whole programme is considered as one module and it is broken into level one modules. Level one modules are decomposed into level two submodules. Decomposition is continued until small building blocks are left, which can be easily coded. Further sub modules can be tested independently.

According to Yourdon, the basic principles of SP are:

— Control structures;

— Modular composition;

— Programme format:

— Comments;

— Readability *vs* efficiency;

— Step wise refinement; and

— Programme verification.

Gilbert listed three important qualities of SP text. They are:

— easy to understand;

— easy to demonstrate; and

— easy to maintain or modify.

The benefits of structured programme are:

— more readable;

— intelligible;

— systematic verification;

— possibility of less bugs;

— clarity;

— easy maintenance; and

— easy to modify.

Cost of Software. Software packages (software and documentation) are available in the market. Any organization can buy such software if it is useful to their requirements. Few software companies do alter or modify the package to suit to the needs of users, provided the changes are not major. Otherwise, software has to be developed specially for the organization, which will be costly compared to that or readily available.

Cost of software is at two stages

— development stage; and

— maintenance stage.

Development cost is non-recurring and maintenance cost is recurring. Maintenance cost is several times more than development cost. A study by Boehm estimates that U.S. Air Force System cost $30 per instruction to develop and $4000 per instruction for maintenance in its life time.

Sommerville listed factors for maintenance cost:

Non-technical:

— Application domain;

— Staff stability;

— Programme age;

— External environment; and

— Hardware stability:

Technical

— Module independence;

— Programming languages;

— Programming style;

— Programme validation; and

— Documentation.

As the large software system is costly to develop and maintain, it is necessary for the organization to assess the returns in terms of:

— finance;

— time; and

— accuracy.

If the returns are satisfactory or beneficial over cost, the software can either be purchased or developed.

Development of Large Software System. Developing a large software system needs lot of effort, knowledge and work. The main steps for development and use of software could be grouped into three phases:

— Design;

— Implementation; and

— Maintenance.

Gilbert had given sequence of seven steps for development of software system. The steps are:

— Requirement analysis,

— Programme specification,

— Design including analyzing the specification,

— Coding of individual modules,

— Testing of individual modules,

— Integration of individual modules, and

— Validation of system performance.

The detailed description of each stage can be seen in next sections.

While developing the software, the support of Computer Aided Software Engineering (CASE) tools are necessary.

CASE. CASE provides support to software engineers with automated tools. The case tools are also known as CASE work bench. The work bench components are:

— Diagram editing system;

— Design analysis and checking;

— Query language facilities;

— Data dictionary facilities;

— Report generation facilities;

— Forms generation facilities;

— Import/export facilities.

Design

Design is a plan or scheme of action which outlines how a desired programme will perform its included function. Thirty percent of time is spent on designing a programme.

In this phase, important decisions are to be taken. Design phase also previews the characteristics of the intended programme. This phase includes planning, understanding requirements, identification of solutions, etc. Forethought, curiosity and quality are essential in design.

The principles of design are listed by Gilbert, as follows:

— Confirm requirements;

— Keep the future in mind;

— Divide and conquer;

— Evaluate for improvement.

Further according to Gilbert every design should answer

— What tasks must be performed.

— How can each task be done.

— How various solutions be connected to gather to form a system.

Various stages in design phase are as follows.

Requirement Analysis. To design the software, it is necessary to understand the problem. It is also necessary to know the intent of the system, possible modifications. The designer has to prepare a set of c questions, which must be posed to the system for which the software is being developed. The questions should answer the intent of each aspect, rules, etc. Ultimately, we should be able to derive the users, original requirements. Once the requirements are known, they may be summarized to prepare requirement document.

On the basis of requirements, precise specifications have to be formulated. Specification is the description of what the system is supposed to do in order to meet the requirements. To prepare specifications may be difficult as the requirements are specified by the user in one or two sentences, *e.g.*, automatization of customer services in a super market. To prepare specifications, whole concept of supermarket and its service are to be analyzed by the experts.

Rammurthy et al had suggested that at least three factors must be taken into account when users want to introduce a LSS. The factors are:

— Problem purification;

— Future characteristic analysis; and

— Safety analysis.

Problem purification is the analysis of the current solution to determine what are the real problems that have to be solved. Purification also includes examination of drawbacks and inconvenience of the present system. By decomposing the problem continuously until it is reduced to bare factors, purification is possible. It also gives clear idea of the requirements of the system and avoids misunderstanding. Future characteristic analysis is to examine and predict change of these problems in future. This phase needs lot of expertise in the subject.

Safety analysis is to prevent the destruction and malfunction that can be caused by the new system. In this stage analysis of the problems by malfunction of the system are to be identified. The alternative ways have to be developed to cope with malfunction.

Specification Analysis. In this phase, the system data flow and algorithms are to be planned. Even the system has to be organized into modules. The designer starts searching for solutions in this stage. Gilbert had suggested following steps for large software system.

— Specification analysis to break down the desired functions to uncover inconsistencies in the specification;

— Improvement of specification by providing for modification and good communication facilities between user and problem., and

— Development of detailed final programme specification.

To design LSS, a specification model can be chosen. Specification generation is difficult to prepare on the basis of informal requirements. It is also difficult to do manually. The existing models that are similar to programme behaviour may be chosen.

Rammurthy *et al* listed the systems that emphasize or, models. For example, Data Structure System Design emphasizes on data flow oriented model.

Specification should also include

— non functional requirements such as performance, reliability, and user friendliness; and

— changing specifications which are common in the life time of the software.

The design also could be either knowledge-based or system. Knowledge-based is algorithm design and system design includes decomposition of the system into modules.

According to Gilbert every solution involves three decisions: What information must be stored for task;

— What use will the programme make of the stored information;

— What data blocks must be used and what is their form.

Further the author also stated that the design should answer:

— What tasks must be performed;

— How can each task behave; and

— How can various solutions be connected together to form a system.

This stage is important in design of software.

Data Flow. Data flow is the scheme of movement of data between programme's data objects and processing actions. On the basis of data flow, the software system can be categorized into the following:

Embedded System. In this system, inputs flow from another system and outputs to another system. In this format, data flow between systems is to be considered.

Updating System. In this, the data is kept for systems, use and updating the data at each execution.

Data flow techniques help designer to build iterations piece by piece. Additional objects are determined at each iteration. The objects can be linked by their appropriate actions. The data flow based design is used in both OS and software. On the basis of the data flow, data flow diagram has to be drawn. Data flow diagram helps in design of the system. Data flow diagram is defined by Gilbert as a diagram of a programme in terms of its data objects (such as files or arrays or flags and its processing actions, showing what data used by each action and where each action places data. It has to be developed by repeated considerations of what data objects are needed and what actions are performed on these objects.

Design Proposal. The designer has to achieve the design. In the process, the designer makes assumptions about

— Characteristics of inputs;

— Overall approach; and

— Analysis of critical actions.

These assumptions are to be documented. The documented assumptions are evaluated for further coding.

Coding and Integration. At this stage, coding can be made. It can be done for each independent module, if it is module programming. Once the coding is finished every module has to be tested. Testing is part of coding and at this stage the necessary changes could be made in coding.

In modular programming, after coding these modules have to be integrated into a cohesive system. After integration it is necessary to test. To integrate and test, top-down method is used. While coding and testing, the qualities of a good programme are to be incorporated. These qualities will help to maintain acceptable level of quality. Rammurthy et al had defined software quality as the totality .of features and characteristics of a product or service that bear on the ability to satisfy given needs. Further, the factors such as reliability, reusability and efficiency are to be taken care of.

Evaluation of Design. Every software should meet the quality parameters alid specifications. The deficiencies of the system could be identified oy evaluation. The correctness can be evaluated either by the designer or a group of evaluators or reviewers. In this, the software is tested to know whether it can handle the situation and achieve tasks or not. The evaluation could be done phase by phase to identity the deficiencies and errors. At the end of each phase, necessary, corrections can be made.

Software Lite Cycle. The software systems pass through many stages during their life cycle. Life cycle begins when someone gives the requirements and until it dies or becomes obsolete. Re phases of life cycle had been divided into two parts.

Development Phase. It includes all the activities from the point the need of the product is identified to the point when implemented product is listed and delivered for operation.

Operations and Maintenance Phase. This part includes all activities after delivery, such as fixing bugs discovered during operation and performance enhancements.

Various models of life cycle had been proposed to describe the activities during the development phase. Important models had been described by Rammurthy et al. They are:

Waterfall Model. It is the most traditional one. Life cycle is divided into requirements, design, coding, testing and maintenance. The software goes from one phase to another sequentially.

Rapid Prototype. This model is in two stages. Prototype development identifies the feasibility and ensures understanding between the customer and developer about the expected functionality of the system. Production quality software development phase is concerned with the actual system development.

Automatic Programming. It is in two stages. Specification development which includes maintenance changes and machine assisted.

Reusability Model. This model recommends searching of reusable components. These reusable components need not be developed again. More appropriate ones are picked and used. In this, the reusability factor is important. This model recommends to develop tools to make software reusable. The models help in designing the software and the software developed is delivered for implementation.

Implementation

The software development is developed by a team of programmers in consultation with managers. While development, several precautions art, taken to. meet the requirements. The software has to be implemented in real situation and has to be evaluated in terms of its performance. Implementation has to be followed by verification of the software.

Verification. While developing the programme, there is a possibility of errors. Elimination of errors is necessary. At least the errors may be reduced to acceptable levels so that the system operates as per specifications. Verification of the programme helps to identify such errors and their elimination is possible. Verification of the programme can be of two stages: Testing debugging.

Testing. Testing is checking the programme, whether it is correct or not and whether it can do what it is supposed to do. At this stage, the software is integrated and exercised. Testing is also determination of properties of programme by using sequence of experiments. Each experiment with selected input has to be presented to the programme. Programme is to be executed and the output has to be observed. This method of observation is testing. Each experiment may be known as test case. By repeating tests at every point the errors can be found out and the same can be eliminated. There is every possibility of bypassing the errors. Testing provides information about programme's behaviour in actual environment or real situation. According to Dijkstra testing shows the presence, not the absence of bugs. At this stage, software developer convinces the buyer, by demonstrating the software working. Elimination of errors at this stage will help to avoid future expensive and troublesome elimination process.

Debugging. French defines bug as a fault that causes a programme to fail during testing or after programme is commissioned. The process of finding and getting number of bugs is debugging. Gilbert defines debugging as a process of finding and repairing the errors. Debugging is inevitable as errors are found in large software system due to their complexities. The errors are to be detected while testing and the same should be isolated for elimination. Good design helps for debugging.

Yourdon suggested a technique known as anti-bugging, which refers to writing programmes in such a way as to make bugs less likely to occur. Whenever they occur, they should be easily noticeable by user and programmers. Testing and debugging are key factors in implementation of software system. The recent news in computing shows how the mistakes or errors effect organizations.

Computing reported that a computing error caused 0.1% mistake in the retail price index. This blunder costed the Government £12 millions in compensation to pension and benefit loosers, donations to charities and administrative costs.

Maintenance

Software is designed and implemented by the programmers. Once implementation is done, the user makes use of the software. To use the software, it has to be maintained. What is maintenance? Maintenance is continuing or retaining the use of software, to enable to achieve the specified objectives of using it. Further 50 percent of total programming effort is to maintain existing systems.

Generally maintenance includes:

— error correction;

— fulfilment changes in requirements;

— system testing;

— incorporating modifications; and

— minimizing programme corruption.

Categories of Maintenance. Somerville categorized maintenance into three types:

Perfective Maintenance. This includes the changes demanded by the users or the system programmer; which improve the system in some way without changing its functionality. Sixty five percent of maintenance comes under this category.

Adaptive Maintenance. It is maintenance due to changes in environment of the programme. This category constitutes 18 percent of maintenance.

Corrective Maintenance. It is correction of undiscovered system errors. This category constitutes 17 percent of maintenance.

Software maintenance can be categorized into four areas:

— General maintenance,

— Internal requirements,

— Additional requirements; and

— External influence.

General Maintenance. The programme performance may be effected due to power failure, errors, "bugs or operational problems. These are to be taken care if we are to use the software. They are general in nature. These can be managed either by software engineers or programmers.

Internal Requirement. in a large system there could be changes in its processes, procedures and input/output formats. The changes may occur over a period of time. To retain the software, the changes have to be incorporated.

Additional Requirements. Every dynamic system develops and new requirements are demanded. To meet the new and additional requirements of the system, software has to be planned.

External Influence. External forces such as virus influence on the software. These forces have to be controlled.

Computing reported that due to virus, the data in the European Community offices in Luxemburg was corrupted. This influenced the performance of storage calculations.

Networking and Resource Sharing

A Public Library System is an important organ of the state, entrusted with the responsibility of maintaining organised collection of books and other reading, material in the service of the public. The system is designed to serve the twin purposes of providing educational support to the under privileged in the society as well as a means of continuing education for the. working class who have no opportunity for formal schooling and education. It is, therefore, apparent that the public library system has a major role to play in propagating literacy, in supporting formal education of the weaker sections, and in providing facilities for continuing education for the working class. It is a pity that nearly half a century after the nation became independent our country has a very poor system of public libraries, even in those states where formal library legislation has been introduced and public are levied of a library cess. The resources so accruing to the state combined with the matching grants made by the Government are too meagre to sustain the existing public library services, not to speak of promoting a healthy growth in their acquisitions.

The economic scenario prevailing in. the country at present makes it abundantly clear that no enhanced allocations to the public library sector will be coming forth from the Government and the libraries themselves will have to find the ways and means of augmenting and supplementing their resources. One way of doing this is to arrive at a satisfactory arrangement of pooling and sharing their available resources, both men and material, first at the local level, then at district level, next at the state level and finally at the national level. Such a system pooling of the resources would enhance the information resources of the public libraries indirectly, at the same time preventing avoidable duplication.

Resource sharing may then be defined as a mode of operation whereby, functions are shared in common by a number of participants having the same objective or goal in mind. In the context of public libraries, resource sharing means the sharing of the information resources available in one library by the clientele served by other libraries, when they are unable to get their requirements met from the local library. Resources here connote reading/audio visual material that is of information value. In fact the modem concept of resource sharing overflows the boundaries as defined above and encompasses other spheres of activities like cooperative acquisitioning, cataloguing and classification; cooperation in the training and development of the professional workers in public libraries and cooperative acquisitioning of equipment and machines which, are extensively employed in the activity of information dissemination and which are too expensive for individual libraries to acquire on their own. While resource sharing activity has at its heart, the goal of maximising the availability and utilisation of information resources and services at minimum cost, some of the essential prerequisites for effective resources sharing are: *(1)* Possession of sharable resources by the participating libraries; *(2)* Willingness to share the resources; *(3)* A planned mechanism of sharing; *(4)* Precise understanding of the use and information potential of their respective collections; and *(5)* A common bibliographic access to the collections of the participating libraries.

No library would be financially strong enough to be self sufficient as far as information resources are concerned. Hence, the concept of resource sharing becomes the central theme of any networking system. The. rise in the cost of publications, lack of adequate manpower to organise the same and the location of libraries at distant and remote places have necessiated the need for networking. The networking of libraries then is one way of achieving maximum results with minimum input.

Although evolving the lasting and permanent arrangement for a mechanism to foster resource sharing among libraries is an ideal and long term goal, there are some immediate factors which make it necessary for libraries to enter into an arrangement for resource sharing at various levels. The most important among them is a resources crunch, *i.e.*, non-availability of funds for non-plan expenditure. With the main thrust of budget allocation by the Government being in the direction of industrial and agricultural development, the libraries are obliged to plan their acquisitions, keeping in view the resources available in other libraries in the area, so that they can get maximum number of books and publications that are not available in other libraries in their geographic proximity. The everincreasing cost of books and publications coupled with the exponential growth in the publishing of books and other reading material, has been the immediate factor in compelling libraries to enter into arrangements for resource sharing. Other factors like increasing needs of the user, easy accessibility of reprographic facilities to the libraries, and the general awareness among the public of the need to share the resources are the other factors which help resource sharing in an indirect manner.

Rapid advances made in the information technology have ushered in a number of advanced information products, technologies and services that can be conveniently harnessed by the librarian community for achieving the objective of networking. These are the computers, the vast communication network developed in the country with STD facility and the T.V. with its own national hookup via satellite and microwave links.

Development of Network

Networking of libraries/information centres using computer and communication facilities became a reality in 1970's. Networks of all types, *i.e.*, local, national, regional and global are operating in the world today. Though the computerisation of information activities started in India in mid 60's, the development of computerised library networks did not gather momentum till recently.

National Network. Over the last ten years the country has successfully seen the emergence of a number of networks like I-NET, NICNET, INDONET, ERNET, INFLIBNET, etc., and some local area networks like the CALIBNET, DELNET, MALIBNET, HYLIBNET, etc. Brief particulars of some of these networks are given below:

I-NET. The Department of Telecommunications has introduced a network called "I-NET". This is the new packet switched public data network. It provides cost effective services to the Government as well as private organisations. The X28 dial up mode is the cheapest connection that many public libraries in the country would be able to afford.

INDONET. In India, the CMC Limited has setup INDONET which is a national computer network with main frame computers being setup at Bombay, Calcutta, Delhi, Hyderabad, Madras, Bangalore and Pune with distributed data processing facility. Databases available at any of these INDONET nodes can be accessed on-line from remote terminals.

NICNET. This is a computer network setup by the National Informatics Centre (NIC), Government of India, for providing information to central and state government departments to draw plans for efficient utilisation of resources thus ensuring uniform socioeconomic development throughout the country.

It is being expanded as a dedicated network covering 22 state capitals and 400 districts to address the rapidly growing awareness to computerisation in different sectors of the Government. Its headquarters is at New Delhi with regional centres at Pune, Hyderabad and Bhubaneswar. Although NICNET is principally meant for use by Government departments, it does have the potential for use by the library and information community.

ERNET. ERNET is a computer network for academic and research community in India.

INFLIBNET. INFLIBNET is envisaged as a computer communications network linking libraries in universities and colleges in the country and libraries in institutions affiliated to the CSIR, ICMR, ICAR, DRDO and Government departments. When full-fledged it is envisaged that INFLIBNET will network 184 universities and 23 institutions deemed to be universities, 7200 colleges and 200 libraries affiliated to other organizations. INFLIBNET is designed to operate at four different levels, viz., national, regional, sectoral and local.

DELNET. DELNET will network 35 libraries in the Delhi area.

CALIBNET. CALIBNET will network 38 science and technology libraries in the Calcutta metropolitan area.

International Networks. Apart from the above national networks, the apex body of the public library network namely the National Library can have access to the number of specialised international databases like INIS, AGRIS, MEDLARS, INSPEC, etc. through some of the international and regional networks like the TELENET, TYMNET, DIALNET, ESA/IRS, BLAISE, EURONET, etc.

In India, among the various types of libraries, the public libraries are the most neglected ones. This is in spite of the fact that they are. the oldest ones in terms of existence. Of late, there is a growing recognition of their services not only in eradication of illiteracy and promotion of adult literacy programmes but also in socioeconomic development of the nation. Public libraries cover a wide range of user groups: illiterates, neo-literates, children, disadvantaged groups like the blind, housewives, students, artisans, labourers and many others engaged in a variety of professions and vocations. To put it in a nutshell, all individuals residing in the area of jurisdiction of a public library may be either its actual users or potential users.

In the earlier days, public libraries were thought to be self-sufficient in terms of acquisition and preservation of all the documents that are required by its user communities and also for provision of free and easy access to its literature/collection. But, of late, it is being felt that no public library can afford to operate in isolation; it has to join the mainstream along with academic and special libraries and go in for modernisation and networking to provide effective and efficient services to its varied and demanding clientele.

The present state of Indian public libraries is deplorable. While other types of libraries such as academic and special libraries are in the process of modernisation through use of computers and communication technologies, the public libraries are lurching. It appears that there is no perceivable impact of modern technology on Indian public libraries. The possible reasons for this sad state of affairs are many. Some of these are:

— lack of realisation of the benefits of modernisation of public libraries;

— lack of political will for public library development.

— under-estimation by the political leadership of the potential of public libraries in nation-building process.

The term 'Network' is used in the present times in place of 'Resource Sharing' or 'Cooperative Systems'. It is because of two important reasons: Potential improvement of library and information operations by interconnecting individual library systems with the more recently developed facilities for data and information transfer; and The significant role played by the computers, telecommunications and new reprographic techniques.

Networking and modernisation are becoming very important in all types of libraries as they enable the users to have access to the resources of many other libraries in addition to their own one. The public libraries are also likely to benefit themselves by participating in networks. The benefits that accrue from networking of public libraries are:

(i) Preparation of union catalogues;

(ii) Provision of cataloguing data/catalogue cards for the publications available in the network libraries;

(iii) Provision of bibliographies;

(iv) Optimum utilisation of rare collections;

(v) Cooperative acquisition of documents;

(vi) Cooperative exchange and distribution;

(vii) Cooperative storage of documents;

(viii) Savings, both of technical work and collections; and

(ix) Minimises cost of the library services in the long run.

Above all, networks offer provision of more number of materials, that is, comprehensively, at less cost and quickly.

With rapid advancements in the various technologies such as telecommunicatjons, satellite communications, microprocessors, computers, etc., several networks are either presently functional or in the formative stage in India. They can be grouped into:

A. **General Networks.** NICNET, INDO NET, VIKRAM.

B. **Subject Networks.** VIDYANET, BTISNET, SIRNET INELIBNET, ERNET.

C. **Specialised/Business Networks.** BANKNET, COALNET, RAILNET, TOURNET, SAILNET.

D. **Geographical Networks.** CALIBNET, DELNET, HYLIBNET, PUNENET, BONET, etc.

A brief note on the purpose and participating libraries of each of the above networks is given below:

NICNET is a Government of India network aimed at providing information to support planning, decision-making and monitoring Government schemes and programmes. It links all the districts and states with the headquarters at New Delhi.

INDONET is a commercial computer network developed by the Computer Maintenance Corporation Ltd. (CMC), New Delhi. It is expected to have about 100 centres in several parts of the country like Calcutta, Bombay, Madras, Bangalore, Ahmedabad, Bangalore, Pune, Hyderabad, etc.

VIKRAM is a packet switched public data network being developed by the Department of Telecommunications, Government of India. The network's main centre is located in Delhi and would link to 8 switching modes. While NICNET is meant solely for the use of Government departments, INDONET and VIKRAM are public networks.

SIRET is a computer communication network of CSIR aimed at linking about 40 CSIR laboratories spread throughout India.

BTISNET, set up by the Department of Biotechnology, Government of India, is a specialised network linking the information centres in genetic engineering, cell culture, biology, etc.

DESINET, developed by the DESIDOC for the DRDO units, covers the defence scientific and research information, and connects all the DRDO laboratories, scattered throughout India.

ERNET is a network meant for the academic and research community. It links 5 IITs, IISc, NCST and DOE.

INFLIBNET (Information and Library Network), being developed by the UGC, will link the institutions of higher learning covering all disciplines, R & D institutions and other national organisations like CSIR, WAR, DRDO, ICSSR, etc.

VIDYANET links several research institutions and laboratories, universities and higher education institutions, research centres of industrial and other commercial organisations.

CALIBNET (Calcutta Library Network), DELNET (Delhi Library Network), HYLIBNET (Hyderabad Library Network), PUNENET (Pune Libraries Network) and BONET (Bombay Libraries Networks) are the library networks linking the library and information centres located in their respective geographical regions.

CALIBNET is a metropolitan network linking 38 libraries in the Calcutta metropolitan area. The libraries or the institutions linked in this network are either scientific research institutions like Bose Institute, Saha Institute of Nuclear Physics or the higher learning institutions like Jadhavpur University, etc.

DELNET links All-India Institute of Medical Sciences, DESIDOC, DST, India International Centre, IIPA, INSDOC, JNU, NPL and NASSDOC.

It is clearly evident from the above that in none of the networks mentioned including the geographical area networks, not even a single public library has been included.

In fact, no sincere and worthwhile efforts have been made in India for public library networking. Recognition of the importance of resource sharing among the public libraries can be traced as far back as to 1919. Shri Suri Venkata Narsimha Sastry, a pioneer in the library movement in Andhra Pradesh, had emphasised the importance of resource sharing among the public libraries at the VI Annual Conference of the Granthalaya Sangham held at Madras in 1919.

No library can be entirely self-sufficient and selfreliant. Therefore, libraries in any region have necessarily to develop interdependence and depend on each other. In the matter of acquisition of a collection, it may be appropriate for a library to concentrate on one or more disciplines or areas of knowledge by building up a strong and comprehensive collection supported by some books generally recognised required in other areas. Occasionally when need arises one could draw on the book stock of another library strong in another field. Such an arrangement results in available resources being utilised more economically and a larger book stock being used by readers in the region.

All the libraries within a state should form part of a network extending from the community library of the village through intermediary levels to the district and to the state central library The state network should eventually connect with the national level.

But, unfortunately, this report is lying in cold storage for the past 8 years. As a result, we do not still have a national policy on library and information system even after 46 years of attaining Independence. This has seriously affected the modernisation and networking of Indian public libraries.

Computer Aided Instruction is a powerful tool in instructing students. CAI has not made much impact in India, in subjects other than Computer Science where we come across many such packages in the form of 'tutors'. As the capabilities of CAI are not restricted to the field of Computer Science and Computer Applications alone, there is wide and promising scope for its application in general education. CAI can be classified as one of the audio visual materials in education. It can be used both in formal and non-formal education.

Metaphorically, they can be called 'Electronic books'. In fact, there is a class of books called 'programmed text books' designed on the lines of CAI packages, which use basically a non-linear model of presentation of lessons. Further, CAI could be used by libraries and information centres in orienting the library users. Use of CAI can be enhanced by providing it as an on.line service in any of the proposed networks. S.M. Rawlines observes that, "Results of the recently conducted surveys indicate that on-line computer assisted instruction is equal or superior to traditional method of training new student library workers. While costing the same, the system frees staff members for other duties. Students response to CAI has been favourable. Staff members have welcomed the free time CAI permits for other projects and more individual attention to students."

According to K.L; Zinn, "Computer Assisted Instruction refers to the use of computers to present drills, practice exercises, and tutorial sequences to the student, and perhaps to engage the student in dialog about the substance of the instruction. A CAI (tutorial) dialog is achieved between computer programme and student when the responses derived from the programme are highly responsive to the questions, answers, and directives given by the student, while at the same time the dialog advances the goals and merns established by the author of the curriculum materials. He further adds that the most visible use of computers in instruction is to provide direct assistance to learners and to assist teachers, administrators and educational technologists in helping learners. The users may work individually or in groups using a device directly connected to computer.

The types of CAI material could be classified into the following:

Drills

Skills practice

Programmed tutorials

Testing and diagnosis

Dialog tutorial

Simulation

Gaming

Information retrieval process Computation

Problem solving

The following guidelines have been identified after examining a few CAI (packages and also with the experience gained in developing one such software called SOCRATES. In fact, these guidelines could be used as bench marks in selecting some of the available CAI software or shells. The selection basically depends on the user requirements and affordability.

Shells *vs.* Prepackaged Lessons. One of the advantages of tutorials with builtin lessons is that the teachers need not worry about lesson preparation and presentation design. However, they are rigid and closed systems. On the contrary, CAI shells offer much desired flexibility and allows teachers to tailor the lesson depending on his evaluation of the students and the feedback. Once the lessons are prepared, they become as good as tutorials with prepackaged lessons, Yet they offer flexibility to update the lessons periodically in tune with the changes in curricula, method of presentation and feedback.

Novice-Friendly. The phrase 'novice friendly' is preferred to the widely used phrase 'user friendly'. We personally believe that user friendly software should offer powerful functions with case of use. Many user friendly software trade off power to simplicity. If a software does not demand prior knowledge of computers, it could be categorized as novice friendly, which may not mean less powerful. One of the widespread notions about UNIX operating system is that it is not user friendly. However, we feel, UNIX is user friendly and provides so many facilities for the user to accomplish varied tasks, though it requires effort on the part of the user in learning the usage of its utilities. In other words, UNIX is user friendly and perhaps is not novice friendly. Many of the so called user friendly software provide layers of menus. But once the user is familiar with the software, he may consider it tedious to reach a particular menu, if it is not one of the first few menus. This prompted many software developers to give options for both menus and command driven functions. Menu driven programmes need not be user friendly programmes but definitely be novice friendly. In the case of CAI packages, it is normally expected that the user might not have prior exposure to the computers and it should be novice friendly. In conclusion, it is ideal to have option for command driven and menu driven.

System Configuration. It is ideal to have a CAI package which runs on a system with minimum configuration. However, this may limit the programmer introducing many beneficial audio, visual effects, especially in the case of graphics presentations. CAl packages in general (exception being Hypertext) do not require much computing power. But the presentation of pictures poses a different problem, as there is no unanimity in the choice of display adopter cards. The adopter cards come in monochrome and in colour modes and in colour with different screen resolutions. However, this problem could be solved if the software provides install able device drivers, so that only the relevant driver is loaded at the time of installation of the package. It is suggested that a fairly good CAI software could be brought on an IBM PC compatible with the following configuration: IBM PC or its clone with 640 KB main memory; 360 KB Floppy disk drive; CGA/HGA switchable card; preferably a colour monitor. However, for a CAI package to be used on an online network, the package should have provision for multi-user access.

Audiovisual Effects. It is attractive if the presentation of lessons are sugared with audiovisual effects. Graphics image presentation, animation sound bring any CAI package near to the video presentation with an added advantage of the interaction with the system. In video presentation, the user becomes a passive observer and his presence or absence makes no difference. An intelligent CAI software can interact with the user and will not proceed further, unless the user wishes so. This could be best achieved by hypertext technology. However, the required hardware configuration and software may cost more.

Evaluation. Presently, only a few systems have the capability of assigning scores to the students. It is desirable if the system could evaluate a user on the basis of certain criteria, like the number of correct answers, the number of times the user has attempted to get the correct answer, the time taken by the student to answer a question. In such cases, the software should have some way of identifying the user so that it keeps track of his usage or discourse with the system.

Keeping these guidelines the authors have developed a CAI package called SOCRATES (Software for Computer Assisted Teaching System). Socrates is a CAI shell and is distinct from the tutors that are in wide use. One of the important problems with these tutors is that the lessons are prewritten as a part of the source code and compiled. In order to alter or modify or add a lesson, one should have access to the source code, which is not the case normally, as we get only an executable modules and overlay files which are binary files. This problem prompted the design model of Socrates to separate the executable module from the lessons and the lessons are ASCII flies. The basic model design is that of 'Learn' package of the UNIX system.

Unlike 'Learn', Socrates is menu driven. It displays horizontal menus of two modules, one for student and the other for teachers. The student is shown a popmenu of subjects on which the lessons are provided with. Once he moves the cursor on to the desired subject and presses return, he will be shown the list of lessons. He can either start with the first lesson or choose a lesson which he left off in his previous interaction with Socrates. The student is asked a question on the lesson he read with multiple choice answers. These answers are presented in window, and the student can choose the likely answer by moving a scroll bar and pressing the return key. Depending on the choice of the correctness of the answer, the student may be presented the same lesson or a previous lesson or the next lesson. Socrates has provision for teachers to modify, add., delete and even change the sequence of lessons. In order to perform these operations, Socrates offers a Screen Oriented Word Processor. This word processor is distinct from the common word processors' which we prefer to call 'Printer Oriented Word Processors'. The word processor of Socrates is programmed for Colour Graphics

Adapter (CGA) and Extended Colour Graphic Adapter (EGA) cards. Although, the software could be run on monochrome and Hercules Graphics Adapter (HGA) cards, its visual effects could only be realized with CGA and EGA cards. The word processor allows teachers to present definitions or technical terms, etc. in distinct colours and colour backgrounds. However, graphical presentation and music are not provided in Socrates. It is the responsibility of the teachers to prepare lessons and design the sequence of presentation. They can present questions with multiple answers and can direct the system to present another lesson depending on the choice of his answer.

Current Technology in the Library

CD-ROM is a growing and advancing technology that holds great promise for libraries and as an alternative for both online database and printed sources. It permits the lowest cost for information provision, that is, to distribute information in bulk and at a comparatively low cost. CD-ROM is an up-and-coming technology in the library world. Librarians must understand and appreciate CD-ROM if they are to make informed decisions regarding its place and application in the library. There is no doubt that CD-ROM can work very well for large static databases. One thing that would like to say with certainity concerning CD-ROM products is that there is constant developments taking place continuously. As librarians, we must have to identify the potential and worth of this new information product.

The history of CD-ROM has recently begun. Philips and Sony the patent holders for basic compact disc (CD) technology established the specifications for compact disc in the Red Book Actually, CD-ROM has been built on the success of CD. Philips and Sony later produced the Yellow Book with a set of licensed standards for CD-ROM.

The two companies first exhibited CD-ROM players at COMDEX (The Computer Dealers Exposition) in November 1984. Later Microsoft proclaimed the importance of CD-ROM in 1985 and sponsored the Microsoft First International Conference on CD-ROM in March 1986 in Seattle, Washington. Microsoft also published the book "CD-ROM: The New Papyrus" Microsoft's first real CD-ROM product, Bookhelf came to market in 1987. The first commercial CD-ROM product was marketed only to libraries.

The first CD-ROM product produced by the Library Corporation contained MARC (Machine Readable Catalogue) records. Silver Platter delivered CD-ROM products to the library reference market. The Educational Resources Information Centre (ERIC) database was introduced in mid 1986 by Silver Platter, in late 1986 by Dialog and in early 1987 by OCLC. At present a number of interesting developments are under way which make the product more effective and efficient to use the number of published CD-ROM, titles and drive installations has grown dramatically over the last two to three years. A recent survey claimed that 3,88,000 CD-ROM drives were installed worldwide by March 1990. It is predicted that it will increase to 4.3 million by the end of 1993. According to IMO Statistics the United States produced approximately three quarters of all CD-ROM products.

CD-ROM stands for Compact Disc Read Only Memory. The Information Technology Handbook describes CD-ROM as follows:

"CD-ROM, short for compact disc read only memory, refers to the use of audio compact disks for computer storage. Like a laser vision disk, information on a CDROM disk is read by bouncing a laser beam off its surface. Unlike a laser vision disk, the information is stored in digital form. The pits are very small, and the function of the laser beam is merely to detect the presence or absence of a pit, indicating a binary 1 or a binary 0.

The Dictionary of Computing explains CD-ROM as:

"The predominant form of read only (ROM) optical disk. Both disk and drive are based on the compact audio consumer product. The disk is 120 mm in diameter, single sided and holds upto 660 megabytes of data. The data is enclosed in the form of a spiral of minute bumps impressed into the surface of the disk at the time of manufacture, and cannot subsequently be altered. Many commercial databases are now available on CD-ROM, often as an alternative to an online service."

Squeezing 660,00 bytes on to a single floppy disk using the nine tracks per inch format of a standard MS-DOS 360K diskette would require a diskette approximately 800 feet across. Therefore, one CD-ROM is equivalent to ten COMPUTER MAGNETIC TAPES, hundreds of pages of microfiche or million of pages of text.

Now let us look into some details about the critical elements that make up the CD-ROM optical disc medium. The CD-ROM disc is a simple circle of a plastic made of bullet proof polycarbonate of the size 4.72 "in diameter with a center hole of 0.59". One side of the plastic is embosed with pattern of recessed pits. This side is metal coated with Aluminium which is approximately 1000A thick. The Aluminium metal is coated with a transport lacquer for protection.

How CD ROM Works

Data is stored on the disc as a spiral track of microscopic pits. Machine readable information is stored on the disc as a series of pits. When inserted into a CD-ROM drive, these microscopic pits appear as bumps from beneath the disc and scatter the light from the laser beam. Lands, that is, the areas between the pits, reflect the light from the laser. This is called the translation of "pits to bits". Intermittent busts of light are deflected into light-detector laser diodes through light polarization techniques that convert the light into electronic signals and decode them as one-off binary bits-ones and zeros. CD-ROM drives read the information contained on disc by focussing low-powered laser beams on the microscopic pits. An optical unit measures the pit's reflectivity and the CD-ROM drives semiconductors translates that reflectivity back into a binary signal that can be read by a computer. CQ-ROM spins at a constant linear rate of 75 data blocks per second which yields a 150 k byte/second data transfer rate. The rotation speed of disc varies as the head moves from inner to outer tracks, so that a constant number of blocks are read every second during reading.

The International Standards Organisation (ISO) 9660 Volume and File structure of CD-ROM Information Interchange (ISO 9660 CD-ROM standard), has originated from a proposal to the ISO by the High-Sierra Group which is an adhoc group of computer vendors including DEC, Apple, Hewlett Packard, Philips, Sony and in cooperation with NISO (National Information Standards Organisation).

CD-ROM drives are computer peripherals. They can be attached to an installed base of host computers or supplied as part of a complete work-station package comprising a host computer, the physical and logical interface and the CD-ROM drive. CD-ROM installations are all based around the IBM/PC/XT/AT and compatibles. Mainframe and minicomputer suppliers are distributing user manuals and documentation on CD-ROM. The performance of the drives is also set to improve as smaller, lighter read laser and better drive motors are employed. The first CD-ROM drives offered average access speeds of 1 second to 2 seconds. In the latest drives this average access speed has come to 0.5 seconds to 1 second. As the size of the CD-ROM drives comes' down, the prices also come down. The Multimedia PC Marketing Council has set a standard for connecting CD-ROM drives to IBM compatible PCs. This eases the customers' fears about incompatibility.

The host computer's operating systems determine the design of the device driver and file server software needed to control a CD-ROM drive and handle it as a peripheral of the host computer. Mostly MSDOS and PCDOS (Disc Operating Systems) are used at present. The file structure creation programme is used to structure and build the directory on the CD-ROM. The device drivers act as a link between the film server software and the CD-ROM controller. Regarding application software, the High Sierra Group's standard is widely adopted for new versions of PC. The application software communicates with the lower system component through 'system calls' defined by the host operating system. System calls allow the application software to tell the system software to do such things like input from the keyboard.

The importance of information in decision making has been recognised by the service organisations, which use it as a vital raw material. It is only recently that information is being recognised as a valuable, saleable commodity. With the availability of CD-ROM, users and producers of information products are confronted with a new information delivery medium and CD-ROM challenges current practices of publishing and integrating information in a fundamental way. Considering the potential of CD-ROM, its feasibilities are limitless. Its high storage capacity is a major advantage, which offers the potential for considerable consumable savings when compared with large microform or paper publications. To quote a few examples, it could be useful for interacting with huge paper collections, for tapping into the world's data banks without the cumulative charges, and for supplying pictures, graphics and other non-text information also with text. It is being used in-house by a range of public and private organisations for data distribution, distributing procedures manuals, reference works, technical manuals, etc. It is also used in a wide range of technical publishing applications in the aerospace, aircraft, automotive, shipbuilding and many more manufacturing environments and to distribute graphic database in the CAD (Computer Aided Design), Desktop publishing and scientific computing fields. The commercial database previously available online are now being distributed through CD-ROM. The Independent, the Times and The Guardian have launched their discs. The Times and The Sunday Times are now fully searchable (full text and retrieval) on CD-ROM which is an emerging alternative to multiple microfilm reels or openended online searches. The software for the CD-ROM edition of The Times and The Sunday Times also permits Boolean searching of all articles. Compton's New Media and Grolier have already come out with CD-ROM encyclopaedias, while the IBM-National Geographical joint venture has released kid targeted disks about mammals and the Presidents of the US.

CD-ROMs being based on CD-audio discs, are rugged, portable media and they are capable of being transported via postal services. Its drive and media costs can be kept low. The more the sales the lower the per unit production costs. Therefore, the most popular material can be produced very cheaply. CD-ROM being a digital storage medium, data can be searched interactively and data can be downloaded into other programmes for processing.

Once a reference material is available on CD-ROM, fully integrated system can be developed. It offers much more flexibility than print does, because of more access points, multi-year access, user friendly software, etc. With networking (Local Area Networks-LAN) and remote access, CD-ROMs can be available to many more users. CD-ROM can provide value added information that is not possible with print, if it can include hybrid indexing /Full-text products which allow increased search access. As we become proficient with optical disc technology and its creative and competitive applications to recent information products, we must also decide on how these products can be best positioned and utilised. Recently the "Magneto Optical" (MO) disc has been developed which not only stores millions of words, pictures, computer data like CD-ROM but it is also capable of erasing and rerecording fresh information over and over again, by the user rather than the manufacturer. The International Serials Data Systems, (ISDS) Register, the world register of International Standard Serial Number, (ISSN) is now available on CDROM under the title ISSN COMPACT. Therefore, more variables may be introduced as users and producers gain experience and confidence with the medium.

CD-ROM in the Library

The largest number of CD-ROM products in the market are aimed at the Library and Information Centres. From the libraries point of view, it requires a more detached perception of our purchasing decisions and smarter buying, we need to develop a built-in bias in favour of change, that is, change of technology and change of service objectives. The first commercially available CD-ROM product, namely, The Library Corporation's Biblio File, was designed and developed specifically for the library market. When first introduced at the 'American Library Associations' (ALA) midwinter meeting in January 1985, Biblio File was a great success. Biblio File contain the complete Library of Congress (LC) MARC (Machine Readable catalogue) database of more than 1,500,000 records. This database includes LC holdings both in English and in foreign languages of books, serials, Government Printing Office publications, maps, fjlms and music scores, It is stored on a minimum of two CD-ROM discs. By 1988 the company reported more than 1000 systems in operation.

This growth was due to its low price and its ability to replace costly automated systems. Other companies such as OCLC, Inc., EBSCO Electronic information, etc. market similar cataloguing systems. Silver Platter Inc. and H.W. Wilson Company market different databases, on CD-ROM. Silver Platter markets topically aligned databases such as MEDLINE and Ca-CD and Compu-index and Software CD. H. W. Wilson Company has their 'Wilson Disc'. Pre Quest Systems from UMI has CD-ROM database packages like 'Periodical Abstracts Ondisc, Newspaper Abstracts Ondisc' and Full Text Newspapers. Laser Quest contains 6.9 million MARC records to meet current as well as retrospective cataloguing needs. Engineering Information Inc., publisher of 'The Engineering Index' and (Ei compendex Plus' now offer a line of disc services on DIALOG On Disc as well as Ei Disc. Meridian Data, Inc. markets Meridians V.R. Publisher which handles premastering needs, that is, we have to prepare any database for preview and test variables before commiting to the final mastered disc. Once the disc is mastered, with Meridian's CD-NET, any CD-ROM is also made available to every one linked with Local Area Network (LAN). CD PACs (CD-ROM Public Access Catalogues) is an inexpensive alternative to Online PACs. Susan K. Charles and Katharine E.Clark conducted a research product to evaluate the feasibility of providing an online updating service to end-users searching . CD-ROM databases. They have found out that end-users are interested in the availability of a low-cost, hybridized CD-ROM / Online updating system. The Aslib survey, The Use of Information Technology by Information Services revealed that a majority of Aslib members were considering searching database on CD-ROM. Grolier Electronic Publishing Inc., has brought out (The 1988 Academic American Encyclopaedia (containing 21 volumes and 9 million words) on a single compact disc with full-text access, which is a valuable addition to libraries. Other notable entrants are Bowker's 'Books in Print' and Silver Platter's 'Library and Information Science Abstracts' (LISA).

ROMARIN is a new CD-ROM, just launched by the World intellectual Property Organization (WIPO). It contains information on all trademarks registered under the Madrid Agreement concerning the international registration of marks in the International Register maintained by WIPO's International Bureau, and which are currently in force.

The ROMARIN CD-ROMs (ROMARIN stands for 'Read-Only-Memory of Marid Actualized Registry Information") have been available since June 1992; they were developed jointly with Jouve Systems d' Information in Paris, France. The CDROMs contain such information (on each mark) as: the serial number of its registration, the mark, itself, the name and address of the owner, and data on exclusions or limitations.

In India, the National Information System for Science and Technology (NISSAT) has established Sectoral Information Centres (SICs) with the object of creating information awareness and to meet the information needs of scientists, technologists, academicians, entrepreneurs, management executives and decision-makers. Out of the ten SICs, 'NICDROM' caters to the information professionals and institutions providing information on CD-ROM, a reference collection of books and journals on CD-ROM, technical specifications, choice and cost of the CD-ROM equipment, CD-ROM database and services. NICDROM services are national in character and the host institution is National Aeronautical Laboratory (NAL), Bangalore.

Compact Disc India Limited is setting up the country's first facility for manufacture of compact discs (CDs) in technical and financial collaboration with Neststal and First Light Technology Inc. of USA.

Compact disc is the new revolutionary recording medium for storing sound, data and video images. Although CDs have worldwide market of more than 900 million discs per annum, India does not have any manufacturing facilities for them.

The main benefits of CD-ROM for the library are:

(a) CD-ROM offers on-disk access to bibliographic database without connect time costs and telecommunication fees.

(b) CD-ROM is physically portable and can be even mailed.

(c) No telecommunication facilities essential.

(d) The physical specifications are standardized. (ISO 9660 International Standards).

(e) Less storage needed for print products because of its high storage capacity.

(f) More service to the end user with all search options and brows ability. It is user friendly (search indexes are available).

(g) CD-ROM databases are more cost effective.

(h) Premastering is possible.

(i) Printing and downloading to hard disk or floppy disk is feasible.

(j) CD-ROM networking helps to share resources through Local Area Networks.

CD-ROM systems resolve many of the retrieval issues of preservation, access, storage and security of libraries and information centres. Since these systems are expensive and beyond the budget of individuals, libraries must make it possible for people to use and become familiar with this media. Libraries must aggressively identify and prioritize those databases that should ideally be converted or created an CD-ROM. Antony W. Brewerton an audiovisual librarian has said that "We should be praising CD-ROM not burying it". David 1. Rait and Ching-Chih-Chin conducted a survey under the auspices of FID (Federation International d' Information et de Documentation) on the use of CD-ROMs and other optical products in public, special, academic, government and other types of libraries in eighteen Western European countries. They feel "on the whole, users completing the FID questionnaire found many CD-ROMs easier, faster, more flexible and more convenient to use than corresponding print and online products. Many CD-ROMs were considered better than print products and were often more comprehensive in coverage." For CD-ROM products to be successful in libraries it is necessary to remove the obstacles for the libraries as well as to guarantee the Information providers a return on their investment.

❒

14

Bibliographical Classification

We have now to consider the bearing of all we have studied up to the present upon library classification. Again and again we have emphasized the fact that the material of classification is the whole of knowledge—that is, the material of knowledge classification. We may now say that a classification of books is as artificial as the ordinary classification of knowledge, but, while the methods of the librarian may vary in important ways from those of scientist and philosopher, they deal with the same unlimited field. In addition to the abstract untrammelled ideas and objects which can be isolated and compounded in thought with which they work, he has to order subjects as they are recorded in books and the physical form of books introduces complications which are the special concern of the librarian. Knowledge classification groups, divides and registers thoughts, things, ideas, in an unlimited manner; but on the other hand-a book is not an idea. In a sense it may be the expression of ideas, but it is infinitely more complex than any idea. For example, in a classification of geological elements the word water conveys a clearly defined simple idea; but a book on water may deal not only with water in the abstract, it may treat of its forms, of glaciers, snow and ice; its chemistry; its movements and mechanics; its relations to astronomy;' the fauna and flora of water; its bibliography; it is a very complex thing. It is impossible, say the philosophers, to classify such a compendium as a book. Of such critics the most potent is Jevons, whose Principles of Science is so important a text-book in our study.

We have apparently undertaken a fearsome and impossible thing in presuming to classify our books; we ought, we suppose, to leave them in unordered arrangement (if that be not a contradiction of terms), with only an author index; and, therefore, to leave them in such manner that they are accessible only to the man who knows every author in the subject in which he is interested, and, when his memory or knowledge fails on this point, inaccessible to him as well! Says L. S. Jast: "This statement of Jevons reminds me of the keeper who went up to the trespassing angler with the remark, 'My man, you can't fish here,' and who received the reply, 'But I am fishing.'" Librarians, in their wisdom or unwisdom, have trespassed on Jevons's precious waters and have shown that they can classify. But, coming as the statement does from so excellent an authority, we must examine it, and clarify our minds in regard to it. From the librarian's standpoint, the hypothetical book may deal, indeed, with all the subjects that Jevons enumerates but it is, after all, a "book on the steam-engine." Remembering the rule that convenience governs all classifications, he asks himself to whom the book will be most useful; for whom, primarily, it is meant; and according to his answer he will place the book—in this case—in engineering. Again, in pure literature, or billes-Iettres, it does not matter much if we do or do not know the qualities of the books included all the subjects of which they treat-because their importance does not lie in their subject-matter, interesting as that often is and must be in works of enduring character, but in their pattern as form or mode of expression; and in classifying them we adopt this characteristic and ignore altogether their subject-matter. We shall come to this question more fully in a moment. We ought to examine Jevons's statement in relation to the time at which it was made, and to the lack of knowledge of libraries which it unfortunately shows. In 1874 there were few reasonably good library schemes; hardly any of the libraries of England were classified, and those that were could not boast of anything wonderful in their arrangement.

One hesitates to accuse so logical and orderly a mind as Jevons of confusion; but he has confused the functions of classification with those of cataloguing. Perhaps this is hardly a fair way of putting it, since his criticism is aimed at the classified catalogue—the actual classifying of books on shelves was a performance of which he had probably never heard. But even here his objection seems to rest upon the belief that only one entry of a book is made in a classified catalogue. A classification of books does not attempt to arrange them by all their subjects, but only by the predominating, or most convenient, subject in each. A book treats of a topic from forty sides; very well, if we had the means, 'and the lack of imagination, we could buy forty copies of the book and place one under each of the forty places on our classified shelves; but I need hardly say that the number of librarians who will achieve such a feat will not be great. On the other hand, our book is a concrete, indivisible thing; which will go into one place only on the shelves; and that place, as I have just affirmed, must be the one must useful to the user of the book. In the catalogue the book can be entered directly, or by reference, under every subject in it in which is of enough importance to justify such entries. There we are handling not the book but written entries—ideas—of it, and these we can multiply as fully as reason and convenience dictate. Jevons's hypothetical book would have to be a remarkably encyclopaedic view of the steam-engine to justify an entry under each of the topics he names. We shall have much to say about the classified catalogue later on.

So, to summarize, experience aiding us, we get back to the position that books can and should be classified; that the order of knowledge and of the sciences is the basis of book classification; the primary difference being that while the knowledge classification arranges knowledge itself and its substances tangible and intangible, a book classification arranges the expression of knowledge in written or other form—the book, print, manuscript or what not. In general it may be said that at least half of the books in the world will fit logically and readily into a knowledge classification if viewed from the standpoint we are now examining; but a good many will not do so, owing to their miscellaneous subject-matter, or to the form in which they are presented. This brings us to the outward and visible difference between the knowledge and the book classification.

Requirements of Book Classification

The study of knowledge classification is essential to the book-classifier who is to understand the making and working of his scheme. We have admitted, and again admit, that many schemes for book-arrangement seem to be the result of the mere scrutiny of books themselves and to be fortuitous in the worst cases and systematic, to some degree, in others; but it never can be admitted that there is no relation between knowledge and its arrangements and books and their arrangement. It may be, in some cases, that the influence of such systems as Bacon, Gesner, and Comte is merely reflected indirectly, but arrangement itself must be logical; all classification must be to make sense. Even if main classes appear in different orders, as widely divergent as are Dewey and Bliss, in the working out of individual classes they tend to approximate at least on broad lines. In short, a classification of books must be a classification of knowledge. Let us, however, recall the point so often made that the Scientists (and Educationists may be added) make the schemes for their individual subjects, and then comes the generalizing Bacon or other philosopher who integrates these various schemes into one system in whatever order seems to him best. His system when completed is therefore a co-ordination of many schemes, each with its individual approach, If this is fully understood the principle that "characteristics must be consistent; no two headings must overlap" will not be interpreted as a skilful writer has done to mean that a single characteristic must be pursued undeviatingly and without change from the Universe to every individual thought or thing classified, which would be manifestly absurd. Book-classification uses many approaches to individual classes, many characteristics to arrange individual sub-classes and sections. The whole point is that every single act of classifying every subject, array or series must itself be divided consistently.

Whether this assumption is accepted or not, there are requirements of bibliographical classification which rise from the subject, books themselves. Books are written representations of thought in general or in particular; they may cover, rarely, the whole of knowledge as a universal encyclopaedia is expected to do; they may deal with several subjects; they may take certain literary patterns, as dictionaries, essays, journals, or as poetry or drama; they may be of a certain age or about that age; be of various physical sizes; shapes and in significant printing types, have illustrations or not which matter. The likenesses and differences may be multiplied and add to the complexity of the book-classification so greatly that the tendency of some librarians, overwhelmed with the magnitude of the task of classifying a library or not convinced that the resulting advantages would compensate for the immense labour, have solved the problem by not classifying, or doing it only in the broadest manner.

While all these considerations are vital ones, we practical librarians know that at least sixty out of every hundred books in non-fiction that pass through our hands are in their bulk about subjects and most of them about one subject that can be recognized although it is not always apparent at a glance. We know, too, that the average serious reader thinks of them as subject representations however many aberrations from this general rule may be known to us.

Having reached that conclusion, we go on to choose according to the practical virtues of schemes: their accessibility, hospitality, and the means they possess of differentiating the various sorts of books and their sizes, forms and modes of treatment. Although it is an accident, cross-dividing all books, size is the first and principal factor in book arrangement. Mere economy of space the most valuable commodity in the modern library makes it obvious that books of elephant folio size cannot stand with octavos and certainly not with duodecimos on shelves: every scheme of arrangement is therefore a series of parallels governed in the first place by the size of the books. This difficulty may be recognized at once. The value of classifying books may indeed be reduced but is by no means destroyed by such considerations.

The Generalia Class

We may consider first the Generalia class which every book classification possesses. In Dewey and Cutter this is called General Works; in Brown, Generalia; in the Quinn-Brown and various older classifications it is called Miscellaneous Works, Miscellany, or Ana. It is often called in the slang of Librarians the waste-paper basket of the classification; from which we may not infer that it is a merely chaotic class. It is certainly not that; it is rather a class for containing works which are so varied in their content that they will not fit into any class of the scheme that deals with a subject, but overlap all or many departments of knowledge. Sometimes Generalia is called a "form class," the form of the works fitting into it being their formlessness; but this is a mere juggling with language. The content of Generalia has form; it includes general encyclopaedias, general periodicals, transactions of general societies, and collected works; works, then, which within one cover range over the whole field of knowledge, or over several parts. Emphasis must be laid upon the general nature of all the parts of generalia; otherwise in practical work error will be frequent. It is clear that The Times, The Enclopadia Britannica, The Spectator and The Quarterly Review are entirely general in their scope; there is no subject in the universe of things or thought which may not properly come within their purview. To class anyone of them as Sociology, Science, History or in any other specific class would be to ignore all the other subjects; it must inevitably, then, go in the Generalia class.

This leads us to the GENERALIA DIVISION, which is entirely distinct, because it is part of a subject class. In this connexion the word "division" does not mean a sub-division of a generalia class, but a sub-division of a subject class. In regard to periodicals we can easily illustrate this: The Times covers all knowledge; but the periodical Nature is a scientific Periodical. But Nature in its turn covers all science, mathematical, natural and physical. Thus in relation to all knowledge Nature is a special periodical devoted to one subject; while in relation to science it is quite general. We may carry this still further. The Journal of the Chemical Society covers every phase of chemistry, is general in regard to that subject; but it is special in relation to Science, in relation to Nature. Only in a loose classification of scientific periodicals could it stand beside Nature on the shelves. Other examples will occur to you of periodicals which deal with special subjects in a general way. These have all, to be provided for in a book-classification, and it is fair to assume that Jevons did not contemplate any such provision when he inveighed against the classification of books.

Brown has given a much more comprehensive and controversial connotation to his Generalia. He includes in it all subjects which are general, and adds to them all such subjects as are pervasive of other classes; that is, subjects which are necessary to the study of every subject in greater or less degree, and without which the arts, etc., cannot be. That is his contention, and his Generalia includes such subjects as Education, Logic, Mathematics, the Graphic and Plastic Arts, and General Science. All these things, by his theory, are involved in the study of other subjects, and, in the modern developments of knowledge some of the sciences which seemed once distinct have been so interwoven that the former clear-cut distinctions have become more formal than real, but Brown's "pervasive" classes in several cases really belong elsewhere. When we come to study the Subject Classification in detail we shall have some criticisms to make of this theory and its application; but it is useful for us to realize this revolutionary experiment in classification at this point. There are also interesting variations in the Bliss scheme which can be discussed more conveniently when we come to consider that scheme.

Catalogue Versus Classification

It will be recognized in regard to Generalia classes and divisions that the catalogue possesses enormous superiority over classification on the shelves as an exhaustive method of treating books. The periodical, encyclopredia, or set of transactions can be shelved in one place only in our library. Thus its use is limited; we know nothing about it except its outer form; any view of the subjects it contains is impossible, except by the examining of the individual volume; a time-wasting process which would deter any but the most enthusiastic worker; and even he, after hours of avoidable labour, is never quite certain that he has not missed something. It is a very important problem for librarians, seeing that knowledge as presented in periodicals is said to be on the average at least four years in advance of books. The perfectly catalogued library may be made to bring all these articles to light if the periodicals are analysed and entries of the articles are made under their appropriate class headings in the catalogue.

This has been done on a co-operative basis by such invaluable works as the Library Association Index to Periodicals, in which some scores of periodicals, general and special, are analysed under appropriate subject-headings. Few libraries, unfortunately, are able to do this work for themselves; the cost in time and money would be too great.

Form Classes

Generalia, then, is roughly a form class; but the form classes proper are those which cover what Jevons, Brunet, and the earlier classifiers call Belles-Lettres and what we have called the fine art of writing. This class is called Literature in most classifications, and is named Literary Forms in the Subject Classification. It ignores the subjects of the books and arranges them into broad groups which show their form; thus we get the divisions Poetry, Drama, Fiction, Essays, Oratory, Letters, and so forth. Now these have very diverse subject-matter; for example, Dante's Divina Commedia is one of the revelations of medireval theology, Shakespeare's Hamlet is a great contribution to human psychology, Browning's Strafford is the great political drama of the seventeenth century, while Tennyson's Becket and Eliot's Murder in the Cathedral are varied versions of the life of the great Saint-Archbishop and his times. Again, Addison's Sir Roger de Coverley essays' reveal the social history of the Queen Anne period more vividly than a hundred formal histories; and I need not add examples of how novels present and illuminate actual things, places, periods and persons. They form, incidentally, material for the student of history, manners, topography and what not, but they are not specially intended for the student of literature. Their subjects are but subsidiary when one considers the purpose of these works, and the people who want to read them. The form and not the subject is the important consideration. So we construct our schedules for Belles-Lettres arbitrarily by the outward form in which the works are cast; metrical form makes poetry for us; drama is simply literary matter written in acts and scenes in poetry or prose of its relation to life and the dramatic unities we take no cognizance; and similarly throughout. But it may not be superfluous to say in regard to the divisions Essays, Oratory and Letters that we must be sure that only books which are interesting for their form merely or are general in character are placed here; and not essays, letters or speeches on specific subjects. We can place in the form division Augustine Birrell's Obiter Dicta and E. V. Lucas's Domesticities, because they deal with no particular subject; but not Butcher's Essays on Greek Drama, or that at one time very famous book, Essays and Reviews, which dealt with the theological position in its day. These latter books are on special subjects and are interesting from the points of view of Drama and Theology. Letters, as a general rule, would be much better if they were considered to be "the man's life in the letters of the man" as they are the best illuminants of Biography and should be classed there. The placing of them in literary forms is a Dewey expedient and it has its justification only when the letters have a very strong literary interest and not always then. The famous letters of Gray, Cowper, Horace Walpole and Lady Mary Wortley Montague come into the latter category, but those of the Brownings and of most other folk ought not to do so. In any case neither class takes such works as the Marquis of Dufferin's Letters from High Latitudes, which recounts travel experiences in Spitsbergen, and Cobbett's Letters on French Grammar both specific treatments of specific subjects, travel book and grammar in the accidental form of letters; they must be classed with the subjects. Thus too, with speeches and other divisions of this class.

The master rule of the classifier is: classify first by subject and then by form, except in the form classes, in which form is paramount. It must be said, too, that some classifiers have made interesting attempts to classify pure literature by subject. Wordsworth, it will be remembered, classified his poems as poems of imagination, sentiment, reflection, narrative, and so on; but few are satisfied with the arrangement, as it is full of cross-divisions and much of the placing is purely arbitrary. The most common form of experiment is that which attempts to classify fiction by subject: all historical novels by the period they present; all topographical at the country or county; and such novels as Reade's It is Never too Late to Mend, and Marcus Clarke's For the Term of His Natural Life, at penology; Dickens's

Nickolas Nikleby at schools; and so on without limit. This arrangement has an immense interest, and is in many ways a useful one; but as the principal arrangement of the books it is thoroughly bad. For one who is interested in penology, a thousand are interested in the stories which Reade and Marcus Clarke tell; and again the law of convenience must prevail.

Outer and Inner Form

It will have been remarked that the term "outer form" has been used, and I think from the examples I have given that its meaning has been clearly understood. It is a valuable distinction in classification, as there is also an "inner form" which is almost of equal importance, and the understanding of which alone makes the right application of the rule, "classify by topic" and then by "form," possible. We can see this quite easily by setting side by side Dewey's Generalia class and his general divisions (but any other scheme will show us very much the same features):

	Generalia Class.		*Generalia Divisions of*
	General Works.		Science.
010	Bibliography.	501	Philosophy, Theories.
020	Library Economy.	502	Compends, Outlines.
030	General Cyclopaedias.	503	Dictionaries, Cyclopaedias.
040	General Collected Essays.	504	Essays, Lectures, Letters.
050	General Periodicals.	505	Periodicals.
060	General Societies.	506	Societies, Associations.
070	General Newspapers (Journalism).	507	Education, Study, Teaching
080	Special Libraries.	508	Polygraphy, Collections.
090	Book Rarities.	509	History.

If we examine these closely we shall at once see that they are almost alike; the main difference being that the first column represents form divisions of the whole classification—they cover all the tables of the scheme; while those in the second cover only the schedules of the class Science. A careful consideration will show that in the form divisions (the second column) two kinds of form are employed. The outer as represented by Compends, Dictionaries, Essays, Periodicals and Polygraphy and perhaps to a lesser extent by Education; the inner as represented by Philosophy and History. A dictionary, encyclopaedia, periodical or newspaper is clearly a thing having a definite outer form which in a sufficient degree is known to us. Poetry, drama, etc., have also a definite form poetry is words according to a pattern or, if we prefer it, has a metrical shape. In all of these works the form is visible, objective. But it is not so with works which come into our inner form group. History, for example, may be a subject, or it may be a form. In such books as Harrison's A Meaning of History, Croce's Theory and History of Historiography and Burckhardt's Reflections on History it is a subject. But Macaulay's History of England is a record of England in a certain length of time treated historically (by a form) and, clearly, a history of the steam-engine is definitely upon the steam-engine, but in the manner of a history. This gives us the clue that we want. Outer form is physical, as it were, the literary shape in which things are presented; inner form is subjective, the method by which the thing is presented. Thus we may have a book, in fact we may have many books, bearing some such title as The Theory of Science, or The Philosophy of Art, or The Theory of Politics. Each of these is distinctly upon a subject; upon Science, Art, and Politics respectively; but each is viewed in a special manner, from a special standpoint; in short, is in a special form. So with the history of a science, art, or thing in which the science, art or thing is the dominant idea of the book, and the history merely the method; in all these history is form. You will now see the bearing of the rule classify by topic and then by form. In all subject-classes we seek first a place for our book at the most specific heading that will contain it, and afterwards sub-arrange by form. The forms we have discussed are usually set out in separate tables in modern schemes and where they, the forms, have a constant meaning they have also numbers which are constant and by that name Bliss calls them. The tables he calls systematic schedules, which of course is what they are.

Form Classes are Adjustments

A book classification, it may be repeated at the risk of being wearisome, is a classification of knowledge; that is to say, a schedule of the subjects in the universe of literature arranged by definite characteristics, and showing in the arrangement the rules of order and of sub-division which we have discussed at considerable length in our preceding chapters. Generalia and form classes are necessary practical, and in the main accidental and artificial, auxiliaries of that classification called for in the form of books. We stress this again because when new-comers to classification make experiment they quite often do so upon the theory actually expounded to me in these words: "Books as a whole do not fit into a knowledge classification; therefore a book classification must be something entirely different. Let us discard all those supposed relationships of knowledge, and shuffle the subjects in our classification in the way that best helps us to find books on the shelves and aids our memory in so doing. Thus, we are obeying the law of convenience; the essential characteristic of their arrangement being not the subjects of the books themselves, but something exterior, some accidental fact about those subjects." As a result of such reasoning we get the theory quite seriously enunciated and quite attractive; moreover, partly true: It does not matter where we classify a book so long as it is properly indexed. That is to say, in approaching the finding of a book on our shelves we ought first to consult the index-catalogue. (The index-catalogue, you will observe, being thus a necessary tool in the library.) If the subject is indexed, the reference there given will serve every practical purpose.

The Index Versus Classification

This is very specious reasoning and, as I have admitted, it is partly true because a purpose of classification is to make the finding of particular books an easy process. There the advantage, or merit, of a system which places books indifferently and relies upon the index, ends. It is only a small part of the work of classification to make the finding of particular books easy, although admittedly a most convenient and practical part. The accepted definition of classification not only implies this, it implies a cardinal purpose which this ignores the arrangement of books so that the law of union of properties is made visible; that is to say, so that the likeness in subject-matter between them is revealed. Thus a classification cannot justly be called a good one which does not show the sequence of subjects; show on the left of a particular book, or group of books, the books that lead up to it, and on the right the books which lead away from it. This is quite elementary; but the assertion that the index will do the work of classification proper has often been made, and it is most desirable that we should be convinced that classification is primarily arrangement with a definite revealing purpose and not a mere filing of books, irrespective of order, in separate pigeon-holes to which a mere index is a key.

An Index Arrangement, not a Classification

It was this confusion of ideas this belief in the functions of classification as a mere indexing expedient which led an American enthusiast, Robinson Smith, into an interesting experiment in classification construction which was published in The Library World for July, 1919 which he calls an Alphabetical Mnemonic Classification, but which is, strictly speaking, not a classification at all. In these he takes the broad classes of literature, and arranges them alphabetically by the names of the groups. Here is his outline:

A Art.
B Biography.
C Christianity and Judaism.
D Dictionaries.
E English Language and Literature
F Fiction.
G Greek Antiquities.
H History.
N National, Industrial and Social Problems.
O Oriental Languages.
P Philosophy.
Q Quartos.
R Roman Antiquities, Languages and Literatures.
S Science.
T Technology.

I Industries.
J Juveniles.
K Knowledge,
L Law.
M Modern Languages and Literatures.
U Unclassified.
V Voyages and Travels.
W Weeklies and Monthlies.
Y Year Books.
Z Newspapers.

Each of these is subject to alphabetical sub-division as an example will show:

L Law.
LA Administration.
LB Banking, Bankruptcy.
LC Criminal.
LE Ecclesiology.
LF Feudal.
LG Greek.
LH History.
LJ Jurisprudence.

and so on, with alphabetical re-divisions of each.

Every student of classification will see at once that this is not classification at all; it is arrangement for quick-reference; and is an indescribable jumbling of topics, the only relation between them being the alphabetical letters of the class names. It has several cross-divisions, mixes characteristics, jumbles topic and form, and has every theoretical fault we can name. It even has defects as a mnemonic arrangement; we search our minds in vain for the possible place in this scheme of many subjects. In short, it is the best example known to me of a so-called classification in which the compiler has ignored or is not cognizant of the main purpose of classification, and has bent all his efforts to the producing of a scheme in which, as he avers, things are easy to find. His principal argument in its favour is that the notation is definitely related to the name of the subject it represents; and thence we gather that he laboured under the delusion that notation was more important than classification itself. This we can best answer by a consideration of the purpose of classification.

❐

15

Periodical Indexing

The library's holdings of each title are given or, in the case of union lists, the holdings of each library within the group. In addition to holdings details various additional pieces of information may also be included, such as the frequency of publication, the shelf mark or other library locational symbol, and perhaps some indication of subject one of this is not included in the shelf mark. If subject descriptors are given to each periodical title then it becomes possible to produce a subject index to the holdings list a very valuable addition. If the holdings list is to be produced with the need of the library staff in mind, in addition to those of readers then a number of additional items of information can usefully be included for each periodical.

These include the publisher, the dealer from which the library fund it is charged to binding information. and possible the names of any readers to whom the journal is routed. The amount of information included will depend on the uses to which the list is to be put, whether it will be used simply as a holdings list, or whether it will also serve other functions within the periodicals department. In fact a holdings list can come quite close to a periodicals accessioning system in the facilities it can offer. The important difference is that an accessioning system normally performs the several functions automatically in response to the data given to it, whereas a holdings list only assists human librarian in their work. A part from the problems which have been mentioned, a decision between these two types of system might be based on of a library's periodicals holdings in a way analogous to deciding where automate methods of book ordering can be justified. A large-sale operation would justify automation. However, in practice, many large libraries find that automate methods accessioning. But a number of libraries are using computers to produce holdings lists now with the intention of extending their systems to include automated accessioning when a satisfactory method of doing this has been developed.

Each entry in a printed periodicals holdings list corresponds to one record in a machineable file. This is normally kept on magnetic tape. Each magnetic tap record has a structure corresponding to the information which is given in the printed list. Because the list must be printed in order, usually alphabetically by periodical title, provision must be made for sorting machineable records into correct order and inserting new records in the right places. A computer sort programme can be used on periodical titles or, alternatively, each record can be assigned a number and the sorting can be done on this.

Numbers are assigned manually so that ascending numerical sequence corresponds to correct alphabetical order of titles. New records to be inserted into the file are assigned numbers which place them in the correct position in the file in strict numerical and alphabetical sequence. The machine file of periodicals holdings will almost invariably be create from an existing manual file. Because the manual file can be assumed to be in correct alphabetical order no machines setting will be involved in this initial setting up of the file. A record format must be devised which will enable the computer to process the file and produce the various outputs which may be needed.

The amount of information identified in the record will vary, but for a straightforward holdings list the following data elements would be adequate: *(a)* Type of record; *(b)* Sequence number; *(c)* Title; *(d)* Holdings; *(e)* Shelf mark or other locational symbol; *(f)* Publication frequency; *(g)* Subject information; *(h)* Titles or headings from which cross references are to be made, together with their reference number. This information for each in the list is punched either into paper tape or punched cards and verified.

The various categories of data in each record are identified either by specific labels or by means of a standard input format. With paper-tape input the format is specified by patterns of space and line shift characters. With input by means of punched cards the format is specified by column and card numbering. Each card in the decklet for each title is punched with the sequence number for the title, and the position of the card within the decklet is also indicated.

The programme which controls the printing of the magnetic tape file makes use of this standard record format to lay each printed entry .out in the desired manner. It is also possible, for example, to re-sort the file by shelf mark or subject identifier to produce a printed holdings list arrange by subject. Alternatively, a straightforward subject index to the main alphabetical sequence can be compiled.

In addition to records of a library's holdings of a particular title the printed list and the machineable magnetic tape file will also contain records for cross references and earlier forms of titles. Each of these cross reference records must also be assigned a numerical sequence number where these are used for alphabetization purpose. They will be specially marked to indicate that they are not full entries, and the following data elements are typically require:

(a) Type of record.

(b) Sequence number.

(c) Title or heading referred from.

(d) Title referred to.

(e) Sequence number of title referred to.

Entries in the holdings list for periodicals currently being received will be left "open". That is they show when a library's holdings for a title begins, but no terminal data is given. The assumption is that the library holds all volumes and parts published to date.

In time, however, a number of periodicals with open entries in the holdings list will cease publication or change their titles, or the library may stop subscribing to them. The open entries will then have to be closed in order to reflect the changed nature of the library's holdings. The library will also have begun to subscribe to new journals which will require new open entries to be made in the list. With most manual methods of producing a periodicals holdings list it is necessary to keyboard large section of the entire fist in order to include alternations and additions such as these to bring it up to date. But with a computer-produced list it is only necessary to keyboard the alterations and additions together with instructions as to how they are to be added to the file. It is this ease of updating which is one major attraction of computer-produced lists of periodicals.

The procedure for updating the machine file is fairly straightforward. Where a new record is to be added to the file, a sequence number is chosen for it which will place it in the correct position in the file. (When the sequence numbers were assigned to the file in the first place, sufficient numbers were left vacant to allow for subsequent inserts into the file.) The type of record is indicated and the data comprising the record keypunched in the standard format.

When an existing records is to be altered it is identified by means of its sequence number. The type of alteration is specified: whether it is to be a deletion, addition, or replacement, and the section of the original record to be altered is indicated. The actual data which follows can either be the whole of the altered section or simply the information need to make the alteration, depending on the type of alteration and its magnitude.

The kind of list so fat can indicate a library's periodicals holdings by means of closed entries for inactive titles and open entries for titles that are currently being received. It can be brought up date wmparatively easily by human decisions about the additions and changes that nee to be made to it. The instructions and data required for these changes must be converted to machine-readable form and input to a computer run, which updates the magnetic-tape version of the holdings list and prints it.

In contrast, a system for accessioning periodicals automatically updates the holdings list of its own accord, with only a minimum amount of human intervention associate with the clerical procedures for incorporating new issues of periodicals into the library's stock. Updating can be done much more frequently and a variety of outputs is possible. Subscription renewals and the associate accounting procedures can also be included with the system.

The method of operation of an automate periodicals Accessioning system depends fundamentally upon the regular pattern of periodical publication. If a given journal is publi.sh once a month then it is likely to appear with a high degree of regularity each month and probably even on a certain day each month. The same can be said for daily, weekly, quarterly publications, etc. Because of this it becomes possible to forecast with some degree of accuracy which periodicals will arrive in a library over any future period of time. This may require some moderately complex calculations but these can be handled with ease by a computer.

In the system which has so far achieved the greatest popularity, the computer punches a deck of eightycolumn card as a result of this forecasting operation; one card for each periodical part, supplement, title page, index etc., that is expected to arrive in the library during the period of the forecast. In most medium-size libraries one month is a convenient period.

A smaller library might opt for a longer period, while a larger library would probably want to reduce the period to a fortnight in order to keep the file within manageable proportions. Each card in the file is punched and interpreted with data sufficient to enable the corresponding periodical part to be identified and processed.

The work of the periodicals checking-in clerk under such a automated system is as follows. For each periodical issue that is received in the library the corresponding punched card is pulled from the card file, It will contain all necessary instructions for the clerk; the shelf mark to be written on the periodical, the library branch or department where it is to be sent, and possibly any routing instructions that may apply to it. The periodical is sent for despatch to the appropriate destination and its punched card placed into a special "received" file.

Cards in this file representing periodical issues now received in the library can serve a number of purposes. They can be printed to give a daily listing of new periodicals arrive in the library. Cumulated weekly or fortnightly listings can be made, or alternatively, such lists can include only those periodicals which were expected to arrive but have not arrived. Because a periodical's full title is not normally included inn the card in order to save space, a computer run is required if these lists are to contain full titles. Finally, each month, card in this "received" file are used to update the main periodicals holdings file. At this run the next month's batch of cards is punched.

Cards still remaining in the file represent parts that are overdue. Claims can be made for these after they have been considered by the librarian in charge of periodicals. The monthly processing run also reports on volumes that have been complete and are now ready for binding. The programme can arrange to provide an even workload for the library bindery throughout the year rather than create a glut of work at the end of each calendar year, when many periodicals complete volumes.

Central to the operation of the system is the machine-readable file of periodicals holdings. This must contain sufficient information about each title to enable the computer to produce the various outputs required by the system. It consists of a number of separate records, one record for each periodical title or cross reference that appears in the printed holdings list.

It is convenient of records to be fixed length, with overspill record for those few. titles which have an unusually large amount of information associated with them. As in the case of the machineable file for a system producing a straightforward periodic listing of holdings, each record in this file is assigned a reference number. This provides the facility for simple unique identification of each record in the file and may also act as a sorting key for arranging periodical titles in alphabetical order. The data contained in each record in this file must be equivalent to that contained in conventional manual car files, but in addition, it must enable the computer to calculate when to expect new issues.

The following information is therefore likely to be required for each record in the file:

(a) Record identification number.

(b) Coden or other short mnemonic identification.

(c) Title.

(d) Sub-title.

(e) Previous titles which cross references have been made, together with the record identification number of each reference.

(f) Shelf mark or class mark.

(g) Subject descriptors.

(h) Number of copies.

(i) Their library locations and routing.

(j) Complete holdings information including bound and unbound volumes and volumes held as microforms.

(k) Frequency of Publication.

(l) Sample average date of arrival.

(m) Number of issues per volume.

(n) Bookseller or supplier.

(o) Library fund charged to and subscription number (if any).

(p) Annual subscription.

(q) Date when subscription is due for renewal.

(r) Reordering procedure.

(s) Binding instructions including treatments of title page, table of contents index, advertisements, covers, etc.

(t) Discarding procedure (if any).

(u) Other additional information; warnings about parts that are to be delayed or not issued, parts claimed, etc.

Each record can contain a relatively large amount of information, so it is necessary to encode certain categories of data to keep the record within a reasonable size. This can be done conveniently for such items as the bookseller, library found, recording procedure, and other additional information where there are only a limited number of different possibilities.

When the system is being set up in the first instance and whenever new records are being added to the magnetic tape file, a fairly complex clerical process is involved in translating the data on the original old manual record into the form in which it must appear in the machine record. In many cases considerable experience of periodicals librarianship is required for this, so that it becomes realistic to create a temporary record to facilitate the conversion process. A librarian creates written record in exactly the same format as the machine record and a clerk keypunches directly from this.

Each month a computer run punches a deck of cards for the periodical parts that are expected to arrive during the forthcoming month. Since the main file is in alphabetical order by title the cards will also be in that order. Each card must contain sufficient information to enable the periodicals clerk to process the periodical and this must not exceed the eighty characters available on the card. The following data elements are typically required:

— Record identification number.

— Coden or other short mnemonic title abbreviation.

— Series, volume, part, issue number.

— Shelf mark or class mark.

— Library location and/or routing instructions.

Where the journal issue in hand corresponds exactly with the card that is in the file, the card is pulled and place on one side and the periodical processed in the normal way. However, if the issue is not the expected one and the correspondence is not exact, then a cards. This may not be necessary if the issue is a duplicate or has been received in response to a new periodical order, but it remains the basic solution to the difficulty caused by the computer forecast not being fulfilled in practice by the actual pattern of the arrival in the library of periodical parts.

It is a slow procedure to punch an eighty-column card and verify it compared with the relatively quick job off pulling one card from a file. The extent to which the computer forecast is accurate, that is the extent to which the future publication pattern of a periodical is the same as or can be predicted from the preset publication pattern, is a measure of the probable success of a periodicals accessioning system of this type.

The experience of libraries using such a system has been somewhat disappointing. A surprisingly high percentage of irregularities do in fact occur with periodicals. Issues arrive late (seldom early), issues are skipped, two or more issues are published together, unannounced supplements are published. This means that a lot of keypunching must be done to inform the system of these irregular arrivals. The system is geared rigidly to a regular pattern of publication and it is difficult to relate this to the rather flexible, unpredictable pattern of real life.

However, as with other automated library systems, once the data has been put into the system and included in the machineable holdings record, then a number of different outputs can be produced without any further manual intervention. These may well provide the justification for an automated system where they can be shown to be useful.

If the library needs a frequent listing of newly received periodical parts for public consultation, then this can be produced easily by the computer. A computer run is required for this if the eighty-column cards for expected issues do not contain the title in a form readily understood by library users. Such frequent listings can be especially valuable in a library system with a number of branches, in each of which current periodicals are displayed. A listing can then be made for each branch and copies displayed in other branches, or one union list can be made.

One copy of a fully detailed printed holdings list can be kept conveniently at each public service point to facilitate the answering of reader's queries. This is especially valuable in a library with a number of branches, for a card catalogue of the periodical holdings of the library system is not likely to be available at each branch. If a subject index can be prepared for this detailed holdings list, or if it can also be pdnted in subject order, then its value will be considerably enhanced. The facility for automatic notification of volumes that are ready for bindings has already been mentioned. This can be especially valuable in a large library and eliminates manual checking of shelves to see which volumes are ready for binding. It requires a high degree of systematization of binding procedures and cannot, of course, make allowances for volumes from which parts have been borrowed or lost.

One important advantage the system has to offer is that it shows up those periodical issues which have not arrived at the end of each month. Their punched cards will be left in the file of expected arrivals. The periodicals librarian must decide for each of them whether to initiate a claims procedure or to file the card into the new month's file. Cards in each month's arrival file can be colour coded so that it is possible to recognize cards representing issue more than one month overdue. The actual claims notice can either be printed by the computer or prepared manually. It is a simple matter during each monthly computer run to check each record to see if the subscription is due for renewal and if so either to print an order form for the next volume or to inform the periodicals librarian to initiate the appropriate manual routines.

Alternative System Designs

The above automate periodicals accessioning system is unsatisfactory in two major respects. The clerical routines required for checking-in periodicals are scarcely any faster than those of conventional manual systems. Both require the periodical to be processed by hand and both include a file look-up. It is more difficult to read the interpreted punched cards of the computer system than the typed headings on manual.cards, but quicker to pull a card. and place it in the "received" bin than write brief information about the issue in hand onto a manual card. Exceptions to the regular pattern demand a fair amount key-punching effort. Access to the file of expected arrivals is speeded up if, instead of a deck of cards, a printout is made containing roughly the same information for each part that is punched into the cards. It is possible, however, to print the full title of each periodical because the restriction to eighty characters no longer applies. Parts are simply ticked off on a list as they arrive.

At the end of the month only briefest details of parts that have not arrived need be punched, for example the serial number of the part in that have not arrived need be punched, for example the serial number of the part in that monthly printout. But the whole list must be searched to find those parts that have been delayed. When unexpected issues arrive in ,the library, these can be entered manually on the list and keypunch at the end of the month in a highly abbreviate coded form. One possible disadvantage with this type of system is that frequent lists of recently arrived parts cannot be prepared. All other outputs are possible, however, and it is not necessary to use the computer at any time other than when a printout of expected issues is made.

Another alternative provides greater flexibility at the expense of more manual keyboarding. A card, edgepunched with paper-tape code, is punched for each periodical title in the collection. Punched into each card are the title and record identification number of the periodical and written on it is all the information required to process each periodical issue.

The edge-punched card for the title is pulled from the file. It is then run through the reading head of a tape typewriter which causes the data punched into the title card punched into a paper tape. Details of the volume and part umber of the issue in hand are then punch manually into the paper tape and the title card is returned to the file. The paper tape thus contain machiner eadable information about all periodical parts that have been received. It is exactly analogous to the file of punched cards which represent received parts in the standard punched-card system and can be used to provide the same range of outputs.

One disadvantage of the tape system is that periodical parts which do not arrive on time are not represented by cards remaining in the file: the computer must make a special listing of them instead. Considerably more staff time is required for routine checking-in than with the punched-card system. Since manual keyboarding is the regular procedure, irregularities in the arrival patterns of periodicals do not cause the same disturbance as in the punched-card system.

This is dual problem facing any system for accessing periodicals automatically ad a solution that is entirely satisfactory does not yet appear to have emerged. The checking-in procedure must be quick if it is to match the great efficiency in this respect of manual accessing systems. Thus almost all manual keyboarding is ruled out except where it is of very limited extent, and it should preferably be needed only for exceptions to the general rule. Secondly, the system design must be flexible enough to cater easily for the many irregularities which are superimposed on the underlying regular pattern of periodical publication.

❑

16

Indexing in Library

It would be extremely naive for librarians, even those that are proponents of advanced modern technology of information dissemination, to assume that book has and will continue to occupy a place of prominence in the library. It is quite possible that book information by the year 2000 will be predominantly available in some electronic form, but regardless of form, the content will still be arranged in some type of book format. The librarian will still need to be an expert in book selection and have a professional working knowledge of the basic elements involved in book acquisition. All book selection is predicate on the principle of supply and demand. Supply simply refers to the types, titles, and varieties of books available in the marketplace from which to choose. Demand on the other hand, refers, to the kind of books the patrons of a particular library will request or need. This is where the acquisition skills of the professional librarian come to the fore.

The library should not acquire, and in all probability cannot afford, every book published. It is equally important to know which books to accept as well as which to reject. Considering that approximately 30,000 books are published each year, the task of selecting books is by no means easy. The librarian needs to formulate and expound upon the basic elements involved inselecting books for his or her library in order that selection procedures be promulgated on valid principles.

1. ***Philosophy of the Library.*** Although many libraries claim to have a philosophy for selecting books, it is difficult to locate a written statement that can be used as a working. The philosophy for selecting books should include the

purpose of the library and its goals for filling the needs of the community it is created to serve. In adopting a philosophy of book selecting, the librarian needs to consider the best, demand, and least-cost theories of book selection.

2. ***Nature of the Community.*** The librarian needs to know the nature of the community which the library is to serve. In the case of the academic or school librarian, the task of identification is relatively simple, as the curriculum perfunctorily describes the literature needs of students. The librarian of a public library has to develop and of ascertaining the reading needs of its community. Factors such as quality of employment, recrt::ational needs, and unique social, political, cultural, geographical, and historical traits of the community need to be identified.

3. ***Availability of Books from other Agencies.*** It must be determined if other agencies in the community provide similar book services. As an example, textbooks are provided by schools, and the library should not be expected to acquire them. If school textbooks are expected to be included in the library collection, then in all probability they will be presented to the library by the school district. It is also possible that other libraries in the community can work out reciprocal agreements regarding the sharing of books and indeed which kinds of books each will acquire.

4. ***Sociological Trends.*** The librarian needs to be aware of sociological trends that may have a bearing on patron's needs or demands for certain types of books. The influence of movies and television on what people read cannot be underestimated. Cultural events, recreational activities, scientific milestones, and ethnic composition of a community are potent forces on what types of books should be on the library shelf.

5. ***Books Available from Governmental Agencies.*** It should be determined if state or federal agencies have book that

they make available to the public, *e.g.*, books for the blind. It is possible that the local library may want to include books form other governmental agencies in its collection, or it may refer the patron directly to the government agency circulating books.

6. ***Booklists.*** Booklists are invaluable guides in building library collections. They tend to narrow down the range of books that should be included in certain types of collections. But it is the librarian who makes the final decision as to what extent the books listed will be those needed for a particular library community.

7. ***Budget.*** The importance of budgets cannot be overlooked. All book selection lists should be based on priority of need, and books should be purchased within the constrajnts of the existing budgets. It very often happens that the best through out list of books to be selected must undergo revision because of limited availability of funds, hence the need for selection priorities. Budget constraints should be approached with optimism and not considered as ugly ogres inhibiting the development of the' library collection. In the final analysis, the library does not need every book published, and although the budgets mandates how many books the library can afford to acquire, if book selection is done judiciously, as evidenced by the use of the library, expenditures can be well justified and increase in future budgets can be deserved and expected.

These seven basic fundamentals are not intended to be exhaustive but to serve as the basis for developing a sound book selection policy.

When selecting books, the librarian can subscribe, either single or in combinations of varying degrees, to the best book theory the demand book theory, or the least cost book theory. Adherents of the best book theory maintain that the true purpose of the library is to provide its patrons with the best books available. In absolute terms, means that regardless of the needs or desires of patrons, only books identified as being the best in their particular class are chosen.

Obviously, the terms best contains some degree of subjectivity. In general, these books have become classics, been given extremely favorable reviews, or been rated best for the social and cultural needs of the patron. There is no dispute that the classics are best books, for they have obviously stood the test of time and made worth while contributions to mankind.

Books receiving excellent reviews for their literary quality can also warrant high selection consideration.

When books are selected because they are best for the subjective evaluation of the librarian, and this can possible be considered an incursion of censorship. In the final analysis who has the right to decide what is best for the patron? As a result, the best book theory implies the possibility of selecting books that run counter to what the patron will actually read. Of what value is it to have a library of best books if they receive little or no use? This concept will be further explored in the demand theory of book selection. Still another aspects of the best book theory deals with the physical attributes of the book. If a choice is available, the librarian should consider the quality of binding and paper, readability of the print; and the clarity or artwork, graphics, illustrations, and photography.

The Demand Book Theory

Advocates of the demand book theory maintain that a book should be selected only if it can be determined that the patron will want it. Book use becomes the overriding criterion of selection. If this theory is carried to its extreme, the library might house a collection of literary trash, but this is justified by being what the patron demands. Perhaps the philosophy of the library should be nurture the cultural needs of its patrons, and some criterion of censorship should be formulated to eliminate the possibility that the library could degenerate into a purveyor of inferior literature. Obviously, some flexibility is needed in selecting what is best versus what is demanded. The librarian, must be astute to developments and tr~nds in book publishing.

Again, considering that over 30,000 new titles are published annually, there is a need for some sort of sliding scale when selecting best and demand type literature whenever best and demand are not one and the same. It is safe to assume that best books tend to have a lasting quality whereas demand books tend to serve a temporary interest. If this indeed is the case, then perhaps decisions can reside in the physical quality of the books selected, with best books being purchased in the best physical quality, available and demand books being purchased in less durable format. The demand book theory of selection can always be justified in terms of use, it should never be used to sacrifice the library's literary standards, which perhaps is a justification for the best book theory.

The Least-cost Book Theory

Subscribers to the least-cost book theory maintain that both best and demand theories can be entertained if all books are selected with the prime consideration that the least expensive version of a book be purchased. It is contended that by adhering to this theory more titles can be purchased. Unfortunately, a total commitment to this theory could eventually result in a rather shabby book collection in both content an physical quality. Purchasing less expensive books written by lesser known authors could well ensue in literature of less quality.

A renowned author of great literary skill, using primary resources for his work, has to produce a work of immensely superior quality than an author with less literary talent using secondary resources. However, when a work by one author is available in different formats, the least-cost book theory can be validly entertained. There should be an awareness as to why a cost structure exists for the same literary work. Perhaps the least-cost editions are abridged, the esthetic quality of pictorial information has been modified, the physical quality of the book has been reduced, or perhaps it is a less prestigious second printing. Whatever the cause, if the librarian can tolerate sacrifices when obtaining a least-cost version, it should be sincerely considered.

Not a direct corollary to the least book theory but still related to cost is the rent-to-won means of book acquisitions, which is worthy of mention at this point. Briefly, there are book jobbers who rent books to a library for one years periods, after which the librarian a year to determine if a book is worth owning and thus to return books not worthy of or needed in the collection. This in a sense, is a variation of least cost, as books that do not prove themselves in the actual library will incur only a rental cost a total ownership cost and will become deadwood in the collection. The three theories of book selection tend .to form a triad of justification and consideration.

Developing a Book Selection Policy

Having investigated the basic elements involved in the selection of books and formulated an awareness of the implication of the best, demand, and least-cost theories as they affect building a book collection, the librarian needs to development a realistic, workable policy for book acquisition. Depending on the particular library and how many people are actually involved, it may be a sound principle to have the book selection policy in a written form detailing prescribed policy, the possibility of personal preferences and biases interfering with the soundness and quality of selection will be greatly minimized.

This is not to imply that the personal opinions of the librarian are not be entertained; after all the librarian is professionally prepared and should possess a respected expertise in book selection, but a documented book selection policy makes provisions for valid, qualitative book selection procedures. The following suggested policy considerations are not listed in hierarchical order, but rather attempt to be comprehensive. Accompanying each policy item are questions to be considered when developing policy for a particular library book selection programme. Some of the items may appear mundane, however, just such items, when taken for granted and not properly developed could negate the quality of the book selection programme.

1. ***Purpose of the Library.*** The book should not be in conflict with the philosophical goals of the library. Questions: Does the book belong in the library? Does the service provided by the library warrant the inclusion of this type of book?

2. ***Quality.*** The book should be in keeping with the qualitative standards set by the library as regards contents respectability, and physical characteristics.

   Question. Is the book judged to be of the highest quality available for selection? If the book is a translation, is the most accurate available? If book quality is sacrificed, what is the justifiable reason?

3. ***Patron.*** The book should be suitable to the abilities, needs, and interests of patrons.

   Questions. Who are patrons that are entitled to use the library?

4. ***Reviews.*** Reviews should be consulted to assist in the selection.

   Questions. How many reviews should be consulted in making a valid decision? What are the credentials of the reviewers?

   What is the range of reading skills of the patrons? Who will be using this particular book?

5. ***Applicability.*** The book should be analyzed with regard to its applicability to a board or narrow audience and assessed accordingly.

   Questions. If broad applicability, will the book serve the needs of a sufficient cross-section of patron types? If narrow applicability, will the book serve informational needs unavailable by any other means?

6. ***Usability.*** A determination should be made as to minimum anticipated usage. A book may have a short usage expectancy and soon I become obsolete; but if it receives a prescribed number of uses, its acquisition is justified. Conversely, a book may receive rather limited use be of permanent value. A formula could be devised to analyze this problem.

Questions. Will enough patrons read the book to justify its acquisition? Is this a book the patron wants or needs?

7. ***Affiliated Resources.*** A book should not be require if it is conveniently accessible, or should more properly housed in the collection of another community agency.

   Questions. Should another agency purchase the book and, if it is so should they be so informed? Can the library afford to duplicate information more properly available from another agency?

8. ***Selection Aids.*** Selection aids should be consulted in order to assure that the book being considered is indeed the best for the library.

   Questions. How many selection aids need to be consulted? What type of quantitative and qualitative information— should the selection aid provide?

9. ***Cultural Influence.*** The book should support the position of local cultural, political, ethic, religious, or social groups. It is permissible to have a controversial book that informs the reader about a particular sect but it should not hurt, misrepresent, or in any way be unjustly harmful.

   Questions. By whom and for whom is this book recommended? What specific cultural contribution is the book purported to make?

10. ***Censorship.*** Policy regarding censorship should be developed by a committee representative of cross sectional interest of library patrons. Granted that a workable censorship policy can be rather nebulous, it should nevertheless be a policy under which the librarian can function. Any book selected which generates a negative reaction vis-a-vis censorship should be referred to a censorship committee comprised of impartial responsible members for review.

Questions. What genres of information warrant censorship concerns? Is the censorship policy up to date and in keeping with currently accepted mores and morals?

11. ***Alternative Media.*** The consideration of alternative media can greatly influence the direction a library will pursue with regard to the acquisition of print and nonprint media.

    Questions. Is the book the proper medium for the particular information it contains, or would some other from be more appropriate? If another media form is chosen instead of the book, do the library and the patron have the technology to use it?

12. ***Balance of the Book Collection.*** Books selected should keep the library collection properly proportioned according'to patron need and use?

    Questions. What are the proportions of books being allocated to the various parts of the collection? Is there a use or datedness variable that may be a justification for altering existing proportions?

13. ***Selector Objectivity.*** Book should be selected to serve patron needs and not what the librarian personally perceives to be those needs.

    Questions. Are books being selected because of personal bias or prejudice? Is a professional attitude being maintained with regard to book selection?

These criteria are not exhaustive, but they will generate through on constructing a book selection policy. The book will be selected with the needs of the patron in mind and enhance the development and enrichment of the community the library serves.

To institute this book selection policy requires the disciplining of the library with regard to personal opinions on book selection and the use of standard procedures in making decisions. The librarian must perform with objectivity; be thoroughly familiar with various book selection aids, have an awareness of library association book standards; identify with the community served by the library; known the library patron with regard to ethnic, social, cultural, attitudinal, educational, vocational, political, and recreational needs, and work within the parameters of the library's philosophy, operation, and budget. In summary, when involved in selecting books, or any other media forms, the libraricm needs to be both a competent professional capably contributing to the operation of the library and a humanist with an acute awareness of the library community's information needs.

Selecting and Evaluating a Book

Assessing a purticular book considered for acquisition requires an intelligent evaluation conducted by a skilled librarian. It is essential the librarian have a broad knowledge of books and be efficient in performing the selection process. It is not expected, nor is it possible, for the librarian to read each book, however, there are certain key features that need to be examined in making a determination to accept or reject a particular book.

The examination of a book should include *(1)* the title page and the author of the book; *(2)* publication date, copyright date, name of publisher; *(3)* the preface or introduction should always be read, as it gives an indication of the purpose of the book and something about the author's point of view; *(4)* chapter headings should be examined, as they give an idea as to how information is structured; *(5)* if time allows, read the first and last chapters, for they usually given an indication of how the information is treated, also randomly select another chapter, preferably one that may appear somewhat controversial, and see' if the author is consistent in his or her style and if he or she has any fixed biases that either help or hinder the presentation; *(6)* if the book has an index, try if out for accuracy ad completeness.

Looking at these features in particular will give the librarian a rather complete picture as to a book's worth and indicate if it should be acquired for the library's collection. To conduct the evaluation properly, it is helpful for the librarian to use dearly defined criteria upon which to base a decision. The degree to which the book being examined meets the evaluative criteria will determine whether or not it merits selection. The following six criteria need to be understood thoroughly when evaluating books.

1. Authority. Something should be known about the author or editor of the book. The author's credentials should be examined, especially with regard to qualifications for writing a particular book and any experiences he or she may have had that contribute to the quality of the book. It would be wise to take into account the reputation of previous publications and whether the present book is on a topic comparable enough to warrant similar merit. A biases the author may be known to possess should be particularly considered it terms of how they affect the book.

2. Scope. Find out how broadly or narrowly the book handles the topic and how deeply it is developed. Ascertain, what limits were placed on the book with regard to content and information, even though it may be adequate, decide whether it is partial or complete in its presentation. Determine if the book contains any serious omissions or conversely, if any areas are overdeveloped to the degree that it may distort the reader's perspective. Another factor, that would affect the scope is date of publication, which has an important influence on the datedness of the material. Some books may have more than one printing date, which is an indication of their popularity, while other books come out in new editions. In the case of a new edition, it is important to know the difference between it and its predecessor.

3. Treatment. Note how the content is treated. The style can be scholarly or entertaining, which incidentally is not meant to imply that one is better than the other, but that style should be in keeping with the content and the purpose of the author. Didactic presentations can be dull, but an inappropriate style can border on absurdity if applied to the wrong topic. Identify the level of the writing in order to learn what reading skill is require and if indeed the book has appeal to that level of reader. Consider whether the readability makes the book applicable to a broad or a narrow range of readers. Inherent in the treatment is the author's style, which is a reflection of his or her talent to write an interesting manuscript. The book, regardless of the topic, should have vitality and be interesting.

4. Arrangement. The book should have on orderly flow to it. Information should be properly sequenced and there and should be no gaps or serious omissions. Also pertaining to arrangement is balance, and it is necessary to be aware of whether there is too much or too little information or topical development. The content should have an intended, methodical progression and not confuse or disorient the reader. If the content by nature tends to be piecemeal, then the pieces should result in a coherent mosaic of information.

5. Format. Format refers to the physical attributes of the book. This would include: the overall dimensions of the book, number of pages, size and quality of the print, quality of paper and binding; the use, quality, size, color, and arrangement of graphics; quality of the cover; and the overall general physical appeal of the book. In some cases, even the dusljacket should be examined for any appealing traits.

6. Bibliographies. Although not generally applicable to weeks of fiction, bibliographies should be examined for quality, datedness, and completeness. They give an insight to the author's expertise in the topic as well as an indication of his or her use and knowledge of primary and secondary resource. The bibliography could be limited to !ocumenting footnoted information and listing suggested readings or preferable a combination of the two. If the book does contain bibliographic information, determine whether it is at the end of each chapter or grouped at the end of the text. See if the book contains any other reference features.

Exercising these criteria when evaluating a book does not require that the librarian be a subject matter expert, however, broad knowledge and a lifetime exposure to all kinds of books are valuable prerequisites to good selection. The librarian has to enjoy working with books. Through adherence to the criteria developed in this section, a procedure can be followed that provides a methodical evaluation of any book and results in building an excellent library collection.

An added feature of this procedure is it gives the librarian a professional knowledge of the content of the library collection which can be used to defend its merits. Even more important it will prove to be invaluable in assisting the librarian to meet the reading needs of patrons by knowing something about what is on the library shelves.

It is appropriate that this section immediately follow the section on evaluation because the six criteria listed there have their strongest applicability in the selection of reference works, Indeed, the librarian needs to be especially discriminating when selecting reference works; They become tools of the librarian in locating requests for information and when placed in the hands of the patron, they should provide information clearly, quickly, and concisely.

By definition, reference book is essentially a fact finder used to locate precise information that is available either as an overview or a summary. A reference work is usually a good place to initiate for quick enrichment but also can on refer the reader to other sources for further investigation. Still another feature of reference works is their ability to provide answers to specific questions and to confirm inquires or information efficiently and succinctly. Hence it is obvious that when selecting reference works particular attention needs to be give to authority, scope, treatment, arrangement, format, and bibliographies.

It is essential for any library to have a 'well-balanced collection of reference works to serve as information search tools for the professional reference librarian and to accommodate patrons with a wide range of skills who need access to it as well. The basic types of reference works house in the reference section are encyclopaldias, dictionaries, indexes, bibliographies, yearbooks and almanacs, etc. Within each of these types, there are many reference works from which to choose. It is for the librarian to ascertain what each reference tool has to offer with regard to types and amount of information contained, arrangement and ease of locating information, and the Reference Works Evaluation Checklist be used as a systematic means of analysis. It contains the procedure for conducting an orderly and complete evaluation of any reference work being considered for acquisition.

Evaluating Fiction

Fiction encompasses such a wide range of topics it is difficult to apply a basic set of criteria that will work well all fiction types. Nevertheless, it is necessary to apply some basic criteria in order to make fiction selection a valid process, which in turn may make it beneficial to generate subsets of criteria or particular fiction types that will make selection more reliable. Content criteria developed expressly for science fiction may not be applicable to a work of fiction that deals with romance. Therefore, rather than have works of fiction be subjected to fixed basic criteria, it may be better to design criteria to fit each type of fiction.

Developing subsets of criteria could be a time consuming task, the worth of which could be measured only by how well and consistently it serves the librarian. However, by adhering to a policy of using prescribed documented criteria, the librarian can avoid the pitfall of using ambiguous means for evaluating fiction. If the librarian develops, even if only mentally, a personal set of criteria for each work of fiction being evaluated, then it is quite possible that books could be selected on the "how I feel about the book" criterion rather than on well-developed, prescribed criteria. First, it would be well to examine the basic criteria that are generally applicable for evaluating works of fiction and from them generate any subsets of criteria that can be uniquely adapted to any particular types of fiction. The following seven criteria can be considered basic to evaluating works of fiction.

1. Author. Is there something about the author that warrants the acquisition of his work? It could be that the author is popular or represents a particular type of fiction that appeal to a particular type of reader. Perhaps the author is relatively new and has something fresh and stimulating to offer.

2. Style. Some factors to consider are: Is it easy to read? Does it challenge the reader? Is the narrative interestingly worded? Does the vocabulary enhance the work? Generally style is that facet which lends a uniqueness to a work of fiction; well done it not only makes the work enjoyable but also makes it stand out as a means of communication. It is in the author's style literary merit comes to the fore.

3. Theme. The theme, although it does not necessary have to be spelled out, is the message of the work. Here the evaluator must exercise discretion with regard to truthfulness, which for example, in a fairy tale could mean nothing more than acceptability or believability. Perhaps of greater importance is the moral, ethical, and social value of the theme. Here is where the evaluator beings to become involved in censorship by assigning a worth or value to the book as it pertains to the welfare of the patron. When this occurs, the evaluator must become purged of any prejudicial biases that are not beneficial or in the best interest of the patron.

4. Plot. The plot is the fabric in which are woven the style, theme, characters, setting, and purpose of the book. The plot must interestingly hold these component together, and upon its ability to do so rests the success of the book.

5. Setting. To be effective, the information about setting should be conveyed subtly but conclusively. Specificity is essential, which incidentally should not be mistaken for a tight, arrow, detailed description of the setting, but rather be understood as a means of given the reader the information necessary to understand when and where events are happening, as well as what influence it has upon the characters.

6. Characters. The characters should give the reader insight and information as to what the book is all about. The characters should be interesting in and of themselves and generate a sense of realness or believability. Above all, the characters should not be static but should develop as the entire book develops. The success of characterization depends not only on what the person is but on what he or she represents.

7. Reviews. Although not part of the book, reviews can provide guidance in selection. However, it is necessary to know something of the reviewers credentials for criticizing a particular type of fiction.

From these seven basic criteria subsets of criteria can be evolved with which particular types of fiction can be evaluated. The subsets are in effect modifications of the basic criteria and serve as an attempt to make them more applicable to particular fiction types. To keep the development of subset criteria manageable, a matrix can be devised to provide a consistent means of selection.

On the vertical exist are listed the types of fiction, while on the horizontal the selection criteria. Assigning a value to each criterion (very low, low, high, very high) gives an immediate indication as to what is important in evaluating a particular type of fiction. As an example, authenticity may be of very high value in selecting a historical novel but be of very low value in selecting a fairy tale. The matrix is not filled out because assigning values, even though they may vary only slight, could produce enough variance over the entire matrix to invalidate its use for a particular library.

Therefore, it is suggested that the reader assign values to the matrix that will be more in keeping with the needs of the final word of judgment, it is a guide to the selection of fiction whose value is measured by its usefulness. With the criteria for evaluating works of fiction and, if necessary, the fiction subset criteria matrix, the fiction selection essentials are now available to be incorporated into a fiction evaluation from. As with all evaluation forms, it should be concise and easy to use and require only that information which will actually be used in making a selection decision. The fiction evaluation form appearing here is a suggestion of format.

Evaluation Nonfiction

Oftentimes, when selecting a book of fiction or nonfiction, a decision is made by judging the book's popularity, the assumption being that if the book is popular it must therefore be good. Using popularity as the sole criterion may more. often then not be safe for selecting fiction books of temporary value nut popularity should not be the major criterion in selecting a book of nonfiction. A work of nonfiction must have genuine intrinsic merit to justify its acquisition. If is necessary to do research to determine if a nonfiction book is of any value of the library collection.

The research is predicated upon criteria that objectively analyze the worth of a book. Ideally, the appraisal of a nonfiction book that receives approval should result in it meeting all specified criteria; but because of the varied scope of nonfiction works, it may be possible to have a book meet one criterion with such a high degree of perfection that its acquisition is warranted. Conversely, it is also possible to have a nonfiction book fail so. miserably on one criterion that it is rejected. The criteria used for evaluating works of nonfiction need to emphasize authenticity and accuracy.

The prime purpose of nonfiction is to present information in a well-organized, understandable fashion. If the book is also interesting and enjoyable, those become additional strengths to merit acquisition. The librarian needs to be especially alert in selecting works of nonfiction, for it is in such books that the legacy of mankind is recorded and made available to everyone. The librarian must determine who are the best writers of this legacy and by so doing select the works of nonfiction that preserve and embellish the culture of a society. The following criteria for selecting works of nonfiction should be carefully digested, for they not only present a means for objective selection but also alert the reader to philosophical considerations that should be of paramount concern in building a library collection.

1. Authenticity (Authority). The author should be an expert with demonstrated knowledge of the topic. If any information, or the interpretation of facts, is presented with a bias, the author should admit to it, either by expressly stating it in the preface, by informing the reader in the substance of the text, or by a proper footnote that information contrary to his or her bases is knowingly being altered or omitted because it is not in support of the premise of the book. Actually, it is a rare author who would admit to such tactics unless they enhance the writer's objectives; therefore, the evaluator must be particularly aware of purposeful omissions and make certain that the book is genuinely authoritative, trustworthy, reliable, and complete.

2. Accuracy (Authority). Closely related to authenticity is accuracy. Are the events being recorded the author's own experiences, or are they the results of investigating other resources? If other resources are being used, are they primary or secondary? If it is a scholarly work, information from primary and secondary resources should be properly footnoted, and a bibliography should be included to substantiate and document the accuracy of the content as well as provide the reader with information for further investigation. Accuracy is not to be taken lightly. When inaccuracies occur whether by intent, omission, or ignorance, they destroy the value of a nonfiction work.

3. Scope. Scope pertains to how the author handled the topic. It can best be evaluated by considering antonymous terms such as exhaustive-brief, superficial-in-depth, broad-narrow, covers many points-investigates a specific a specific point, introductory-summary, exploratory-advanced. Using these terms when analyzing nonfiction helps to identify the scope with which the content is treated and determine if a book is needed for the library collection.

4. Organization of Material (Treatment, Arrangement). As nonfiction deals with what is true, real, and factual, it is the organization of material that gives it the necessary credibility. Supportive to organization is they style of writing, which can range from scholarly to popular. Whatever the writing style, a work of nonfiction should have vitality and be interesting reading. Information needs to be presented with clarity. The nonfiction book's chapters collectively encompass the overall purpose of the 'book, but each chapter should be complete in and of itself and be identified as a logical, cohesive entity. Indexing, if applicable, is an aid to organization, but it cannot redeem poor organization. A positive attribute of organization, but it cannot redeem poor organization. A positive attribute of organization is that the reader can accumulate knowledge from the book. When a book is properly organized, knowledge obtained early in the text becomes a prerequisite to acquring still more knowledge later on in the book.

5. Graphics (Format). It is often vital to nonfiction works to support them with graphics, especially when they deal with technical data. Graphics help to clarify the content. Visuals should be of proper size, easy to read, help the reader to understand the text better, and convey meaning better than the printed word.

6. Bibliographies. Bibliographies are invaluable in documenting information. Perhaps their greatest valueless in expanding the usefulness of the book by guiding the reader both to resources used in preparing the book and to sources of additional information. Bibliographic entries should be examined for completeness and amount of information offered. In some case, imprint information will suffice, in other situations, annotations and excerpts greatly enhance the value of a nonfiction book.

Once you have used these six criteria in analyzing a nonfiction work, a determination can be made as to who can use the book and for what purpose. The book can apply to a broad or narrow readership with regard to ability, need, and interest. The book can also be categorized as scholarly, popular, interest. The book can also be categorized as scholarly, popular, entertaining, informational, introductory, advanced, partial, complete, etc. Once you have determined the use and purpose, a decision can be made as to whether or not a book should be acquired for the library collection. A nonfiction evaluation form has been designed to be subjective, unlike the fiction evaluation form, which is objective. Either form can be revised vis-a-vis objectivity subjectivity. Textbooks are found primarily in the domain of schools and school libraries. However, public libraries are becoming more involved with communities' ongoing educational needs and do have textbooks in their collections. Colleges are now offering external degrees, (*i.e.*, student can enroll in courses without even setting foot on campus), and as a result the public library is quasi-involved in formal education.

An individual library does not usually choose a particular textbook but decides only whether or not to have it in the collection. The actual selection of textbooks is done by government agencies, *e.g.*, state school board. It is recommended that when selecting a textbook from a prescribed list, the librarian do it with the cooperation of local school officials, *e.g.*, school curriculum textbook committee.

It is difficult to define the term textbook because there is no specific class of books that fits a definition. It would be better to describe what a textbook does in an effort to arrive at a classification. A textbook is any book used as an integral part of the study of a particular curriculum. If a novel by Ernest Hemingway is used as a text for the study of American literature, for all practical purposes it becomes a textbook for that course. In this case, the student reads a Hemingway novel not primarily for pleasure but to learn some specifics of American literature. This is a case where a book written as a novel, because of unique qualities, also serves as a textbook.

Many books are written solely for a particular curriculum or course of study, and it would be advantageous to use this type of book in generating a definition of a textbook, with the emphasis on what it does rather than on what it is. A textbook provides information for a course of study by organising a body of information and presenting it in a prescribed sequence. The author states the parameters of the textbook and develops the content accordingly.

In selecting a textbook, there are several characteristics to be considered beyond those already discussed: *(1)* the table of contents should be detailed and well developed; supporting it should be an index the helps to locate specific information quickly; *(2)* vocabulary should be geared for a specific reading level; *(3)* layout should be arranged for easy reading (textbooks often divide a page into two columns); *(4)* chapters should deal with specific learning objectives and limit discussion solely of them; *(5)* there should be some type of linear progression and organization, *e.g.*, easy-difficult, past-present-future, basic-advanced, generalities-specifics, theory-application. There are other features that enhance the quality of a text book: *(1)* chapter summaries or reviews; *(2)* question and work assignments;

(3) teachers' editions which include answers, methods for using the textbook, and suggested activities; *(4)* supplementary materials, *e.g.*, testbook, workbook, overhead transparencies, ditto masters, laboratory manual; *(5)* appendixes to supplement the text; and *(6)* glossary of terms and definitions.

Textbooks are generally intended for group use, and a good textbook can be used by an entire group. In general, the textbook tends to keep the group together with regard to material being covered at any particular time during the course of instruction. In the past, course were taught using only one textbook; and indeed the textbook was the course. Today, there is a trend toward making the textbook a supplementary aid to the course and using a host of media in conjunction with it, *e.g.*, other books, films, filmstrips, programmed instruction, etc. This trend reflects the realization that there is no such thing as a homogeneous group in which everyone performs equally well with one textbook. Any group is made up of students with a range of individual differences hat can be best administered to by having a variety of learning materials. This trend does not be little the value of the textbook because materials. This trend does not be little the value of the textbook because a good textbook still eliminates the need to use parts of several books to acquire information on a particular topic. When a textbook is used in conjunction with other media, the curriculum is further enriched.

When evaluating textbook, one should be aware of a few characteristic that often times are readily apparent. Textbooks have a tendency to be conservative in that they only consider one opinion or entertain a particular point of view. Often there is little consideration for cultural or ethnic differences, the assumption being that all readers presses the ideals and educational goals of white, meddle class America.

Although the author tries to be accurate, it is impossible to get everything into a text; as a result, editorializing must be done. A textbook can surreptitiously persuade the reader toward a particular philosophical ideal which can be ignorantly accepted because of the lack of complete information. The textbook, in its effort to provide information, can lead the reader to accept conclusions without ever discovering or testing his or her own conclusions.

Perhaps an awareness of these shortcomings is further evidence that although a textbook is geared for a particular course of study and may be its mainline of information, other information sources need to be made available. Textbooks lie more in the realm of the school librarian, and a government agency is usually responsible for their selection. However, the local librarian is responsible for his or her library collection and, although not involved in the selection process, should be vitally involved in the rejection process by making only the best textbook available for patrons.

Selecting Children's Books

Children's book also need to be assessed and withstand the critical scrutiny of the criteria outlined in the section on selection and evaluation developed earlier in this chapter. Beyond this, the librarian needs an awareness of some basic considerations that apply in the selection of children's books. Perhaps to the library novice it may appear convenient to. classify a whole section of the library collection as being children's books and proceed on the premise that it contains low level, simple materials on topics suitable for children.

Such a broad categorization does not take into account the extremely broad range of reading skills children have and the types of books that must cater to those skills. When it is considered that the bulk of popular adult reading material is written pretty much at the eighth-grade reading level and that only more serious and scholarly polished books venture into the use of more sophisticated vocabulary, the selecting of adult books with regard to adult reading ability is not really that difficult a task. However, with children's books the reading level ranges from that of a tot unable to read a printed word all the way to that of a sixth-grade child capable of mastering eighth-grade reading material.

The librarian should be aware of the child's general disposition toward reading. At present, there are many criticisms that "Johnny can't read," and the society is creating a generation of nonreaders.

Accusations have been leveled at television, for discouraging reading, and at schools for not giving enough attention to the problems of reading. It would be ridiculous to deny that there are any reading problems, especially when there are presently in the United States over 20 million adults classified as functionally. illiterate (*i.e.*, unable to read a classified ad or fill our a job application). But the solution to the reading problem resides not in placing blame but in seeking solutions. The children's librarian can make an invaluable contribution toward achieving the solution. First and foremost, the children's librarian should be aware that children possess an uninhibited and insatiable curiosity, they are yearning to investigate and explore their big, wonderful world. The children's library can do much to nourish this enthusiasm with fine literature. For the very young nonreader and for the child beginning to master the intricacies of reading, there is enjoyment in having someone read them stories.

Story telling is an art, that which practice can be easily mastered and will hold a child spellbound. The library needs a wide collection of books that can be read to children and initiate them to the adventures of reading. In addition to books read to children, there are books young readers can "read" for themselves. This type of book needs of be well illustrated and aurally and is eager to master visually. The visuals help the child make the transition from nonreader. Visuals need to have clarity of communication by almost spelling out pictorially what they are saying.

The book collection should contain a gradient of picture books, with books having many illustrations and few words and gradually inverting the proportion to many words and few illustrations. The objective is to challenge and motivate the child to want to learn to read and provide materials that will foster the growth and rewards of reading skills. It is important to remember that the child has a natural curiosity, and it is necessary to use it to its greatest advantage. Parallel to selecting books on a pictorial-print gradient is the consideration of interest.

The pictorial-print gradient challenges the child, but the content must stimulate or interest him or her. Hence there is another gradient to consider, that of the child's growing world. Initially, the child's real world is egocentric and limited pretty much to family and home. Gradually, the child's real world expands to include neighbor-hood, library, school, and an ever enlarging world community.

Obviously, the child's reading interests will grow accordingly, and the library needs to be ready to minister to them. The child also has a imaginary, make-believe world, much at time can become quite "read." The library can foster reading development by including in the collection books that appeal to the child's sense of adventure. Still another consideration that cannot be overlooking is the child's personal vocabulary. Critics accuse television of propagating a society of illiterates, but it cannot be denied that a child from the television era has mastered a far greater vocabulary than his pretelevision predecessor.

This means that when the child is ready to read, it is not the Dick and Jane books that will have appeal, but books that contain a more adult vocabulary. Furthermore, with regard to the pros and cons of television's effect upon reading ability, it has been found that at around age 10 the intelligent child who has had an oversized diet of television becomes somewhat saturated with the medium and seeks other channels of communication, namely the printed word. With less intelligent children, this phenomenon occurs a little later.

It is for the library to be ready to capitalize on this regenerated interest in reading by having literature of suitable level and interest. Rather than criticizing television and crusading against it, the librarian should use it as a means of promoting reading and filing a void that cannot be achieved by the television tube. May be for the group of children who have drifted away from reading but now have a new-found reorientation to it, the librarian will need to be especially aware of books of low level-high interest (*i.e.*, low level vocabulary but more mature content suitable for a 10- to 12-year-old child). The purpose is to have books that can be mastered and still be of interest. Perhaps it would be also wise to take into consideration books that do not take too long to read, for television has conditioned the child to obtaining a complete story in a minimum amount of time.

One other aspect of children's books to consider is that of format. Printing should be large enough for the child to read easily, illustrations need to be colorful, pages durable and easy to turn, and bindings extremely durable. Children tend to be hare on books and give them punishing use. If books do receive heavy use, then. the library should consider the advantages and disadvantages of prebinding.

Basically there are four types of prebinding: *(1)* reinforced in the publisher's original covers when the book is bound, *(2)* original binding is resewn with stronger stitching, (3) resewn and reinforced with buckram covers, which can have the publisher's original design, and (4) resewn and rebound in buckram, plastic, or fabrickoid. Obviously, prebinding cost more, but the book will last much longer and will not need rebinding which involves removing it from the collection. However, i a book is to be prebound the original pages should be strong and durable (*i.e.*, as strong as the heavier binding). Most of the concerns and considerations discussed here go beyond selection and evaluation and have a profound influence on the success of the library collection. The children's collection should be a treasure for the child, but it must be in a form whereby its wealth can be readily recognized, used, and appreciated.

Assessing and Constructing Book Reviews

There is a twofold purpose discussed here: *(1)* to know how to assess book reviews and *(2)* to be able to actually construct a book review. In the process of selecting books, the skilled librarian refers to book reviews for assistance in making acquisition decisions. The librarian does not have time to meticulously read every book acquired, but by following the selection criteria set forth in this chapter, he or she can develop an efficient selection technique, and published reviews help to guide and reaffirm judgment.

To be able to construct a book reviews help to did arid reaffirm judgments. To be able to construct a book review not only helps to analyze them better, but also provides an indispensable service to library patrons. It is indeed a fortunate patron who has the services of a librarian in selecting a book for a particular requirement and who is able to give an assessment as to how well a book can fill a need. With regard to assessing book reviews, it is important for the review first to. provide a comment on what the book is about. Now the comment about a book is not to be confused with a book report. Often book reviews that are nothing more than glamorized book reports mislead the reader by presenting superficial descriptions of content and fail to reveal more valuable and intrinsic insights.

Attention needs to be given to the scope of the book and the manner in which information is treated. A review should give information as to the broadness or narrowness of the topic, as well as the vehicle by which content is developed and characterizations are used to convey meaning. Next the book review should describe the book's attributes and its literary merits. The reviewer should tell how well the book is put together and the .degree to which it achieves its intended propose. Here is where the reviewer present a case for the book's strengths and deficiencies. Something should be said of the author's writing style and its contribution to the particular work being assessed. Along with the author's style, reference should be made of the author's credentials as they relate to the particular book being reviewed. A statement of the author's experience, authority, and knowledge of the book's topic help to qualify its value. As the author's credential are not usually found in the context of the book, it is beneficial for the reviewer to document his or her source information. Also, if warranted, information regarding the reputation of the publisher can be given. Some mention should be made of the book's physical characteristic, *e.g.*, dimensions, number of pages, quality of print and illustrations, and, if applicable, the quality of pages, quality of print and illustrations, and, if applicable, the quality of indexes and bibliographies.

Finally, the reviewer should make an unequivocal statement bout the book as a discrete entity. If they are applicable, the reviewer can also include external factors. For example, the reviewer may compare the book to any of the author's previous works or compare it to similar works by other authors. Mention should be made of the book's current and future value. Recommendations should be made as to the type of reader who would most benefit from reading the book and for what purpose.

Although they do not pertain directly to the book being reviews, the librarian should known something of the reviewer's credentials and reputation. The reviewer should have read the book and know something of the topic. The reviewer should also be responsible for good literary from in the review per se. The review should be authoritative, comprehensive, informative, easy to read, and (it is hoped) free of prejudicial biases. On occasion, the librarian may find it helpful to construct a book review. Basically there are three reason for doing so: *(1)* there is no review available on the book; *(2)* the librarian disagrees with existing reviews; or *(3)* a review has to be written for a particular type of reader, *e.g.*, reviewers of children's book write their reviews for adult readers when in actuality a great service would be provided if they were written for children to provide them with guidance as to whether or not the book is worth reading. It is important to remember when writing book reviews that the purpose is to enlighten the reader as to his or her possible desire, interest, or need to read the book.

For the book review to be valid and reliable, the reviewer should read the entire book. A second-best method would be to skim the book, nut a review predicated on the skimming technique should be done only by a person extremely skilled in skim reading. If the review is accomplished in this fashion, the reviewer should admit that the review was constructed from knowledge obtained from skimming or a cursory overview.

Obviously, the standards used to analyze book reviews can serve as a guide in constructing them as well. However there are additional factors to take into consideration. When constructing a book review, it is always necessary to keep in mind the importance of comprehensiveness and completeness while at the same time being concise and brief.

An extensive treatise, regardless of how well done, is seldom appreciated. It is a good practice after completing a book review to reread it to see if it can be further improved by editing it further down. There is actually no prescribed order in which information has to be presented; what is given head is a logical sequence intended to inform, not confuse, the reader. The review must contain a complete bibliographic entry. Something should be said about the type of book being reviewed. If it is a work fiction, the review should indicate what the plot is about, the theme of the book and how it is conveyed, the setting(s) in which the book takes place, the use of symbolism, what the characters contribute to the book, and the general pace and development of the book.

With a work of nonfiction, mention should be made of the contribution the book makes, the accuracy and completeness of information, the scope or emphasis given to exploration of content, and the parameters the book entails. Some insights should be given regarding the author and his writing ability. The review should react to and take a definite stand on any particular positions or points of view advocated by the author. This should be a statement of what the author is attempting to do with regard to how the content is treated and how it can affect or influence the reader. It is important to mention something of the author's writing style. Oftentimes, this can be achieved by quoting a passage from the text; but when this is done, the passage should be representative of the writing style of the entire book.

An assessment need to be made of the book's literary merit. Depending on the reviewer's own disposition and writing style, all this information can be conveyed either objectively or subjectively. Some reviewers find it difficult not to intersperse personal opinion throughout the entire review. But regardless of the reviewer's writing style, the review should conclude with an appraisal of why the book is liked or not liked, as well as a recommendation as to what kind of person would benefit from reading it and why he or she would appreciate it.

❑